DATE DUE

~~MY 1 01~~			
~~AG 8 '01~~			

DEMCO 38-296

UNITED STATES ELECTORAL SYSTEMS

UNITED STATES ELECTORAL SYSTEMS

Their Impact on Women and Minorities

Edited by WILMA RULE and
JOSEPH F. ZIMMERMAN

PRAEGER

New York
Westport, Connecticut
London

Library of Congress Cataloging-in-Publication Data

United States electoral systems : their impact on women and minorities
  /   edited by Wilma Rule and Joseph F. Zimmerman.
       p.   cm.
    Includes bibliographical references and index.
    ISBN 0–275–94240–6 (pbk. : alk. paper)
    1. Representative government and representation—United States.
    2. Elections—United States.   3. Minorities—United States—
    Political activity.   4. Women in politics—United States.
    I. Rule, Wilma.   II. Zimmerman, Joseph Francis, 1928– .
    JF1063.U6U55   1992
    324.973—dc20   91–29608

British Library Cataloguing in Publication Data is available.

A hardcover edition of *United States Electoral Systems* is available from the Greenwood Press
imprint of Greenwood Publishing Group, Inc. (Contributions in Political Science, Number 294,
ISBN 0–313–27730–3)

Library of Congress Catalog Card Number: 91–29608
ISBN: 0–275–94240–6

First published in 1992

Praeger Publishers, One Madison Avenue, New York, NY 10010
An imprint of Greenwood Publishing Group, Inc.

Printed in the United States of America

The paper used in this book complies with the
Permanent Paper Standard issued by the National
Information Standards Organization (Z39.48–1984).

10 9 8 7 6 5 4 3 2 1

Copyright Acknowledgment

An earlier version of Chapter 3 by Bernard Grofman and Lisa Handley appeared in *American
Politics Quarterly* 17, no. 4, pp. 436–45, copyright © 1989 by Sage Publications, Inc. Reprinted
by permission of Sage Publications, Inc.

FOR LEON WEAVER

Contents

Preface

Important demographic changes are occurring in the United States. America's minority population is growing appreciably and in some cases dramatically. The Latino and Asian populations have at least doubled in the last decade in California and other regions of the West. African-Americans continue to increase their proportions throughout the South and industrial areas of the North. All will continue to do so as we move into the 21st century. Many members of racial and ethnic groups aspire to elect their members to the decision-making bodies of our nation. The Voting Rights Act of 1965, as amended, continues to help make that dream a reality for blacks and specified language minority groups in a number of cities, counties, states, and congressional delegations. But there is still much to be done, since minorities remain grossly underrepresented relative to their population.

There are today new actors on the political stage: minority and Anglo women are entering elective government in greater numbers. They compose over 50 percent of the nation and at most average 20 percent of all elected officers. Women bring to office a perspective that has been largely absent in the male-dominated elected bodies of the past. Formidable obstacles still exist and need to be removed or reformed to achieve increased political opportunity for minority and Anglo women.

It is against this backdrop that this anthology took form. The Section on Representation and Electoral Systems of the American Political Science Association sponsored a workshop on minorities and women at the 1989 annual meeting of the association. The workshop participants presented working papers of how electoral systems affected black and Latino men and women as well as Anglo women. It was the first time that a scholarly workshop had considered black and Hispanic women's chances for election separately from black and

Hispanic men's prospects for election. Minority women were previously invisible in electoral system research; they had been merged either with their ethnic group or into the women's category.

From this start, we envisioned a book that would present the expanded case studies of the workshop together with an overall analysis of the general situation. The case studies, we thought, would be useful to those looking for practical ways to provide representation for minorities and women. The chapters with the case material present real-life experiences with different electoral systems instead of the theory of how the systems might work. Concrete electoral arrangements that impede and those that facilitate electoral opportunities for African-Americans, Latinos, and Anglo women are presented, based on solid scholarly work. The barriers that exist and how they can be overcome are also treated on the basis of careful study by leading experts. Throughout the editing process that followed, we tried to make each chapter understandable to the many people who are interested in making government more representative, inclusive, and responsive.

In Part I, Joseph F. Zimmerman provides an overview of the volume and presents six criteria for evaluating the equity of electoral systems. Part II, on Congress, begins with an insightful introductory chapter by Georgia A. Persons. Bernard Grofman and Lisa Handley present their thorough analyses of black and Hispanic congressional districts. Wilma Rule and Pippa Norris conclude the section by analyzing the deleterious effects on women of the single-member district system of electing members of the United States House of Representatives.

Wilma Rule's study of recruitment opportunities for minority and Anglo men and women in the 50 state legislatures opens Part III. Her article is followed by five fascinating case studies—Pennsylvania by Sandra A. Featherman, Florida by Anita Pritchard, Maryland by M. Margaret Conway, Illinois by David H. Everson, and Arizona by Michelle A. Saint-Germain. The concluding chapter in Part III, by Richard L. Engstrom, examines how alternative election systems can be employed in judicial elections.

Part IV opens with a pathbreaking study of minorities and women in county government by Victor DeSantis and Tari Renner. Susan Welch and Rebekah Herrick give us a comprehensive view of the election of minority men and women in larger cities, followed by Susan A. MacManus and Charles S. Bullock's survey of women elected officials in small cities of Florida. Edward Still shows us the results of a remarkable experiment in alternative election systems in Alabama, and Leon Weaver and Judith Baum lay out the pros and cons of New York City's proportional representation system for electing community school boards.

Options for increasing direct representation for minorities and women are presented in the two chapters that conclude the book. Joseph F. Zimmerman spells out how various electoral systems can reform unfair procedures in local governments. And R. Darcy's chapter presents data from the United States and other countries to document his conclusions for increasing women's proportions in legislatures.

The coeditors thank the contributors for their patient and willing revisions to their manuscripts. In a few instances, the coeditors disagree with the contributors' analyses and recommendations. All the chapters are of high standard, and we leave it to the reader to compare them and to decide which measures are needed to provide more electoral opportunities for minorities and women.

We also thank our respective universities for assistance. A special word of gratitude goes to our dedicated typists, Maxine H. Morman and Addie Napolitano, who valiantly struggled through many table and text revisions and made them all neatly and correctly.

Finally, we would like to acknowledge the outstanding job done by our Greenwood Press copyeditor, D. Teddy Diggs. The manuscript was greatly improved as a result of her efforts.

This volume is dedicated to Leon Weaver, who had a long-standing interest in the fairness of electoral systems for all groups in our society, and particularly women and minorities. This concern is reflected in his chapter with Judith Baum on the effect of the proportional representation system employed to elect members of community school boards in New York City. Professor Weaver encouraged others, especially those with recent degrees, to study electoral systems. He was a founder of the sections on Representation and Electoral Systems of the American and International Political Science Associations and was active in both groups until shortly before his death. His wise counsel and assistance will be sorely missed.

PART I

INTRODUCTION

1

Fair Representation for Minorities and Women

Joseph F. Zimmerman

Unrepresentative governing bodies have long been a problem in the United States, with blacks and women having been the most grossly underrepresented group. More recently, the rapidly growing Hispanic population has replaced blacks as the most underrepresented group. In addition, both minority and Anglo (non-minority) women have the lowest proportions elected to public office relative to their populations and compared with the men in their respective group. Cultural, legal, and political barriers, singly or in combination, have limited the number of blacks, Hispanics, and women elected to public offices.

In a democratic system of government based on majority rule, there is an unavoidable clash between the views of the majority and those of the minorities on numerous issues. To ensure that minorities have direct input into the policy-making process, it is essential that minority groups above a "critical" mass be provided full opportunity to elect some of their members to office.

Chapters in this volume: (1) highlight the problems women and minority candidates face in seeking election to Congress under the single-member district electoral system; (2) present case studies of the impact of different electoral systems on women and minority candidates' opportunities for election to state legislatures; and (3) offer insights into the relationships between the election of women and minority candidates to local government offices under the single-member district, multimember district, at-large, cumulative voting, limited voting, and proportional representation electoral systems.

All members of Congress are elected by the single-member district system, as are most members of state legislatures and many members of local governing bodies. Under this system, which favors male candidates, only one representative is elected in each district.

The multimember district system, employed to elect some state legislators and local governing council members, provides for the election of two or more candidates in each electoral district. As most of the chapters in this book demonstrate, this system improves the election prospects of women and certain minority candidates compared to the single-member district system.

Cumulative voting, limited voting, and proportional representation systems, which are explained in detail in chapter 17, facilitate the election of women and minority candidates to public office. Cumulative voting was used in Illinois until 1982 (see the chapter by Everson). This system allows an elector to cast more than one vote for a single candidate up to the number of officials to be elected. By allowing an ethnic or party minority or women to cast more than one vote for their candidates, the system enables these groups to elect some representatives. The same result may be achieved by using the limited voting system, which authorizes an elector to vote for more than one candidate but less than the number of seats to be filled (see the chapter by Still).

There are two types of proportional representation (PR)—the party list system and the single-transferable vote system. Both are favorable for women and minorities (see the chapters by Rule and Norris and by Weaver and Baum). The party list type is used in Europe but not in the United States. The number of representatives elected from each party's list of candidates is determined by each party's proportion of the total votes cast in the election.

The single-transferable vote system is currently used to elect 32 community school boards in New York City and the city council and school committee in Cambridge, Massachusetts. Voters express their preferences for candidates by placing a number next to the names of their first, second, third, etc., choice. Based on the number of valid ballots cast and the number of representatives to be elected, a quota sufficient for election is determined by a formula detailed in chapter 17. The single-transferable vote system results in representation by parties or groups in accordance with their respective shares of the votes cast.

This chapter identifies major barriers to the election of minorities and women to public offices, outlines several possible electoral solutions for their underrepresentation, and concludes with criteria for measuring the fairness of various electoral systems.

BARRIERS TO ELECTION

Political scientists have identified the following as barriers to the election of blacks, Hispanics, and/or women to public office: the voting system, the second or runoff election, incumbents seeking reelection to office, inadequate campaign funds for challengers, and election laws making it difficult for potential candidates to have their names placed on the ballot. It should be noted that each barrier may affect a specific minority group or women in a different manner and that two or more barriers may be interrelated.

The Voting System

The issue of the best election system for city councils was a prime concern of the municipal reform movement that originated in the late 19th century. The reformers were convinced that the ward system of election promoted and perpetuated "invisible" city councils controlled by corrupt political machines, and resulted in councils that did not represent the best interests of the citizenry at large. The movement sought to replace a large, bicameral city council with a small, "visible," unicameral council, ward elections with at-large elections, and partisan elections with nonpartisan elections. The reformers were generally successful by the middle of the 20th century in replacing ward elections with at-large elections, which promoted the candidacies of middle-class white males. The municipal reform model was reassessed in the 1960s by a number of observers who were convinced that the quality of municipal government had been generally improved by the reforms but concerned that the city council elected by the at-large plurality system was insensitive to the special needs and desires of blacks and Hispanics because the council tended to reflect white middle-class values.[1]

As a result of the implementation of the Voting Rights Act of 1965 by the United States Department of Justice, many cities covered by the act readopted the single-member district system in order to promote the election of blacks to the city council.[2] One of the problems associated with this system is gerrymandering, and the United States Supreme Court in 1977 upheld as constitutional the creation of a New York State Assembly district in Brooklyn with a 65 percent black population.[3]

Experience with single-member districts, as Herrick and Welch explain in this volume, promotes the election of blacks to office because they tend to be geographically concentrated. Grofman and Handley demonstrate in their chapter that black members of Congress are elected from black plurality districts in which the combined black and Hispanic population exceeds 50 percent. Similarly, Pritchard in this volume reports that there was an increase in the number of blacks elected to the Florida State Legislature subsequent to the adoption of the single-member district system in 1982. Persons explains in her chapter that exploitation of the single-member district system by minorities is not without tradeoffs and limitations.

Not surprisingly, each electoral system may affect a group differently. Rule in this volume shows that the single-member district system limits the opportunity for Anglo and minority women candidates to be elected to state legislatures and the United States Congress. DeSantis and Renner in this volume report that district elections at the county level do not strongly promote the election of black men to county legislatures. And Welch and Herrick conclude in this volume that multimember and at-large elections favor the candidacies of black and Hispanic women to city councils.

The at-large plurality system disadvantages black male candidates unless blacks constitute a majority of the residents within the multimember district. On the other hand, Rule reports in this volume that state legislatures employing multimember districts have higher percentages of black women members than state legislatures employing single-member districts. The Conway chapter also reveals that multimember districts for the Maryland House of Delegates elections improve the election chances of black women and men candidates. Darcy in this volume reaches a similar conclusion in his chapter.

The dilutive effects of at-large elections on black male candidates can be offset by the adoption of cumulative voting or limited voting, as Engstrom and Still document in their chapters. And Everson reports in his chapter that cumulative voting in Illinois over a 110-year period was effective in providing minority party representation.

The Second or Runoff Election

The election law in several states and a number of city charters provide for a runoff primary election or a runoff general election in the event no candidate receives a majority of the votes cast. If three or more candidates split the vote to the extent that no candidate receives a majority of the votes and the plurality candidate is black, the runoff primary or general election will involve a contest between the black candidate and a white candidate. If there is racial polarization in voting, the runoff election will ensure the election of the white candidate unless blacks constitute a majority of the voters.

Rule in this volume reports that the runoff primary election is responsible in part for African-Americans, Hispanic men, and Anglo women in a number of states achieving lower legislative proportions relative to their proportions of the general population.

Incumbency

Incumbents seeking reelection are a major barrier to most other candidates unless the incumbents have been engaged in activities reflecting adversely on their character or unless their national political party is blamed by the public for an event or scandal, such as the Vietnam War or Watergate. Featherman reports in this volume that the high salary paid to Pennsylvania state legislators encourages incumbency and thereby limits opportunities for the election of black and women candidates. And Saint-Germain in her chapter documents the power of incumbency in the Arizona State Legislature.

Incumbent state legislators in a number of states and members of Congress employ large staffs that may devote part of their time and efforts to promoting the reelection of the incumbents. Furthermore, incumbents are in the public spotlight as they make speeches and attend private and public functions. Incumbents also communicate with constituents through newsletters prepared and mailed at public expense and may make public-service announcements that generate or reinforce their name recognition. In fairness to incumbents, it must be pointed out that incumbents have an obligation to keep their constituents informed and to provide assistance when requested. Nevertheless, the potential for abuse in employing public resources to assist reelection campaigns exists.

Darcy notes in his chapter in this volume that term limits for incumbents will probably promote the election of women to office. In 1990, voters in California, Colorado, and Oklahoma approved constitutional amendments limiting the number of terms that state legislators may serve. Pritchard reports that Anglo women candidates in Florida benefited not only from the change to single-member districts but also from the large decennial population growth, which encouraged a number of incumbents to retire. She also documents the considerable increase in incumbency that occurred since Florida switched to single-member districts in 1982. Pritchard's finding is corroborated in Rule's state legislative study. Rule found significantly greater incumbency in the 35 single-member district state legislatures and less in the 15 multimember district state legislatures as of 1989.

Campaign Finance

Numerous studies reveal that incumbents have a decided advantage over challengers in terms of fund-raising for election campaigns. Candidates for state and national offices, as well as candidates for offices in large cities, often need substantial sums of money to finance their campaigns, which rely heavily on expensive television and print media advertising. Major contributors tend to donate funds to the probable winners of elections, typically the incumbents. As a consequence, challengers usually are able to raise only a fraction of the funds that incumbents raise. MacManus and Bullock, however, report in this volume that women council members in small Florida municipalities did not perceive lack of campaign funds to be a significant barrier to the election of women to office.

If the term of office is only two years, incumbents frequently engage in fund-raising activities throughout the term of office and may not completely separate their fund-raising activities from their official activities. The New York State Commission on Government Integrity in 1989 pointed out, "off-year fund-raising is a particularly effective way to discourage potential challenges, the political version of a 'preemptive strike.' "[4]

All states and the national government have corrupt practices acts that limit the amount of funds that may be contributed by individuals and organizations to election campaigns and also the amount of funds that may be expended by candidates for public office. Enforcement of such laws typically is lax and may involve little more than the release of unaudited campaign receipts and the requirement that candidates periodically file expenditures reports during the election campaign. The principal beneficiaries of the lax enforcement of laws usually are the incumbents.

Complex Election Laws

The election laws in a state may make the playing field for incumbents and challengers uneven. The problem is most acute in partisan elections, since the state committees of the two major parties often influence the nature of the election laws and seek to include in the laws provisions facilitating the removal of the names of challengers from the primary election ballots.

The New York State Commission on Government Integrity reported in 1988 that the complex procedural requirements in the state's election law often necessitate that candidates who collect more than the required number of signatures must "participate in expensive, time-consuming litigation in order to defend their right to run for office."[5]

Strong candidates may be prevented from running for public offices by technical failures to comply with all provisions of the election laws. Furthermore, the complex legal obstacles to ballot access may discourage other competent individuals from seeking election to public office.

POSSIBLE SOLUTIONS

The effectiveness of each barrier in hindering the election of minorities and women to public office varies from jurisdiction to jurisdiction, as does the difficulty of removing the barriers. This volume places heavy emphasis on the types of election systems employed in the United States and their role in promoting or hindering the election of blacks, Hispanics, and women to public offices.

As reported in the chapters by Still and Zimmerman, three electoral systems— cumulative voting, limited voting, and proportional representation—have been adopted by a small number of local governments and have been successful in facilitating the election of minorities and/or women to public office. Baum and Weaver in their chapter conclude that proportional representation in New York City has been successful in electing community school boards reflecting the ethnic, racial, and sex composition of the respective populations.

The barrier to the election of minorities and women posed by the second or runoff election is difficult to eliminate. Adoption of the preferential voting system, also known as the alternative vote, would have the advantage of eliminating the runoff election, with its low voter participation, but may not promote the election of a minority or a woman candidate, since the successful candidate is determined by the majority vote rule.

In a preferential voting election, the voter indicates his/her preferences for candidates for a single office, such as mayor, by placing a number after the name of each candidate, with number "1" indicating first preference, number "2" second preference, etc. If no candidate receives a majority of the number "1" votes, the candidate with the smallest number of "1" votes is declared defeated and his/her ballots are transferred to the remaining candidates according to second preferences. If no candidate receives a majority of the number "1" and number "2" votes, the candidate with the fewest votes is declared defeated and his/her votes are transferred to the other candidates. This process is continued until one candidate receives a majority of the votes.

Prospects for limiting the terms of incumbents are best in the 23 states with constitutional provisions authorizing one or more types of initiatives.[6] It is improbable that a majority of the members of the state legislatures in the other 27 states will vote to limit the number of terms that a member may serve.

The only solution for the campaign finance problems is the adoption of laws providing for public financing of election campaigns. Prospects for the enactment of such laws, however, are slim.

Reform of state election laws, where needed, also will be difficult to achieve, since the laws are designed to protect incumbent legislators. If election law abuses are publicized widely in a state with the initiative, citizen resentment may produce a petition drive to place a new election law on the referendum ballot.

In general, the chapters in this volume indicate that the campaign to increase the numbers of blacks, Hispanics, and women elected to public office should be a multifaceted one that encourages more members of these groups to seek elective office, promotes a change in the election system, encourages the voluntary retirement of long-term incumbent elected officials, seeks to limit the number of terms an incumbent may serve, supports the enactment of public financing of election campaigns, and works for the simplification of complex election laws hindering the access of challengers to the ballot.

This chapter concludes by offering criteria for measuring the degree of representational equity produced by various electoral systems.

CRITERIA FOR FAIR REPRESENTATION

In a polity where there are no legal or other impediments to adult citizens registering and voting in elections, the following six canons of a good electoral system can be employed to assess the equity of representation produced by various electoral systems. The canons, or criteria, are interrelated and overlapping rather than discrete.

Effectiveness of Ballots Cast

The effectiveness canon measures the potency of each ballot cast by a registered voter and indicates that a nondiscriminatory electoral system does not cancel or invidiously dilute the effectiveness of ballots cast by any citizen or group of citizens. In the eyes of a minority group, the election must be more than a type of periodic consultation ritual that is meaningless to the group members because their ballots are rendered ineffective by the design of the electoral system. If a minority group perceives that the electoral system makes the group powerless, group participation in the political process will be low, and the public interest will suffer accordingly.

Maximization of Participation

A fair electoral system encourages the enrollment of eligible voters because they can visualize that their exercise of the franchise will be effective in helping to determine one or more winners in an election contest. Logically, voter turnout by members of a group in an election will be in direct relation to the possible influence that the group can exert. Low voter registration and turnout on election day may be the product of alienation—a sense of powerlessness—rather than apathy.

Representation of Competing Interests

An important feature of a good electoral system that is functioning properly is elected officials who have a special sensitivity to the needs of ethnic and racial groups, including minority and Anglo women. A truly representative legislative body will treat all citizens fairly in the process of accommodating competing interests. An electoral system that guarantees direct representation on a legislative body for women and members of minority groups will facilitate the necessary political accommodation and help to ensure responsiveness by the legislators to the needs of the minority groups and women.

Maximization of Access to Decision Makers

A proper system of voting will result in the selection of legislators who are willing to listen to, and seek out, the views of all groups in the polity. Consultation with constituents must be genuine and not *pro forma*, or alienation and cynicism will be promoted.

Equity in Group Members' Representation

Fairness in representation is the hallmark of a democratic political system. If members of a group are underrepresented in terms of their population strength in a legislature, or other elected offices, the election system should guarantee that they will be able to elect more members of their group to bring their direct representation closer to parity. Direct representation for minorities and women— in approximate accordance with their proportions in the population—should be deliberate and not a product of happenstance.

Legitimization of the Legislative Body

An important function of an electoral system is to legitimize the legislative body in the eyes of the citizenry, thereby facilitating the implementation of policy decision. The effectiveness of a government's policies depends in many instances on the active cooperation and support of citizens. A widespread view that the electoral system is deliberately designed to favor one group over another and the legislators fail adequately to represent citizens will seriously weaken the perceived legitimacy of the policymakers.

NOTES

1. For an example, see Edward C. Banfield and James Q. Wilson, *City Politics* (Cambridge, Mass.: Harvard University Press and M.I.T. Press, 1963), pp. 139–42.

2. Voting Rights Act of 1965, 79 Stat. 437, 42 U.S.C. § 1973.

3. *United Jewish Organizations of Williamsburg, Inc., v. Carey*, 430 U.S. 144 at 156 and 159–60 (1977).

4. *The Midas Touch: Campaign Finance Practices of Statewide Officeholders* (New York: New York State Commission on Government Integrity, 1989), p. 4.

5. *Access of the Ballot in Primary Elections: The Need for Fundamental Reform* (New York: New York State Commission on Government Integrity, 1988), p. 1.

6. Joseph F. Zimmerman, *Participatory Democracy: Populism Revived* (New York: Praeger Publishers, 1986), pp. 68–104.

PART II

SENDING WOMEN AND MINORITIES TO CONGRESS

2

Electing Minorities and Women to Congress

Georgia A. Persons

The focus of this chapter is the descriptive representation of minorities and women and is directed toward illuminating the impact of electoral systems on electing minorities and women to Congress and the related question of why these groups are greatly underrepresented in the national legislature.

THE CONCEPT OF REPRESENTATION

The composition of elective bodies is an important factor in assessing their representativeness and in evaluating the legitimacy of the processes of governance. However, measuring or assessing the representativeness of elective bodies is not a straightforward process except in the extreme case when a group is excluded totally and when political significance attaches to such exclusion. As a general measure, political scientists use the proportional representation of major groups in the population as the standard against which to assess the representativeness of elective bodies. Using this measure for African-Americans, Hispanics, and women, we conclude that Congress is grossly unrepresentative. However, population proportions are not a totally objective standard for assessing a group's representation.

Pitkin's analysis and definitional operationalization reflect the relative and subjective nature of representation.[1] Pitkin defines four variants of representation, including descriptive and substantive representation, which are particularly applicable to electoral bodies. Descriptive representation occurs when an elected official mirrors his or her constituency in terms of salient social characteristics such as race, ethnicity, religion, etc. In regard to an elective body, the descriptive characteristics become highly visible indicators of the extent to which the social diversity of the populace is reflected in institutions of government. Substantive representation occurs when an elected official represents the interests of his or her constituency in terms of policies advocated, positions taken, voting behavior, and similar matters.

Whereas substantive representation is largely policy-oriented, descriptive representation is symbolically significant. However, there is the very strong assumption in politics, significantly borne out by experiences of several groups over time, that substantive representation is enhanced greatly by and parallels descriptive representation. This assumption, however, embodies an overstatement in regard to the implied concurrence among members of a given group in regard to the nature and locus of the group's interests, appropriate strategies for advancing the group's interests, and general philosophical predispositions and ideological perspectives. In short, descriptive representation does not, a priori, equal substantive representation.

Concern about the representation of women and minorities reflects the social and political realities of our times. Relative to African-Americans and women, these concerns have historical antecedents in organized social movements and political conflicts dating to the founding of the Union. However, the politically relevant groups and concerns of minorities have expanded over time as the substantive interests of specific racial and ethnic groups have been identified as being distinct and thus politically relevant. We make reference to the largest minority groups when we use the term *minority* to include African Americans, people of Hispanic origins, and, increasingly, people of Asian origins. The latter two groups are extremely diverse. Only in the case of African Americans is there a largely unambiguous situation of a distinct subset of substantive interests and conditions embraced by and applicable to the group as a whole. This situation derives from a historical exclusion and continuing discrimination, and a resultant subordinate status based on skin color. Thus, in terms of its social and political significance, the ethnicity of blacks is fundamentally an ascriptive condition that has in turn fueled a political (counter-) mobilization.

The situation of Hispanics is similar, yet different in important ways. Individuals of Hispanic origins may be of any race, experiences of discrimination are not as widely shared among members of the group, and self-identification with a minority status is not as widely shared within the group in politically significant ways. In the case of Asian-Americans, it is even less clear that distinct cultural differences shared within the various Asian groups are seen by these groups as constituting the basis for a distinct politics based on distinct substantive interests. This situation may or may not change over time. Analysts have found that immigrants of similar ethnic origins from diverse locations may not initially form a self-conscious, unified group, but rather the consciousness of a bond between persons of common descent may develop gradually as a result of stimulation by political elites.[2]

Hispanics and Asians face problems of ''pan'' nationalism or the necessity of developing a consciousness that overrides and embraces distinct subidentities.

In the case of some Hispanic group members, particular circumstances and social conditions—such as low-income status—have fueled the development of group identity and consciousness and in turn led to social action and mobilization. With respect to Asians as a collective, a politically significant ethnic consciousness may develop as a strategic choice in recognition of the significance of ethnicity as a strategic requirement of political and social mobilization in the modern state. For Hispanics, language clearly serves as the main pillar in the identification of "pan-nationality" and subsequently ethnic consciousness. There is no commonly shared language among Asians, and one would expect that geographic region of origin, and common experiences in the United States, might serve as the pillars of a shared ethnic identity of political consequence.

As a society, we do not seek to evaluate the extent to which the total racial/ethnic/cultural diversity of the population is reflected in elective bodies. We do not attribute, for example, significance to the presence or absence of individuals of Ethiopian, Armenian, Asian Indian, Vietnamese, or Aleutian descent in representative bodies. On the one hand, we effectively use the presence or absence of members of certain minority groups as indicators of the openness of the political system. On the other hand, as a society we have not attributed political relevance to the minority status of many groups, and possibly will not. This fact is part of the ambiguity of representation.

In focusing on the descriptive representation of women, we are making the implicit and explicit assertion that gender is politically significant in ways cutting across and transcending other descriptive characteristics, such as class, race, ethnicity, religion, etc. Although this assertion is not shared by all women in its total meaning, the assertion is valid due to several factors: the historical denial to women of political rights extended to the male population (even technically to African American males by way of the Fifteenth Amendment) and the resulting exclusion of women from representation in elective bodies; the subordinate status of women politically, socially, and economically; and the organization of women around issues that have largely grown out of their subordinate status in society. Thus, the common denominator in the representation of minorities and women, though not consistently or absolutely so, is a subordinate status in American society and resulting sets of substantive interests that compose distinct politics.

Table 2.1 summarizes the descriptive representation in Congress since 1975. Before the 1970 edition of the *Statistical Abstract of the United States*, there was no breakdown of members of Congress by race or gender, and only a partisan breakdown was given. In the 91st Congress in 1969, there were 10 females in the House of Representatives and one in the Senate. A full 20 years later there had been little more than a doubling in the total representation for each group, with 31 females and 26 blacks. In 1990, two women served in the Senate, but there has been no black member of the Senate since 1978. By 1989, Hispanics had been added as a new category of minorities in the *Statistical Abstract*, with 10 members in the House of Representatives.

Table 2.1
Members of Congress, Selected Characteristics, 1975–90

Representatives

Congress	Year	Male	Female	Black	Hispanic
94th	1975	416	19	15	7
95th	1977	417	18	16	5
96th	1979	417	16	16	5
97th	1981	416	19	17	6
98th	1983	413	21	21	8
99th	1985	412	22	20	10
100th	1987	412	23	23	11
101st	1989	410	25	24	10
102nd	1990	406	29	26	10

Senators

Congress	Year	Male	Female	Black	Hispanic
94th	1975	100	–	1	1
95th	1977	100	–	1	1
96th	1979	99	1	–	–
97th	1981	98	2	–	–
98th	1983	98	2	–	–
99th	1985	98	2	–	–
100th	1987	98	2	–	–
101st	1989	98	2	–	–
102nd	1990	98	2	–	–

Source: United States Bureau of the Census, *Statistical Abstract of the United States, 1990* (Washington, D.C.: United States Government Printing Office, 1990) p. 257, and *Congressional Quarterly Weekly Report*, November 10, 1990, p. 3835.

ELECTING AFRICAN-AMERICANS TO CONGRESS

Relative to single-member districts that structure elections to the House, the most important issues are apportionment and the drawing of district lines. Apportionment must be considered after the decennial census in addition to the constitutional requirement of allocating representatives on the basis of population, the United States Supreme Court's "one person, one vote" dictum requires that each district be of approximately equal population size. Also, the Voting Rights Act of 1965 prohibits voting practices that dilute the voting strength of minority voters and requires covered jurisdictions to preclear changes in election systems with the United States attorney general or the District Court for the District of Columbia.[3] The act has demonstrably contributed to major increases in the number of black elected officials and to enhancing Hispanic political participation. The act also has combined with increased salience of minority concerns and traditional concerns about electoral politics to increase greatly the stakes involved in reapportioning congressional districts. It is a persistent fact of American life that minority electoral gains are disproportionately tied to the availability of safe seats as defined by majority or near-majority black or Hispanic election districts. Thus, the fate of minority representation in the House lies in the reapportionment process and the drawing of district lines. If election districts are drawn to preserve majority black or Hispanic populations, minority representatives are likely, though not guaranteed, to be elected.

Only eight blacks were elected to Congress before enactment of the Voting Rights Act. The first post-Reconstruction election of a black to Congress occurred in 1928 with the election of Oscar DePriest from the south side of Chicago. This district has had the longest continuous black representation of any congressional district and has elected, in addition to DePriest (1928–34), Arthur Mitchell (1934–42), William Dawson (1942–70), Ralph Metcalf (1970–78), Harold Washington (1978–83), and Charles Hayes, the incumbent for the 101st Congress.[4] Adam Clayton Powell was elected to represent Harlem in New York City in 1944, thereby producing a total of two blacks in Congress. Blacks, in turn, were elected from Detroit (Mich. 13th) in 1954, Philadelphia (Pa. 2nd) in 1958, California (29th) in 1962, and Detroit (Mich. 1st) in 1964. Thus, it took 36 years to reach a total of a half dozen blacks in Congress at one time. These blacks each represented a majority black district, and each was elected from a district outside the South. The first black elected from a southern district was Andrew Young, who was elected in 1972 to represent the Georgia 5th district, which was only 29.5 percent black.

Before the 1990 elections there had been five black women elected to the United States House: Shirley Chisholm of New York, Barbara Johnson of Texas, Yvonne Braithwaite Burke of California, and Cordiss Collins of Illinois, who were elected in the mid–1970s; and Katie Hall of Indiana, who served briefly from 1982 to 1984. During the 101st Congress, Cordiss Collins was the lone black woman in Congress. In the 1990 elections, three black women were elected to the House. However, they did not break totally new ground in that each was elected to replace a black male incumbent. Maxine Waters replaced Augustus Hawkins in the California 29th, Barbara Rose Collins replaced George Crockett in the Michigan 13th, and Eleanor Holmes Norton replaced Walter Fauntroy as the at-large delegate from the District of Columbia.

In the 1990 elections there was a net gain of two black members of Congress, for a total of 26, with the election of William Jefferson in the Louisiana 2nd and Gary Franks representing the Connecticut 5th. Franks became the first black Republican in the House since Oscar DePriest's departure in 1935, and his district has the smallest number of blacks (4 percent) of any black representative.

The District of Columbia and 16 states have the largest concentrations of black citizens—Alabama, Arkansas, Delaware, Florida, Georgia, Louisiana, Illinois, Maryland, Michigan, Mississippi, New York, North Carolina, South Carolina, Tennessee, Texas, and Virginia. Although approximately 58 percent (15) of the black members of Congress are elected from these states, New York, Illinois,

Table 2.2
Congressional Districts Represented by Blacks, 1990

MEMBER OF CONGRESS	DISTRICT	PRINCIPAL CITY	PERCENT BLACK IN DISTRICT	PERCENT WHITE IN DISTRICT	PERCENT HISPANIC IN DISTRICT
Dellums(D-CA)	8	Oakland	27	60	7
Dixon(D-CA)	28	Los Angeles	39	38	28
Dymally(D-CA)	31	Compton	34	42	25
Waters (D-CA)	29	Los Angeles	50	32	37
Franks (R-CT	5	Waterbury	4	93	3
Norton (D-DC)	At-Large	Washington,DC	70	31	3
Lewis(D-GA)	5	Atlanta	65	34	1
Collins(D-IL)	7	Chicago	67	29	4
Savage(D-IL)	2	Chicago	70	25	7
Hayes(D-IL)	1	Chicago	92	6	1
Jefferson(D-LA)	2	New Orleans	52	44	3
Mfume(D-MD)	7	Baltimore	73	25	1
Conyers(D-MI)	1	Detroit	71	27	2
Collins(D-MI)	13	Detroit	71	26	3
Espy(D-MS)	2	Greenville	58	41	1
Clay(D-MO)	1	St. Louis	52	48	1
Wheat(D-MO)	5	Kansas City	23	75	3
Payne(D-NJ)	10	Newark	58	34	14
Flake(D-NY)	6	Jamaica	50	44	9
Towns(D-NY)	12	New York	47	29	38
Owens(D-NY)	12	Brooklyn	80	13	10
Rangel(D-NY)	16	New York	49	25	38
Stokes(D-OH)	21	Cleveland	62	36	1
Gray(D-PA)	2	Philadelphia	80	18	1
Ford(D-TN)	9	Memphis	57	42	1
Washington (D-TX)	18	Houston	39	41	27

Note: Numbers may not add to 100 percent because Asian-Americans are not included, and according to the Bureau of the Census, persons of Spanish origin may be of any race.

Source: *National Roster of Black Elected Officials, 1990* (Washington, D.C.: Joint Center for Political Studies, 1990). Data on the November 1990 elections will be published in the 1991 *Roster*.

and Michigan contribute almost 35 percent of the total. California, which has only a 7 percent black population, elected four blacks to Congress, or 17 percent of the total. These numbers and their distribution indicate the undue reliance of black candidates on concentrated black population bases for election to Congress. This observation is borne out by the data in table 2.2, which show that 20 black congress-persons were elected from districts with at least a 47 percent black population base. What we also see from table 2.2 is that of those eight districts that do not have at least a 50 percent black population base, in only three do the combined black and Hispanic populations equal less than fifty percent of the total population. In only three districts (Dellums of California, Wheat of Missouri, and Franks of Connecticut) are blacks clearly elected by majority white constituencies. The only black senator since the Reconstruction era was Edward Brooke of Massachusetts, who was elected in 1966 and served until 1979.

With a primary precondition of concentrated black population bases, there remains very little slack in the system in regard to districts from which blacks will likely be elected (before changes in the post–1990 redistricting). Of the 25 congressional districts with the highest percentages of black population, only seven are not represented by a black. One of these districts, NY–18th, is represented by a Hispanic. The 1st district in Indiana (Gary) was represented in 1983–85 by a black, Katie Hall. That district has a 24 percent black and 8 percent Hispanic population and again should elect a minority person to Congress.[5] Given the pattern of electing blacks to Congress with a very clear dependency on concentrated majority or near-majority black populations, the black population has significantly maximized its presence in Congress within the context of the single-member district electoral system. Much of this success is attributable to the mobilization of the black population, with critical support from Hispanic voters in some instances and, in fewer instances, critical support from white voters. The fact that all black members of Congress are in the House attests to the difficulty black candidates experience in white settings.

ELECTING HISPANICS TO CONGRESS

Hispanics were elected to Congress as early as 1822, and subsequently a total of 47 Hispanics have been elected to Congress, including two to the Senate. The total includes 15 nonvoting delegates elected to the House over the years from the territories of Puerto Rico, Guam, and the Virgin Islands. In the 101st Congress, there were 10 full-fledged voting members of the House who were of Hispanic origins. There are three nonvoting delegates from Puerto Rico, Guam, and the Virgin Islands. With the exception of Representative Henry Gonzales, these members composed the Congressional Hispanic Caucus.

The term *Hispanic* is used broadly and includes individuals of many nationalities, including Mexicans, Puerto Ricans, Cubans, Spaniards, and Spanish-speaking individuals of countries of Central and South America who may be of any race. The growth of the Hispanic population in the United States has been nothing less than spectacular, exceeding the 20 million mark in 1989. The Hispanic population grew by more than 60 percent in the decade of the 1970s and by 39 percent in the decade of the 1980s, resulting in a doubling in the size of the Hispanic population in the period 1970–90. Immigration contributed about one-half of the growth of the Hispanic population, compared with 21 percent of the growth of the non-Hispanic population.

The top 10 states in terms of Hispanic population based on 1980 census data are Arizona, California, Colorado, Florida, Hawaii, Nevada, New Jersey, New Mexico, New York, and Texas. All nine voting Hispanic members of Congress come from Texas (4), California (3), Florida (1), and New York (1). The Hispanic congresswoman from Florida in the 101st Congress, Iliana Ros-Lehtinen, was

Table 2.3
Population Characteristics of Hispanic Congressional Districts, 1990 (in Percent)

MEMBER	DISTRICT	HISPANIC	ASIAN	BLACK
E. Roybal	California −25	57	8	10
Martinez	California −30	48	9	1
Torres	California −34	42	4	2
de la Garza	Texas −15	66	−	1
Gonzales	Texas −20	56	1	9
Bustamante	Texas −23	51	1	4
Ortiz	Texas −27	55	−	3
Ros-Lehtinen	Florida −18	50	1	13
Richardson	New Mexico −3	37	−	1
Serrano	New York −18	49	1	44

Source: *Almanac of American Politics, 1990* (Washington, D.C.: National Journal Incorporated, 1990).

elected in a 1989 special election to succeed the late Claude Pepper, who had long represented the 18th district. That district was 50 percent Hispanic and 13 percent black in 1989, and in November 1990 Ros-Lehtinen was elected to a full term. The most glaring absence of Hispanic representation is in New Mexico, where Hispanics compose over one-third of the state's population. The three congressional districts in New Mexico have Hispanic populations of 33, 29, and 37 percent, respectively. However, New Mexico elected two Hispanic senators, Chavez in 1935–62 and Montoya in 1964–77, suggesting that there was once within New Mexico a mobilization that favored the election of Hispanic candidates to national office.

Table 2.3 depicts population characteristics of Hispanic congressional districts. The obvious conclusion is that Hispanics are elected from districts with majority or near-majority Hispanic populations. Grofman and Handley found that a slightly higher population concentration of Hispanics is necessary to ensure Hispanic success in electing one of their own to Congress than is necessary in electing a black.[6] Like blacks, Hispanics need to exploit their population concentrations to elect one of their own to succeed a retiring popular white member of Congress. Such elections occurred in the cases of Bustamante of Texas and Ros-Lehtinen of Florida, who first were elected in 1985 and 1989, respectively.

ELECTING ASIANS TO CONGRESS

The United States Bureau of the Census combines Asians and Pacific Islanders (API) as a common population grouping. This grouping includes a broad diversity of groups differing in origin, culture, language, and recentness of immigration. In regard to this and other racial/ethnic categories, the bureau offers the explanation that its classification primarily reflects self-identification of respondents.

Although the API population is widely dispersed across the country, members are disproportionately concentrated in the western United States. The distribution of the Asian population is due in part to the policy of sponsorship established by the federal government under the Refugee Resettlement Program. In 1980, three states had an Asian population of more than 300,000: California (1,246,654, or 36 percent), Hawaii (452,951, or 13 percent), and New York (327,499, or 9.4 percent). Pacific Islanders also lived disproportionately in the West, with the overwhelming majority residing in Hawaii (137,696, or 53 percent) and California (66,171, or 25.5 percent). Other states with more than 4,000 Pacific Islanders were Washington, Texas, and Utah.

Politically, Asians have made their presence felt, especially in areas where they have been historically settled. However, we cannot speak of Asian politics as a national social movement. There is no Asian caucus in the Congress, in part because the number of Asian members of Congress does not warrant such an organization. Indeed two of the four Asian members of Congress do not represent majority Asian districts. Representatives Robert Matsui (D-Calif. 3rd) and Norman Mineta (D-Calif. 13th), Americans of Japanese descent, represent districts with Asian populations of only 6 percent. In only one California congressional district (12th) do Asians compose 20 percent of the population. That district was represented in the 101st Congress by a white female. In Hawaii, Asians and Pacific Islanders composed 61 percent of the population in 1980. And Hawaii had two Asian representatives, Congresswoman Patricia Saiki and Senator Daniel Inouye, in the 101st Congress. The appointed replacement for the late Senator Spark Matsunaga (Asian) was Daniel Akaka, a Hawaiian, who won in a contest against Saiki in the 1990 election.

In regard to the election of Asians to Congress, only limited conclusions can be based on the very different cases of California and Hawaii. The California case leads to the conclusion that the election of Asians to Congress is not tied to their majority or near-majority presence in election districts, and this conclusion certainly sets them apart from other minority groups in the United States. Although there is strong ethnic consciousness within the various subpopulation groups of Asians, it is not clear that these groups consider themselves as minorities in ways intended to reflect or bestow political significance upon them. In the case of Hawaii, the state's politics reflects the political dynamics of the indigenous population, white settlers, and the large numbers of Asians and Pacific Islanders. In terms of future projections regarding the API population, given the growing economic clout of various Asian groups, we might expect that over time, impressive numbers of this grouping will emerge in major political positions. However, their route to political prominence will probably be different from that pursued by other minority groups.

ELECTING WOMEN TO CONGRESS

An assessment of efforts to elect women to Congress necessitates an approach and discussion differing substantially from assessments of electing minorities. For example, one would not look for majority female population clusterings or consider the percentage of women in a given election district. On the other hand, there is a major factor of commonality that joins the two assessments: the issue of subordinate status in regard to the similar positions of (some) minorities, and women within the overarching social structure. In regard to most minorities, status is determined by social stigma based on race or ethnicity. Politically, the status of minorities is amenable to limited alteration by their strength in concentrated numbers in strategic population clusterings. This concentration of population, generally driven by social rejection, has enabled African-Americans and Hispanics to a lesser degree to optimize their political positions in the drawing of electoral district lines and in subsequent electoral contests. For women, subordinate status has been determined by gender-based biases transcending racial and ethnic lines, biases that have defined the range of roles acceptable for pursuit by women. Although alteration of their status has not been unrelated to their numbers in the population, the politics of drawing electoral districts or defining electoral systems have not directly affected the political fortunes of women. Thus, as women are incorporated, albeit differentially, into the political and social structure of their specific racial or ethnic groups, it is primarily in the pursuit of common goals or common interests as defined by their commonly shared subordinate status that we realize something that we can characterize as women's issues or feminist politics, which, in turn, accords a unique political significance to women as a group.

After the 1990 elections, there were 29 female members in the House and two in the Senate, the highest number ever to serve at any one time since the first woman was elected to Congress in 1916. There were 24 Anglo women and seven minority women—four African-Americans, one Hispanic, and two Asian. There has never been a black, Hispanic, or Asian woman elected to the United States Senate. There are many explanations for the small number of women in Congress and in elective office generally, including personality differences between male and female candidates, situational factors associated with being female in a male-dominated society, and biases based on sexual stereotyping, which influences voter preferences.[7] An important explanation is that smaller numbers of women generally pursue elective office. One must hasten to add that the comparative reluctance of women to pursue elective office stems from their overall subordinate status and the social marginalization of women who pursue nontraditional roles and other structural reasons set forth in chapters in this volume.

An excellent explanation of the conditions of social marginality as it pertains to women is offered by Githens and Prestage, who explained that women have traditionally been taught that involvement in politics meant participation in the role of voter, at best with emphasis on playing supportive roles in civic matters affecting home and family life, in service-directed positions, and in male-dominated organizations and institutions.[8] Women who have attempted to break out of this ascribed role have frequently experienced a marginalized status ensuing from the conflicting demands of role identification and two distinct groups: women and politicians. The woman as politician must reject several values and norms of the traditional woman's role, yet the politician group does not fully accept her and frequently accepts her only in a subordinate and differential manner. The political woman does not belong fully to either group but exists in a marginalized status vis-à-vis both groups. As a consequence, many women have chosen not to pursue elective office.

The women's movement has provided a more issue-oriented context for viewing women candidates for political office. However, as a system-challenging sociopolitical movement, the women's movement induces both support and some degree of backlash and also induces a certain ambiguity among women politicians in regard to being identified with this movement. Carroll found that a significant number of women candidates who were committed to feminist issues kept such commitments hidden from public view, particularly in their campaign activities.[9] Voters assume that women candidates generally are presumed to be social reformers with regard to a certain set of women's movement issues. Both minority candidates and women candidates are seen disproportionately as agents of sociopolitical change, and justifiably so.

Since 1977, the concerns and embodiment of the women's movement have been manifested within Congress by the Congressional Caucus for Women's Issues, a bipartisan legislative service organization dedicated to promoting women's economic and legal rights. The caucus has focused on economically based issues such as pay equity, family leave, dependent care, pension reform, child-support enforcement, educational equity, and civil rights. Women members of Congress generally have a special interest in these types of issues, which become part of the political canvas against which the voters view them. In short, women candidates for Congress seem to the voters to be, at least tangentially, part of a broader sociopolitical movement.

How do women fare in their efforts to win election to Congress? A study undertaken by the Women's Campaign Research Fund (WCRF) in 1984 provides very useful insights into how women have fared as candidates.[10] Since money in the form of campaign contributions is the mother's milk of modern congressional campaigns,[11] the study focused on the issue of fund-raising to determine whether women candidates had a reasonable chance of winning elective office. The study analyzed campaign receipts reported to the Federal Election Commission for all 3,271 major party candidates, male and female, who ran for the House from 1976 to 1982.

The study found that women have made considerable and consistent progress since 1976 in terms of fund-raising for their campaigns. In 1976, the average female candidate raised only two-thirds as much as the average male candidate. However, women did progressively better in each subsequent election cycle. In 1978, women's average campaign funds were 77 percent of men's average. In 1980, women increased their average to 86 percent of the men's average. In 1982, the average female candidate raised 93 percent as much as the average male candidate, and the average female challenger raised 99 percent as much as the average male challenger. The study also found that by 1982, women candidates were able to raise campaign funds in virtually the same manner and from the same sources—high donors, major parties, and political action committees (PACs)—as their male counterparts. These findings mirror those of other analysts who discovered that women candidates fare well in terms of PAC contributions, whereas black candidates are comparatively underfunded from PAC contributions.[12]

Finally, the WCRF study asked the compelling question: If women candidates can raise money on a basis essentially equal to their male counterparts, why are there so few women in Congress? The WCRF study offered two responses to that question. First, relatively few women ran for a seat in the House during the four election cycles studied: 54 women candidates in 1976; 46 in 1978; 51 in 1980; and 55 in 1982. Women have to run to win. However, starting effectively as outsiders, women face the formidable task of running as challengers for seats in an institution in which the success rate of incumbents in recent elections has been approximately 98 percent. Additional information on this subject is included in the chapter by Rule in this volume.

WCRF also found that women tend to run for the more difficult open seats, where their opponent's party had a very high percent of the vote in previous elections. Overall, approximately 60 percent of the women were challengers or were running for difficult open seats, compared with 45 percent of the men. WCRF's assessment of House races and the distribution of male and female candidates in each category over the four election cycles studied are given in table 2.4. Unlike the situation of campaign funding, the difficulty of races in which women candidates run does not improve over time.

SUMMARY

Rules, procedures, and the systems that they form are never neutral in effect and impact. However, one can make a very convincing argument that the single-member district system is not in and of itself the primary discriminatory factor in the election of minorities to Congress. The primary impediment to increasing the number of minorities in Congress is social bias and the continued refusal of the white majority to vote in sizable numbers for African-American and Hispanic

Table 2.4

Categories in Which Congressional Candidates Ran, 1976–82

TYPE OF RACE	MEN	NUMBER OF CANDIDATES	WOMEN	NUMBER OF CANDIDATES
1976				
Incumbents	47%	359	28%	15
Open seats	14%	109	13%	7
Challengers	39%	299	59%	32
TOTAL	100%		100%	
1978				
Incumbents	46%	354	35%	16
Open seats	14%	109	11%	1
Challengers	40%	302	54%	25
TOTAL	100%		100%	
1980				
Incumbents	49%	375	29%	15
Open seats	9%	74	12%	6
Challengers	42%	322	59%	30
TOTAL	100%		100%	
1982				
Incumbents	48%	364	31%	17
Open seats	12%	93	22%	12
Challengers	40%	305	47%	26
TOTAL	100%		100%	

Source: Perception and Reality: A Study of Women Candidates and Fund-Raising (Washington, D.C.: Women's Campaign Research Fund, 1984), pp. 47–51.

candidates. This bias and the social rejection that it entails have led to residential segregation of African-Americans and many Hispanics and has fueled a substantially ethnic consciousness and a concomitant political mobilization. The result is that African-Americans and Hispanics have substantially maximized the political clout ensuring from their concentrated population patterns and have been able to exploit the single-member district election system.

The exploitation of the single-member district system by minorities is not without trade-offs, limitations, and ambiguities, given that the major precondition for the election of African-Americans and Hispanics to Congress is their presence in concentrated population clusters. If members of these groups disperse too much in their residential patterns, they stand to lose their chance at descriptive representation, at least, and quite possibly substantive representation as well.

Because of the continuing pervasiveness of social and political bias, the need for racial- or ethnic-based mobilization becomes an imperative for some minorities. This imperative, in turn, leads to an emphasis on scoring, in which descriptive representation becomes the symbol of success and, a priori, is seen as equalling or maximizing substantive representation. Although descriptive representation satisfies some demands and needs of a given racial/ethnic group, the assumptions about maximizing substantive representation may not always be valid. Former Representative Peter Rodino, an American of Italian descent, for example, was widely viewed as providing substantive representation of his majority black constituent base in an outstanding manner. Yet for largely symbolic reasons, he was targeted for removal, primarily and initially, by some African-American activists external to his district. However, the voters returned Rodino to Congress until he decided to retire in 1988. This situation illustrates the ambiguity of representation within a racial or ethnic context.

Viewed as a means of overcoming social and political bias against minorities, the single-member district system clearly can be an impediment to obtaining a level of representational diversity in the future. If single-member districts have to be used to overcome bias, it follows that specific ethnic groups will have to seek majority, near-majority, or some "critical mass" status within election districts in order to be elected. The redistricting processes also will have to be sensitive to such population configurations.

In the case of the representational status of women, many of the issues regarding descriptive versus substantive representation of minorities apply. On the one hand, we can assert that more women running for elective office is the major precondition to increasing their numbers. On the other hand, well-ingrained social biases regarding acceptable roles and role expectations, which transcend race and ethnicity, continue to restrict the number of women for whom the pursuit of elective office is a personally viable option. As in the case of minorities, for women the basic impediment lies deeply embedded within the social system rather than being a product of electoral systems, unless, of course, one offers an alternative electoral system. A proportional representation system, for example, would ensure specific representational levels based on race, ethnicity, and gender for dispersed groups voting as blocs.

NOTES

1. Hannah Pitkin, *The Concept of Representation* (Berkeley: University of California Press, 1972).

2. Helena Lapata, "The Functions of Voluntary Associations in an Ethnic Community: Polonia," in Ernest Burgess and Donald Bogue, eds., *Contributions in Urban Sociology* (Chicago: University of Chicago Press, 1964).

3. Joseph F. Zimmerman, "The Federal Voting Rights Act and Alternative Election Systems," *William and Mary Law Review*, Summer 1978, pp. 621–60, and Armand Derfner, "Vote Dilution and the Voting Rights Amendments of 1982," in Chandler Davidson, ed., *Minority Vote Dilution* (Washington, D.C.: Howard University Press, 1984).

4. Bernard Grofman and Lisa Handley, "Preconditions of Black and Hispanic

Congressional Success,'' paper presented at the Conference on Electoral Geography, University of Southern California, Los Angeles, April 1988.

5. Robert Caitlin, "Organizational Effectiveness and Black Political Participation: The Case of Katie Hall," *Phylon*, Summer 1985, pp. 179–92. See also the chapter by Grofman and Handley in this volume.

6. Grofman and Handley, "Black and Hispanic Congressional Success."

7. Emmy Werner and L. M. Bachtold, "Personality Characteristics of Women in Politics," in Jane Jacquette, ed., *Women in Politics* (New York: Wiley Press, 1974); Paula Dubcek, "Women and Access to Political Office: A Comparison of Female and Male Legislators," *Sociological Quarterly*, Winter 1976, pp. 42–52; and Laura E. Eckstrand and William Eckert, "The Impact of Candidates' Sex on Voters' Choice," *Western Political Quarterly*, March 1981, pp. 78–87.

8. Marianne Githens and Jewel L. Prestage, "Marginality: Women in Politics," in Marianne Githens and Jewel L. Prestage, eds., *A Portrait of Marginality: The Political Behavior of the American Woman* (New York: David McKay, 1977).

9. Susan J. Carroll, *Women as Candidates in American Politics* (Bloomington: Indiana University Press, 1985).

10. *Perception and Reality: A Study of Women Candidates and Fund-Raising* (Washington, D.C.: Women's Campaign Research Fund, 1984). See also Carole Uhlaner and Kay Schlozman, "Candidate Gender and Congressional Campaign Receipts," *Journal of Politics*, February 1986, pp. 30–50.

11. Gary Jacobson, *Money in Congressional Elections* (New Haven: Yale University Press, 1980).

12. Allen Wilhite and John Thielman, "Women, Blacks, and PAC Discrimination," *Social Science Quarterly*, June 1986, pp. 283–98.

3

Preconditions for Black and Hispanic Congressional Success

Bernard Grofman and Lisa Handley

Our purposes are to examine preconditions for black and Hispanic congressional success and to account for differences in minority congressional representation by region. Our chief explanatory variable is electoral geography—the geographic distribution of black and Hispanic voting strength within states and across states. In particular, we show that there are major regional differences in the nature of minority population concentrations. We also show that, without a significant (combined) minority population concentration approaching 50 percent, minority electoral success at the congressional level is highly improbable. Furthermore, we show that such sizable minority population concentrations (roughly a quarter of a million persons) rarely are found outside of urban areas.

BLACK CONGRESSIONAL SUCCESS BY REGION

If we look at black population as of 1980, we find that more than half of all blacks resided in southern or border states—52.2 percent to be precise (13,598,881 of 26,046,119, not including the District of Columbia). The southern population is 18.2 percent black, whereas nonsouthern population is 8.2 percent black. In contrast, there were in 1988 only five southern or border-state congresspersons, compared with 18 from the smaller black population in the non-South. Of course, there are fewer members of Congress elected from the South (there are only 142 southern congresspersons, compared with 293 from the non-South), but 3.5 percent of southern members of Congress are black while 6.5 percent of nonsouthern members of Congress are black. "Why are there so few black members of Congress from the South?" would seem a natural question.

Geographic Concentration of Black South Versus Non-South

Of the states with black population over 400,000, 11 are found in the South and nine in the non-South. There are six states in the non-South and six states in the South with a population exceeding one million blacks, although only in the non-South is there a state with above two million blacks (New York). Such slight differences in black population concentrations at the state level would not appear to account for differences in black congressional success rates in these two parts of the country. Indeed, the six states in the non-South with above one million blacks elected in 1990 15 black congresspersons, whereas the six southern states with above one million elected only two black congresspersons. In particular, four of the six southern states with above one million blacks failed to elect a black member of Congress. Thus, we need another explanation of lower rates of black congressional success in the South than statewide black population figures.

At the municipal level, black population is much more concentrated in the non-South than in the South. We develop in table 3.1 a number of indices of the relationship between black urban concentration and black congressional succeṡs in the South and non-South. We have created parallel tables for black population standard metropolitan areas (SMAs), but the results are so similar that we have omitted these tables.

Table 3.1 reveals that 13 of the 19 black non-South congresspersons came from cities with more than 500,000 blacks. These cities (New York, Chicago, Detroit, Philadelphia, and Los Angeles) have at least one black congressperson. Moreover, four of the five black members of Congress from the South come from districts containing cities (Houston, Baltimore, and Memphis) that are above 300,000 black in population. Similarly, all 18 nonsouthern congresspersons and five of the six southern congresspersons come from districts containing cities with at least 100,000 blacks. Most of these cities are large enough in total population to comprise at least one congressional district (Atlanta, Kansas City, Newark, Oakland, and St. Louis are the only exceptions), but most black congresspersons (18 of 22) are elected from districts whose principal city is not majority black in population (the exceptions are from Atlanta, Baltimore, Detroit, and Newark).

Table 3.1 also reveals that every city with at least 500,000 blacks elects at least one black congressperson but only six of the 18 cities with between 100,000 and 299,999 blacks are the basis for districts that elect a black congressperson (33 percent). Note there are no differences in the election rates of black members of Congress between southern and nonsouthern cities with very substantial black populations because there are *no* southern cities with more than 500,000 blacks and *no* nonsouthern cities with between 300,000 and 499,999 blacks. Looking only at cities with between 100,000 and 299,999 blacks, we see that differences in black electoral success between the South and the non-South are not statistically significant—five out of 12 (42 percent) versus one out of six (17 percent) cities

Table 3.1
**Black Congressional Representation as a Function of Black Population
Concentration in Cities, South and Non-South,* 1980**

	BLACK CONGRESSIONAL SEATS			
	NON-SOUTH		SOUTH	
CITIES CLASSIFIED BY BLACK POPULATION	YES	NO	YES	NO
Cities with above 500,000 blacks	5(13)	0	–	–
Cities with between 300,000 and 499,999 blacks (Washington, D.C. omitted)	–	–	4(4)	1
Cities with between 200,000 and 299,999 blacks	2(2)	0	1(1)	1
Cities with between 100,000 and 199,999 blacks	3(3)	7	0	4

	CITIES WITH AT LEAST ONE BLACK MEMBER OF CONGRESS	
	NON-SOUTH	SOUTH
CITIES CLASSIFIED BY BLACK POPULATION	PERCENT	PERCENT
Cities with above 500,000 blacks	100	–
Cities with between 300,000 and 499,999 blacks	–	100
Cities with between 100,000 and 299,999 blacks	42	17

*The number in parentheses is the total number of black congresspersons representing those cities.

in the South elect blacks. In short, *once we control for the size of (urban) black population concentrations*, differences between the South and the non-South are small, albeit the few differences suggest that, even holding black population constant, the South is slightly less apt to elect black congresspersons.

The South versus non-South differences in number of black congressional seats are due to a compositional effect. Nearly seven million nonsouthern blacks (6,843,745) are found in cities with over 100,000 blacks; in contrast, not even three million southern blacks (2,861,282) are located in such urban concentrations. Thus, a much higher percentage of nonsouthern blacks than of southern blacks are found in cities with over 100,000 blacks (55.0 percent as compared to 20.4 percent).

Why should differences in geographic dispersion be such an important factor in accounting for different rates of black success in different parts of the country?

To answer that question, we must understand how the proportion of minority population in a district affects the probability of black congressional success.

Population Proportion and Black Congressional Success

Frank Parker of the Lawyers Committee for Civil Rights under Law, a noted civil rights attorney, claimed that blacks are denied the opportunity to elect a candidate of their choice without a district that is 65 percent black. The essential argument is that, because of lower levels of black registration and turnout and a lower proportion of blacks who are of voting age, a district that is 50 percent black in population will not be anywhere near 50 percent black in turnout on election day. Thus, it may take a black population at or above 65 percent to provide "effective voting equality."[1] Also, blacks may be more willing to vote for whites than vice versa, and incumbents are apt to be white and thus have a double advantage against black challengers (race and the value of incumbency). Moreover, inexperience with campaigning, difficulties in raising funds, and lack of a large pool of candidates with strong records of previous governmental service all serve to handicap blacks who seek office.

We can look directly at the validity of Parker's claim for Congress. In Table 3.2 we show 1980s black congresspersons and the proportion black in the districts that elected them. Only districts that were over 65 percent black elected black congresspersons in every one of the five elections from 1982 to 1990; the Georgia 5th—which is exactly 65 percent black—elected a black to office now but did not always do so in the early 1980s. In the districts with between 50 percent and 64 percent black, only half (three of six) elected a black congressperson in 1982; but by 1990, all of these districts were electing blacks to Congress.

If we look only at the 1990 election districts, every district above 45.2 percent black elected a black member of Congress. Furthermore, only 15 of the 25 black congresspersons in 1990 were elected from majority black districts; five of the remaining nine black representatives were elected from districts that were 40 to 50 percent black (there are nine congressional districts with black populations falling in this range, hence half of them elected blacks), and the other four black members of Congress were elected from districts with less than 40 percent black populations (in the California 8th and 31st, the Missouri 5th, and the Connecticut 5th). However, six of nine of the nonmajority black districts that elected a black to Congress had substantial Hispanic populations, ranging from 25.1 percent to 38.0 percent.

We believe it important to distinguish between the minority population proportion needed to create "safe seats" and that needed to provide minority candidates a "realistic chance of elections"—that is, a probability well above 50 percent but still rather less than certainty. For Congress, it seems apparent that black population percentages as low as 45 percent can provide black candidates a near certain chance of election. Of course, we must be very careful in interpreting the percentages in table 3.2. A percentage of blacks sufficient to elect a

Table 3.2
Black and Hispanic Populations in Congressional Districts and Black
Congressional Representation, 1982–86

DISTRICT	POPULATION		BLACK ELECTED				
	BLACK 1982	HISPANIC 1982	1982	1984	1986	1988	1990
Illinois 1	92.1	1.1	yes	yes	yes	yes	yes
New York 12	80.1	10.1	yes	yes	yes	yes	yes
Pennsylvania 2	80.0	1.2	yes	yes	yes	yes	yes
Maryland 7	73.3	1.0	yes	yes	yes	yes	yes
Michigan 13	71.1	3.1	yes	yes	yes	yes	yes
Michigan 1	70.7	2.1	yes	yes	yes	yes	yes
Illinois 2	70.3	7.4	yes	yes	yes	yes	yes
Illinois 7	66.9	4.7	yes	yes	yes	yes	yes
Georgia 5	65.0	1.1	no	no	yes	yes	yes
Ohio 21	62.3	1.0	yes	yes	yes	yes	yes
Tennessee 9	57.2	1.0	yes	yes	yes	yes	yes
New Jersey 10	54.8	13.8	no	no	no	yes	yes
Mississippi 2	53.7	1.1	no	no	yes	yes	yes
Missouri 1	51.5	1.0	yes	yes	yes	yes	yes
New York 6	50.3	9.4	no	no	yes	yes	yes
New York 16	48.5	37.9	yes	yes	yes	yes	yes
New York 11	47.1	38.0	yes	yes	yes	yes	yes
California 29	46.6	32.3	yes	yes	yes	yes	yes
Mississippi 4	45.2	1.0	no	no	no	no	no
Louisiana 2	44.5	3.5	no	no	no	no	yes
New York 18*	43.7	51.3	no	no	no	no	no
California 28	43.0	19.6	yes	yes	yes	yes	yes
S. Carolina 6	40.9	1.1	no	no	no	no	no
Texas 18	40.8	31.2	yes	yes	yes	yes	yes
N. Carolina 2	40.1	1.0	no	no	no	no	no
California 31	33.7	25.1	yes	yes	yes	yes	yes
California 8	26.5	6.5	yes	yes	yes	yes	yes
Indiana 1	24.2	8.2	yes	no	no	no	no
Missouri 5	22.9	2.8	yes	yes	yes	yes	yes
Connecticut 5	4.2	3.3	no	no	no	no	yes

Note: This list contains the 25 congressional districts with the highest percentage of black residents as of the 98th Congress. At the bottom of the list are four congressional districts that also elected black representatives.

*Elected a Hispanic congressperson in each of these years.

black to Congress in an urban district with a substantial Hispanic minority (i.e., California's 29th) in fact may guarantee defeat for black candidates in a district carved out of Deep South black-belt counties.[2] The easiest way to summarize the results in table 3.2 is to note that *black congresspersons are elected from black plurality districts in which combined black plus Hispanic population is above 50 percent.*

There is another important point that seems to hold for black congressional seats; namely, that once districts above 50 percent black elect a black they appear to continue to do so (see table 3.3).

Table 3.3
Permanency of Black Electoral Success in Districts That Have Elected a Black*

STATE	CONGRESSIONAL DISTRICT	PRINCIPAL CITY	FIRST YEAR A BLACK ELECTED
California	29th	Los Angeles	1962
	8th	Berkeley/Oakland	1970
	28th	Los Angeles	1972
	31st	Compton	1980
Illinois	1st	Chicago	1928
	7th	Chicago	1970
	2nd	Chicago	1980
Maryland	7th	Baltimore	1970
Michigan	13th	Detroit	1954
	1st	Detroit	1964
Mississippi	2nd	"delta district"	1986
Missouri	1st	St. Louis	1968
	5th	Kansas City	1982
New York	16th	Manhattan (Harlem)	1944
	12th	Brooklyn	1968
	11th	New York	1982
	6th	Queens	1986
Ohio	21st	Cleveland	1968
Pennsylvania	2nd	Philadelphia	1958
Tennessee	9th	Memphis	1974
Texas	18th	Houston	1972

*These are the congressional districts that have had continuous representation by a black since a black first was elected. Two congressional districts that have elected blacks have not done so continuously: (1) The Georgia 5th (principal city, Atlanta) first elected a black in 1972, but when Andrew Young resigned the seat in 1977, the seat went to a white, and a black was not elected again until 1986, and (2) the Indiana 1st (principal city, Gary) was served by a black representative for only one term, 1983–85.

HISPANIC CONGRESSIONAL SUCCESS

Hispanics are concentrated more highly in a handful of states than are blacks. In particular, the only two states with more than two million Hispanics, California and Texas, have over one-half (51.6 percent) of all Hispanics in the United States. Indeed, these states accounted for seven of the 10 Hispanic members of Congress elected in 1990. However, Hispanics are slightly less concentrated in large cities than are blacks; 24.8 percent of the Hispanic population is located in cities with more than 200,000 Hispanics, compared with only 29.5 percent of the black population in cities with more than 200,000 blacks. Hispanics within cities also are considerably less segregated than blacks, an important point to note when the system of representation is based on single-member districts.[3]

For Hispanics and blacks, cities with large minority populations tend to elect minority representatives, although the pattern is not quite so clear for Hispanics as for blacks. The two cities (New York and Los Angeles) with more than 500,000 Hispanics elect at least one Hispanic congressperson. However, only one of the two cities with between 400,000 and 499,999 Hispanics is represented by a Hispanic congressperson (San Antonio elected a Hispanic to office in 1990, but Chicago did not). Of the 10 Hispanic congresspersons, seven are from cities with over 100,000 Hispanics, including three from cities with over 500,000 Hispanics. The other three Hispanic members of Congress come from districts centered on cities that have less than 100,000 Hispanics but that are majority Hispanic cities: Laredo, Texas; McAllen, Texas; and Santa Fe, New Mexico.

Hispanic Population Proportions and Hispanic Congressional Success

We show in table 3.4 the percent Hispanic and percent black in the 15 congressional districts with the highest Hispanic population proportions, and the electoral success (or absence thereof) of Hispanic candidates in these districts. There were 10 Hispanic members of Congress in 1990, 2.3 percent of the House, compared with a 1980 United States Hispanic population of 6.4 percent.

As table 3.4 indicates, Hispanics generally are not elected to Congress from districts that are less than 64 percent combined minority except in California and New Mexico. Excluding the California 34th and the New Mexico 3rd, however, it appears that a clear Hispanic majority and a combined minority population greater than 55 percent provides a substantial probability of Hispanic congressional success. To achieve certainty, a 60 percent Hispanic population and a combined minority population near 70 percent appears necessary. These percentages may not need to be as high in California or New Mexico, however.

There are several reasons that the percentages necessary to elect a Hispanic congressperson are higher than the percentages needed to elect a black congressperson. One of the primary reasons is that a much higher proportion of the Hispanic population is noncitizen than is the case for the black population. Therefore a district that is, for example, 60 percent Hispanic in total population may not be 50 percent Hispanic in eligible voters.[4]

As with blacks, once a district with significant minority population elects a Hispanic member of Congress, it continues to do so (only the New Mexico 1st, which first elected a Hispanic in 1968, failed to re-elect a Hispanic in 1990). Also, for Hispanics as for blacks, the principal difference between the 1970s and the 1980s was not in the percentage of minority population needed for

Table 3.4
Hispanic and Black Congressional Districts and Hispanic Congressional
Representation in the 1980s*

DISTRICT	1982 POPULATION (in percent) HISPANIC	BLACK	HISPANIC ELECTED 1982	1984	1986	1988	1990
Texas 15	71.7	1.0	yes	yes	yes	yes	yes
California 25	63.6	9.6	yes	yes	yes	yes	yes
Texas 20	61.7	8.8	yes	yes	yes	yes	yes
Texas 27	61.5	2.7	yes	yes	yes	yes	yes
Texas 16	60.2	3.6	no	no	no	no	no
California 30	54.2	1.1	yes	yes	yes	yes	yes
Texas 23	53.1	4.1	no	yes	yes	yes	yes
New York 18	51.3	43.7	yes	yes	yes	yes	yes
Florida 18	50.7	15.8	no	no	no	no	yes
California 34	47.6	2.3	yes	yes	yes	yes	yes
New Mexico 3	39.0	1.0	yes	yes	yes	yes	yes
New York 11*	38.0	47.1	no	no	no	no	no
New York 16*	37.9	48.5	no	no	no	no	no
New Mexico 1	37.4	2.3	yes	yes	yes	no	no
Arizona 2	35.5	5.6	no	no	no	yes	no

Note: This list contains the 15 congressional districts with the highest percentage of Hispanic residents
    as of the 98th Congress. There are no Hispanic representatives other than those representing
    districts listed above.

*Represented by a black congressman.

Hispanic victory but in the number of districts in which such a percentage could
be found (these data are not shown).

CONCLUSIONS

We have shown how a black plurality and a combined minority population
just barely above 50 percent are sufficient to create a congressional district in
which a black candidate has a realistic opportunity to be elected to Congress
and how a 65 percent district creates a virtual certainty of black success.

Except in a few states, such as California and New Mexico, congressional
districts with a clear Hispanic plurality and a combined minority population
greater than 55 percent are needed to offer a Hispanic candidate a realistic
opportunity to be elected. A district with a 60 percent Hispanic population and
a combined minority population close to 70 percent creates a virtual certainty
of Hispanic success (except perhaps in areas where a very high proportion of
Hispanics are noncitizens).

Using 1980 population figures, we see that the congressional representation
of Hispanics and blacks relative to their populations is quite comparable. Hispanics have a congressional representation of 2.3 percent, compared with a

population of 6.4 percent, for a representation/population ratio of .36 (2.3/6.4). The ratio for blacks is .50 (5.7/11.5). The difference in representation ratios for blacks and Hispanics essentially vanishes when we take into account the Hispanic noncitizen or the nonvoting-age population. However, the ratio of each is less than half of what the population strength would suggest because many minorities are dispersed in rural areas and smaller cities.[5] As noted earlier, single-member districts generally will not provide congressional representation proportional to minority population.

Black and Hispanic congressional representation has been a matter of widespread concern. We believe we have demonstrated the importance of urban concentration in accounting for the relative success rates of blacks in the South as compared with the non-South and of Hispanics as compared with blacks.

NOTES

This chapter is an updated version of our earlier article—"Minority Population Proportion and Black and Hispanic Congressional Success in the 1970s and 1980s"—which was published in the *American Politics Quarterly*, October 1989, pp. 436–45. This research was partially supported by National Science Foundation Grant 85–063–76, Program in Political Science.

1. For a further discussion of these points and of the mathematics underlying the "65 percent rule," see Kimball Brace, Bernard Grofman, Lisa Handley, and Richard Niemi, "Minority Voting Equality: The Sixty-Five Percent Rule in Theory and Practice," *Law and Policy*, January 1988, pp. 43–62.

2. There is no single "magic number" of minorities that is appropriate to all times, places, and types of elections. For a more detailed discussion of this point, see ibid. and Bernard Grofman, Michael Migalski, and Nicholas Noviello, "Effects of Multimember Districts on Black Representation in State Legislatures," *Review of Black Political Economy*, Spring 1986, pp. 65–78.

3. Black residential segregation in most urban areas is quite stark. See Carl E. Tubner, Annemette Sorensen, and Leslie J. Hillingsworth, Jr., "Indexes of Racial Segregation for 109 Cities in the United States, 1940 to 1970," *Sociological Focus*, vol. 17, 1984, pp. 328–35.

4. Not only are there differences in citizenship rates, but there are also important differences in the age structure of Hispanics, blacks, and Anglos. In 1980, 35.5 percent of the Hispanic population was below the age of 18, compared with 36.0 percent of the black population and 26.6 percent of the white population.

5. However, as noted above, representation for minorities in single-member district systems can not be expected to be proportional to population strength in any case.

4

Anglo and Minority Women's Underrepresentation in Congress: Is the Electoral System the Culprit?

Wilma Rule and Pippa Norris

Is the single-member district electoral system largely responsible for limiting women's opportunity to serve in the Congress? The answer is yes. The major culprit for women's underrepresentation is the electoral system, but there are other important political and social causes working in combination with the system. These include the constitutional separation of Congress and the presidency, the political party system, the high rates of incumbency, the cost of campaigns, and unfavorable state environments with low percentages of women state legislators. These factors constitute a system of barriers that explains why women's proportion in Congress is among the world's lowest. Since there are only two Anglo and no minority women in the Senate, this chapter focuses on recruitment to the House of Representatives. We conclude the chapter with suggestions for removing barriers and promoting Anglo and minority women's congressional representation.

HOW DOES WOMEN'S REPRESENTATION COMPARE WITH MEN'S?

Table 4.1 shows Anglo and minority women's and men's proportions in the House compared with their population percentages. Anglo women were 6 percent of the House members in 1989, whereas black, Hispanic, and Asian women comprised less than 1 percent.

Anglo men, who are about 40 percent of the population, held 86 percent of the House seats in 1989. Black men are close to representation/population parity at .94, and Latino men with a rating of .56, hold only about one-half of the seats one would anticipate based on their percentage of the nation's population. Women have miniscule representation/population ratios: Anglos with .15, fol-

Table 4.1
Anglo and Minority Members, United States House of Representatives, 1989
(N = 435)

	ESTIMATED POPULATION PERCENT	NUMBER IN HOUSE	PERCENT IN HOUSE	REPRESENTATION/ POPULATION RATIO
Anglo Women	41.17	26	6.0	.15
Black Women	6.20	1	.2	.03
Hispanic Women	3.73	1	.2	.05
Asian Women	N/A	1	.2	N/A
Anglo Men	39.52	372	85.5	2.16
Black Men	5.64	23	5.3	.94
Hispanic Men	3.73	9	2.1	.55
Asian Men	N/A	2	.2	N/A

Note: The Anglo women category includes four elected in special elections in 1989. The Anglo men category includes one Hawaiian representative. No Asian population data were available for 1989. Population percents in the table above omit Asians and do not sum to 100 because of rounding.

Sources: Center for the American Woman and Politics, Eagleton Institute, Rutgers University; Joint Center for Political Studies; National Association of Latino Elected and Appointed Officials; and United States Bureau of the Census, *Statistical Abstract of the United States, 1990* (Washington, D.C.: United States Government Printing Office, 1990), pp. 14, 16.

lowed by one Hispanic and one black woman with .05 and .03, respectively. In 1990, two additional black women were elected to the House of Representatives, increasing black women's representation/population ratio to .11, or about one-tenth of parity.

HOW DOES THE UNITED STATES COMPARE WITH OTHER COUNTRIES?

Figure 4.1 gives the percent of women elected to 25 lower houses of parliament between 1985 and 1987. Japan had the smallest proportion of women in its lower house—slightly more than 1 percent. The members are chosen by an electoral arrangement that is similar to the single-member district system in the United States. Candidates run and raise campaign funds as individuals and not as a political party team. In Japan's 1989 elections, women's proportion in the lower house remained the same, but the percentage of women in the upper house rose

Figure 4.1
Percentage of Women in Parliament in 25 Democracies, 1985–87

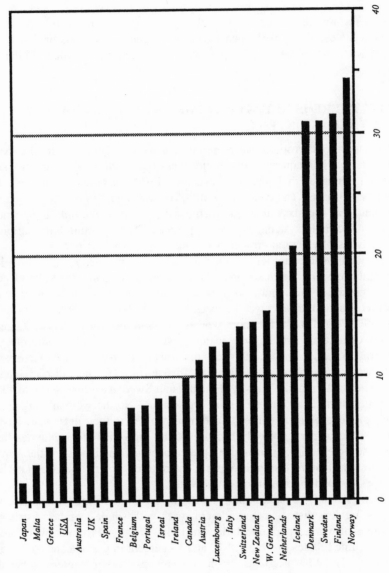

Source: International Centre for Parliamentary Documentation, *Distribution of Seats between Men and Women in National Assemblies* (Geneva, Switzerland: 1987).

to 13 percent, compared with the 2 percent women in the United States Senate. Japan's upper house members are elected by the party list/proportional representation (PL/PR) system described in a subsequent section.[1]

Second lowest in women's members of parliament was Malta, followed by Greece. The United States was the fourth lowest. Austria, Italy, and Luxembourg are in the middle of the chart, with double the percentage of women in the United States. Those parliaments with the largest proportions of women representatives—31 percent to 34 percent—are Denmark, Sweden, Finland, and Norway.

WHY THERE IS GREATER WOMEN'S REPRESENTATION IN OTHER COUNTRIES

The party list/proportional representation system generally results in higher women's parliamentary representation than the single-member district system. Fifteen countries in figure 4.1 have the PL/PR system, and six have single-member districts. The countries with PL/PR average 17 percent women in parliament, and the six with single-member districts average only 8 percent. Germany mixes both systems and has 15 percent. The remaining three nations have other types of electoral arrangements and average only 4 percent.

In the PL/PR countries, women are added to the party list to broaden the general appeal of the ticket and to give them the opportunity to be elected. In these countries the number of representatives elected per district, that is, the district magnitude, averages between two and 13. Generally, the more representatives per district, the more women are nominated and elected. Greece has a low district magnitude, with many constituencies that elect only one or two persons to parliament, and this low magnitude is a major reason Greece has so few women members of parliament. In contrast, the high district magnitude countries of Denmark, Norway, Finland, and Sweden average seven to 13 members per district, and about a third are women. Nordic women's organizations have prodded political parties to add more women to their lists. They have been successful, in part, not only because of the high district magnitudes but also because voters may express their preference for candidates on the list.[2] This preferential feature results in more women voters for the party's slate and increases the party's proportion of the votes.

New Zealand, Canada, France, Australia, the United Kingdom, and the United States are low district magnitude countries with single-member districts. Proportions of women parliamentarians in 1985–87 ranged from a low of 5 percent in the United States to a high of 10 and 14 percent in Canada and New Zealand, respectively. What accounts for the differences among single-member district countries? All but the United States have the parliamentary system of government and unified political parties. Responding to women's groups, several parties in the parliamentary countries have adopted effective plans to nominate and support more women for winnable parliamentary seats. In contrast, America's division of government among the president, Congress, and the states has resulted in fragmented political recruitment groups organized around particular offices.[3] Consequently, there are no unified national party organizations to require and support local parties' recruitment of women to Congress.

Other important factors for women's recruitment to national legislatures include lack of right-wing party dominance, large proportions of women working outside the home, many women professionals and college graduates, a healthy economy, and no dominant religion. The countries with lower proportions of women in figure 4.1 have several of these unfavorable factors that constrain women's parliamentary recruitment. Although most of these contextual variables are favorable in the United States, other political obstacles remain.

CONGRESSIONAL INCUMBENCY AND WOMEN'S POLITICAL OPPORTUNITY

In 1842, Congress mandated the single-member district system of elections for the House of Representatives.[4] Previously, multimember districts and high turnover were common, with first-termers constituting about 50 percent of each new House.[5] Incumbency increased with time, and the number of open seats declined. By 1988, only 6 percent of the mostly Anglo male incumbents declined to run or died in office. Of those remaining, 98 percent were reelected. The number of women has been increasing very slowly under these near static conditions (see table 4.2).

Factors greatly facilitating incumbents' chances for reelection include the perquisites of office—estimated as worth some $1,000,000 each term.[6] Free (franked) mail to constituents, unlimited free telephone calls, and free travel to their districts enable members to campaign informally between elections. They also receive large contributions when the formal campaign for reelection begins and thereafter. In addition, the electorate's low partisanship in voting when the candidate is an incumbent favors incumbents. A simulation of House elections based on present incumbency predicts a decrease of men members to 87 percent by the year 2020, with women's representation increasing to 13 percent.[7]

Another reason for women's underrepresentation is that few run for the extremely small number of open seats. In the 1984 primary election for the House with 24 open seats, there were only 15 women candidates, compared with 130 men contestants. Four women were successful in the primaries, and only one was elected.[8] By 1990, there were 30 open seats, and four women were elected. This slight improvement was not large enough to help women's representation in the House, since the four elected simply replaced four others who had declined to run in 1990.[9] Why don't more women enter open races? One very important reason is the enormous amount of money they must raise to win.

Table 4.2
Incumbency and Women's Election to United States House Seats, Presidential Election Years, 1976–88 (N = 435)

	1972	1976	1980	1984	1988
Number of Incumbents Retiring or Deceased	45	51	37	24	26
Percent Open Seats	10.3	11.7	8.5	5.5	6.0
Number of Incumbent Candidates	390	384	398	411	409
Number of Incumbents Defeated	25	16	37	19	7
Percent Reelected	94	96	91	95	98
Number of Women Elected	16	18	19	22	25
Percent of Women in House	3.7	4.1	4.4	5.1	5.8

Note: The open seats in midterm elections were 44 in 1974, 53 in 1978, 42 in 1982, and 41 in 1986. The percentage of incumbents elected in the following midterm years was 1974, 88%; 1978, 94%; 1982, 90%; and 1986, 98%.

Sources: United States Bureau of the Census, *Statistical Abstract of the United States, 1990* (Washington, D.C.: United States Government Printing Office, 1990), p. 257, and Center for the American Woman and Politics, Eagleton Institute, Rutgers University.

MONEY AS A BARRIER TO WOMEN'S ELECTION

Although there are exceptions, House candidates with the most money generally win.[10] In 1982, successful women candidates spent $228,387 on their campaigns. Three elections later, the amount had more than doubled to $510,000.[11]

The experience of one unsuccessful woman candidate in the 1990 campaign illustrates the role of money in a House campaign. Dissatisfied with the incumbent's lack of attentiveness to the issues she believed important—including education and environment—she decided to challenge him for the seat. The House district sprawled from urban areas in the Sacramento Valley to the sparsely populated mountain counties on California's eastern boundary. Although lacking in legislative experience, the former teacher was an articulate and energetic candidate. She related the following to one of the authors:

Early on I met some influential people in Stockton [valley city where the opponent held a commanding lead] and they asked me if I could raise $1,200,000 for the campaign. That was all they were interested in. . . . I went to Washington and talked with the Democratic party and women's groups and they said I had to raise the money to win. They would supply staff and tell me how to run the campaign. But as I went around the

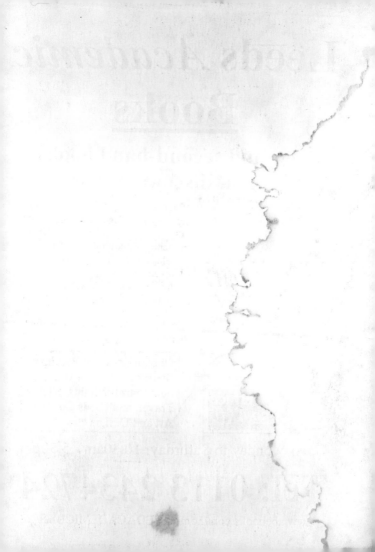

district I found that people felt powerless with the present way campaigns were run. I decided I'd be spending my time raising money to support a professional staff, and I didn't want to do that. Instead, I'd run an all-volunteer, grass roots campaign.[12]

This Democratic party candidate was fortunate in having the incumbent drop out of the race, leaving the seat open. However, an articulate and energetic conservative Republican state senator announced his candidacy. He received over a third of his funds from automobile, retailers, timber, and other commercial and industrial political action committees (PACs) and the remainder from the Republican party and individual contributors. With a total of $500,000, he won a close election, despite his woman opponent's 2,000 enthusiastic volunteers and $200,000 in mostly individual contributions.[13]

About 10 percent of candidates' funds come from the national Republican and Democratic parties, 55 percent from affluent individual contributors inside and outside the district, and the remainder from political action committees. In 1987–88, the Democratic Congressional Committee gave $12.5 million to individual candidates while the Republican counterparts dispensed $33.6 million.[14] But PAC contributions were eight times that of the Democrats' and three times greater than the Republicans'.

Table 4.3 reveals that in 1987–88, $82 million (80 percent) of the $102.3 million raised by PACs went to incumbents. Corporate PACs gave 90 percent of their funds in that year to incumbents; trade PACs donated 87 percent; and labor and others gave 67 percent. The major PAC spending for incumbents, the minor spending by national parties, and the fierce competition for the few open seats make House elections difficult for challengers to win.

Successful women candidates cite raising funds as the major problem of their campaigns.[15] Women especially are handicapped in this task by fewer business and/or professional connections with potential contributors. Although campaign workers sometimes help women make up for this void, money is still essential for television and other advertising.

A change in the federal ethics law may result in more open seats in the 1990s, according to the chair of the Democratic Congressional Committee.[16] After 1992, House incumbents may no longer keep excess campaign funds for personal use, and this change may encourage a number of members to retire. Yet the problem of campaign funding for women challengers and those running in open-seat races will remain.

Emily's List, the National Women's Political Caucus, the National Organization of Women-PAC, the National Abortion Rights League-PAC, and the Women's Campaign Fund are among the women's organizations partially funding women's campaigns, but their money is limited. These organizations, as well as individuals and other PACs, will give funds to candidates who have a good chance of winning—especially women with state legislative or other elective office experience.

Table 4.3
Political Action Committees' Funding of House Candidates, 1983–84, 1987–88 (in Millions of Dollars)

TYPE OF COMMITTEE	TOTAL AMOUNT GIVEN	INCUMBENTS	CHALLENGERS	OPEN SEATS
	1983–84			
All PACs Total	75.5	57	11	7
Corporate	23.4	19	3	2
Trade/Membership/Health	20.4	16	2	2
Labor	19.8	14	4	2
Other	9.1	5	3	1
	1987–88			
All PACs Total	102.3	82	10	10
Corporate	33.5	30	1	2
Trade/Membership/Health	28.6	25	2	2
Labor	26.9	18	5	3
Other	13.3	9	2	2

Note: The table includes amounts given to candidates in elections during the two-year periods. Breakdowns for amounts given to incumbents, challengers, and open-seat candidates may not agree with totals because of rounding. Categories for 1987–88 have been combined.

Source: United States Bureau of the Census, *Statistical Abstract of the United States, 1990* (Washington, D.C.: United States Government Printing Office, 1990), p. 269.

FEW WOMEN ON THE RECRUITMENT LADDERS TO CONGRESS

In 1984, only 10 of the 22 women members of the House of Representatives had held elective office before being elected to the House.[17] Six declined to run again between 1984 and 1989 for various reasons and were replaced by 13 other women. The new members included 10 with elective office experience: four state senators, three state assembly members, one assistant secretary of the state of New York, one former member of the United States House, and one member of a city council—77 percent of the total newcomers. This extraordinary cohort of women outdistances the average group of House members, which has about 55 percent former elective officeholders.

Table 4.4
Population Proportions and Ethnic and Gender Representation in the 50 State Senates, 1989

	ESTIMATED PERCENT OF POPULATION	NUMBER OF STATE SENATORS	PERCENT OF STATE SENATORS
Hispanic Women	3.7	5	.2
Hispanic Men	3.7	36	2.0
Black Women	6.2	18	1.0
Black Men	5.6	74	3.7
Anglo Women	41.2	243	12.2
Anglo Men	39.5	1,619	81.0
TOTALS	99.9*	1,995	100.1*

*Does not total 100% because of rounding.

Note: Anglo figures were computed from the total number of women and men legislators minus the numbers of Hispanic and black legislators. The number of Asian and Pacific state senators was not available.

Sources: The National Association of Latino Elected and Appointed Officials, the Joint Center for Political Studies; Center for the American Woman and Politics, Eagleton Institute, Rutgers University; and the United States Bureau of the Census, *Statistical Abstract of the United States, 1990* (Washington, D.C.: United States Government Printing Office, 1990), pp. 14, 16.

Some readers may be thinking that the answer to women's underrepresentation in the House is simple: recruit more women candidates who are state legislators and other officeholders. However, there are four times as many men as women in elective office. In state assemblies, women representatives were 18 percent in 1989, but in state senates—the most House recruitment–relevant office—their proportion was only 13 percent, including 1 percent minority women (see table 4.4). The 87 percent male senators were mostly Anglos with about 6 percent minority men.

Twenty-one of the 29 women members (72 percent) of the House in 1989 were elected from states with higher proportions of women in the state senates or assemblies. Eight came from states with lower averages of women state legislators. Why are some states favorable and others unfavorable for the election of women?

The three main reasons for women's low state legislative representation are (1) unfavorable state electoral framework, (2) state or local Democratic party dominance and lack of party competition, and (3) unfavorable state socioeconomic context.

The 35 single-member district states in 1989 averaged 12.4 percent women in their state legislatures, whereas the 15 states with multimember districts averaged about 21.8 percent. Thus, single-member districts are a major spoiler of women's state legislative opportunity and eventual congressional chances for election. The same problems—including greater incumbency and costly legislative campaigns in highly populated states—generally prevail within single-member district states as well as at the federal level.

Black and Anglo women are favored in states with multimember legislative districts, and this finding probably applies to other minority women. When voters have two or more representatives to choose, more women run and are elected. However, African-American, Hispanic, and Anglo men are favored when there are single-member districts. But minority men also do well when there is an ethnic majority of voters in districts with two or more state representatives (refer to Conway's and Saint-Germain's chapters on state legislatures in this volume).

Minority candidates as well as Anglo women also are disadvantaged by runoff primaries requiring a majority vote for winning. A single plurality primary would afford them an opportunity to compete in the general elections. Small legislatures also deny minorities election opportunity, since there is less possibility for minority districts if there are fewer seats. This situation also applies to city councils in large cities (see table 13.4 in Welch and Herrick's chapter in this volume).

The single-member district electoral system is the main cause of our two-party system, which, in turn, limits women's options for candidacy support. Lack of party backing is an important reason women are not candidates for state legislatures.[18] The Democratic party has in the past been unfavorable to women's state legislative recruitment. The zero-order correlation between women in state legislatures and Democratic party dominant legislatures was − .40 [p.01] in all states and − .39 [p.01] in the northern states in 1984.[19] Competitive or Republican-dominated states have in the past been best for women's election to state legislatures.

States with fewer African-American and Anglo women college graduates and professionals and fewer women in the work force are unfavorable environments for women state legislators. In these states, women's organizations that markedly contribute to women's state legislative recruitment, such as the National Organization for Women, are fewer in number relative to the states' populations (refer to tables 5.3 and 5.5 in Rule's chapter on state legislatures).

SUMMARY AND CONCLUSIONS

The single-member district electoral system is a major cause of women's low representation in the House of Representatives and in the state legislatures, which are the recruitment ladders to the House. Among 25 Western democracies, the United States is the fourth lowest in women's representation—only 6.6 percent of the House in 1990.

Most favorable for women is the party list/proportional representation system with seven or more representatives per district and a preference arrangement for voters. In parliamentary countries with the PL/PR electoral system—as well as in those with the single-member districts—unified parties prodded by women's groups have successfully promoted women's national legislative recruitment. With the PL/PR system, women run as part of a team, with expenses covered by the party. In the United States, women candidates scramble to raise the enormous amounts of money needed to challenge incumbents or to contest for the nearly nonexistent open seats in the House.

Experience in elective office, particularly in state legislatures, is nearly essential for election to the House. But women are only 17 percent of state legislators. In states with multimember legislative districts, women's proportions are almost double that in states with single-member districts. Women are more apt to run and be elected when voters have two or more representatives to choose. Black, Hispanic, and white men are favored in single-member districts, but minority men also do well in multimember districts with an ethnic majority. Other favorable electoral arrangements for women and minorities include the single primary and larger state legislatures.

The Democratic party—North as well as South—has been a negative factor associated with fewer women in state legislatures. Competitive or Republican parties have facilitated women's recruitment. Important contextual factors include more women college graduates and professionals, more women in the work force, and strong women's organizations. More than 70 percent of House members in 1989 were elected in states that have higher percentages of women legislators. Clearly this link to the House is of critical importance for increased women's congressional representation.

Nondiscriminatory alternatives for changing states' single-member district systems for electing House members, as well as suggestions for other reforms, are given below.

• *Enact a congressional law permitting states to adopt new electoral arrangements consistent with the 1982 amendments to the Voting Rights Act.* Among the alternatives are the following: (1) Combining districts in majority black, Hispanic, or white areas to elect two or more representatives. Legislative districts in Maryland and Arizona are designed this way (see Conway's and Saint-Germain's chapters in this volume). (2) Adopting the single-transferable vote, the cumulative vote, or the party list/proportional representation systems. These nondiscriminatory multimember systems provide minorities and Anglos representation equal to their voting strength. (Refer to Zimmerman's chapter in this volume.) All have been used in the United States except the PL/PR system, which some localities nevertheless might find suitable. PL/PR flexible systems allow the voter to choose particular candidates on the list or to vote a straight party ticket.[20] The more members elected per multimember district, the smaller the proportion of votes needed to elect newcomers and defeat incumbents. Besides increasing turnover, these alternative systems allow more voters to see their candidates elected (see Still's chapter in this book). They also could lessen voter alienation and increase voter participation. Significantly, these systems do not depend on residential segregation to give minorities representation in the United States House.

- *Amend the Voting Rights Act to prohibit denial of the voting rights of women, just as minorities are now protected.* This proposed amendment might be an important step in facilitating the adoption of electoral systems that favor both minority and nonminority women and men.

- *Require disproportionate political party recruitment, support, and funding for women United States Senate and House candidates, state legislature candidates, and candidates for other major elective offices in the states.*[21] This proposal includes providing incentives for local parties promoting women's candidacies, setting a timetable for increases in women's representation until equal representation is obtained, and increasing national parties' fund-raising capabilities.

- *Limit perquisites for members of Congress, and reform campaign finance.* "Perks" enabling incumbents to campaign informally between elections could be disallowed. They amount to continuous public financing of incumbents' reelection, whereas no such public funds are available to challengers or those who run for open seats. A voluntary checkoff on the income tax form for funding House campaigns is one solution. Money from contributors might be severely limited to incumbents and partially limited to challengers. PAC money should continue, since educational, environmental, labor, and women's committee funds are often critical for women's decision to run and conduct successful campaigns. The possibility of public funding of television time for congressional candidates also might be explored.

Two other reforms merit consideration. The first is expanding the size of the United States House by 40 or 50 members after the 1990 census and every 10 years thereafter to keep pace with population growth.[22] (The United Kingdom's Parliament has 650 members and Germany's 519.) A simple statute could institute this reform. A second reform is limiting terms of United States House members and state legislators.

In 1990, California and Oklahoma voters limited the number of terms that state legislators may serve, and Colorado voters limited the tenure of members of the United States House from that state to 12 years. Whether these ceilings violate provisions of the Voting Rights Act, whether only Congress may enact such a law, or whether a constitutional amendment is required are important questions raised by these initiative actions. The California Supreme Court in 1991, however, upheld the state legislative term limitations, and its decision was confirmed by the United States Supreme Court in 1992.[23]

The last reform, if upheld in the courts, would result in the loss of many knowledgeable members of the House. However, it would also create more open seats, as would the increase in the size of the House. These measures could move the United States toward equal representation for white and minority women. The process could be hastened if the two political parties are dedicated to this objective and if other steps are taken along the lines set forth above.

NOTES

The author thanks Pat Ament, Erik Herzik, Irving Krauss, and Kay Larson for contributions to this chapter.

1. Theodore McNelly, "The 1989 House of Councillors Election in Japan," paper presented at the 1989 annual meeting of the American Political Science Association, Atlanta, August 31–September 3, 1989. Australia and Germany, with mixed single-member and multimember systems, elect four times as many women to parliament under the latter system (Wilma Rule, "Electoral Systems, Contextual Factors, and Women's Opportunity for Election to Parliament in Twenty-Three Democracies," *Western Political Quarterly*, September 1987, pp. 477–98). Also see Pippa Norris, "Women's Legislative Participation in Western Europe," *Western European Politics*, October 1985, pp. 90–101.

2. Matthew Soberg Shugart, "Minorities Represented and Unrepresented," unpublished manuscript, 1990, available from Wilma Rule.

3. Joseph A. Schlesinger, "The New American Political Party," *American Political Science Review*, December 1985, pp. 864–67.

4. 5 U.S. Stat. 491 (single-member districting statute, 1842).

5. Gary Jacobson, *Money in Congressional Elections* (New Haven: Yale University Press, 1980), p. 2.

6. Bruce Cain, John Ferejohn, and Morris Fiorina, *The Personal Vote* (Cambridge: Harvard University Press, 1987), p. 174.

7. Kristi Anderson and Stuart Thorson, "Congressional Turnover and the Election of Women," *Western Political Quarterly*, March 1984, pp. 143–56.

8. Barbara C. Burrell, "The Political Opportunity of Women Candidates for the U.S. House of Representatives," *Women and Politics* 8, no. 1, 1988, pp. 51–68.

9. Wilma Rule's telephone interview with the National Women's Political Caucus, November 31, 1990. See also "The 1990 Elections, Congress," *New York Times*, November 8, 1990, pp. 16–17.

10. Jacobson, *Money in Congressional Elections*.

11. Michael Barone and Grant Ujifusa, *The Almanac of American Politics, 1984* (Chicago: R. R. Donnely and Sons, 1983).

12. Wilma Rule's telephone interview with Patricia Malberg, candidate for California's 14th district seat, October 30, 1990. For Representative Louise Slaughter's campaign, see Linda L. Fowler and Robert D. McClure, *Political Ambition* (New Haven: Yale University Press, 1989), pp. 204–17.

13. Wilma Rule's telephone interview with Dave Bauer, treasurer for the John Doolittle Campaign Committee, November 14, 1990.

14. United States Bureau of the Census, *Statistical Abstract of the United States, 1990* (Washington, D.C.: United States Government Printing Office, 1990), p. 266.

15. Susan J. Carroll, *Women as Candidates in American Politics* (Bloomington: University of Indiana Press, 1985), pp. 49–51.

16. "Fazio to Gain Clout as Chief Fund-Raiser," *Sacramento Bee*, November 14, 1990, p. A1.

17. Wilma Rule, "How and Why Do Women and Men's Congressional Recruitment Patterns Differ and What Is the Significance of This Difference, If Any?" paper presented at the annual meeting of the Western Political Science Association, Anaheim, California, March 26–28, 1987.

18. Carroll, *Women as Candidates*, pp. 55–56.

19. Wilma Rule, "Why More Women Are State Legislators," *Western Political Quarterly*, June 1990, p. 442.

20. R. S. Katz, "Intraparty Preference Voting," in Bernard Grofman and Arend

Lijphart, eds., *Electoral Laws and Their Political Consequences* (New York: Agathon Press, 1986), pp. 99–100.

21. See, e.g., Joni Lovenduski and Pippa Norris, "Party Rules and Women's Representation: Reforming the British Labour Party," paper presented at the annual meeting of the American Political Science Association, San Francisco, California, August 30–September 2, 1990.

22. Charles A. Kromkowski, "Why 435?: Rediscovering the Democratic Principle," unpublished manuscript, 1990, available from Kromkowski at the Woodrow Wilson Department of Government and Foreign Affairs, University of Virginia, Charlottesville, VA 22901.

23. *Legislature of the State of California et al. v. March Fong Eu, as Secretary of State et al.* 91 *Daily Journal* D.A.R. 12510 (legislative term and spending limits).

PART III

ELECTING STATE LEGISLATORS AND JUDGES

5

Multimember Legislative Districts: Minority and Anglo Women's and Men's Recruitment Opportunity

Wilma Rule

Electoral systems are of critical importance in democratic countries. They set the framework within which political parties and other political recruitment groups operate and in which voters choose.[1] Particular histories, cultures, and economies in each state influence the adoption and change of electoral systems and rules.

We examine the recruitment opportunity for election to state legislatures which is provided or denied by multimember electoral systems and other contextual factors. In addition to their state governance role, state legislatures are important because they provide experienced candidates for the United States Congress. Our focus is on African-Americans and Latinos—as well as Anglo women and men—and their state legislative inclusion or exclusion.

States' electoral systems may affect blacks, Latinos, and Anglo women and men differently. Hence, we ask: What changes might provide a win-win situation for all, rather than a zero-sum one in which one gender or ethnic group loses and another wins seats in the state legislature?

This chapter reviews previous research, examines direct representation of minority and Anglo men and women in state legislatures, sets forth the data and methods used, and analyzes the impact of multimember legislative systems on African-Americans, Latinos, and Anglos.

INVISIBLE MINORITY WOMEN IN PREVIOUS RESEARCH

Most scholars of electoral systems and minorities have grouped together black men and women and Latino women and men.[2] Similarly, most research on the impact of electoral systems on women's recruitment investigated minority and Anglo women as one group. Consequently, black and Latino women were "invisible'' in studies of the impact of electoral systems on recruitment opportunities. Research on blacks found they were denied legislative recruitment opportunity in multimember legislative districts but not in single-member districts in some states.[3] However, the opposite was found for all women whose legislative recruitment was consistently greater in states (and nations) with multimember legislative districts.[4]

Hispanic women's political recruitment opportunity has received minimal attention. However, Welch and Herrick report in this volume that the at-large election systems in municipalities provide Latino women more political recruitment opportunity. With the exception of Pritchard's and Saint-Germain's studies in this volume, there has been no previous research on the impact of electoral systems on Latinos' state legislative recruitment.

MINORITY AND ANGLO WOMEN'S LEGISLATIVE RECRUITMENT

Relative to their population and compared with their male counterparts, African-American, Hispanic, and Anglo women lack equal recruitment opportunity to state legislatures. They compose over 50 percent of their respective groups. In 1984, black women constituted approximately 6.4 percent and Latino women about 3.6 percent, compared with Anglo women who constituted about 41 percent of the nation's population (see table 5.1).[5] Yet Anglo women were only 11 percent of state legislators in 1984, whereas Anglo men constituted over 82 percent. Less than 1 percent of state legislators were black women in 1985, compared with about 4 percent black men. Latino women were one tenth of one percent of the nation's legislators, whereas Hispanic men constituted 1 percent in 1984.

By 1989, the proportions of minority and Anglo women legislators had increased, and the ratio of men to women was much lower. Comparison of women and men's nationwide legislative representation/population ratios (percent in legislature divided by population percent) reveals the following: Anglo men, 1.87; black men, .67; Hispanic men, .42; Anglo women, .36; black women, .19; and Hispanic women, .05. Thus, women were still very far from having equal legislative recruitment opportunity, as their national representation/population figures show.

DATA AND METHODS

Most socioeconomic data for this research were derived from the 1980 United States Census of Population, since more recent detailed census information was not available. Consequently, this chapter employs the 1984–85 proportions of women and men legislators for each state.[6] The 1989 recruitment data are used where appropriate to compare with the findings for 1984–85.

In 1982, four states—Arkansas, Florida, Hawaii, and Illinois—changed from

Table 5.1

Change in Minority and Anglo Men's and Women's Legislative Representation in the 50 States, 1984, 1985, and 1989

	1984 Population Percent	1984 Number	1984 Percent	1985 Number	1985 Percent	1989 Number	1989 Percent
Hispanic men	3.57	100	1.0	–	–	112	1.5
Hispanic women	3.60	7	0.1	–	–	16	.2
Black* men	5.71	–	–	312	4.20	284	3.8
Black women	6.35	–	–	72	0.97	88	1.2
Anglo** men	39.32	6,117	82.3	–	–	5,795	77.7
Anglo women	41.45	820	11.0	–	–	1,166	15.6

RATIO CHANGES 1984–89:

Hispanic men to Hispanic women legislators: from 14.3:1 to 7:1
Black men to black women legislators: from 4.3:1 to 3.2:1
Anglo men to Anglo women legislators: from 7.5:1 to 4.9:1

Note: — indicates that data were not available.

*Most changes in black representation 1985–89 are the result of *two subsequent elections*—1986 and 1988. However, most changes in Hispanic and Anglo representation in 1984–89 occurred in *three subsequent elections*—1984, 1986, and 1988.

**Anglo figures were computed from the total number of women and men legislators, minus the numbers of Hispanic and black legislators. The number of legislators increased from 7,438 in 1984 to 7,461 in 1989.

Sources: The National Association of Latino Elected and Appointed Officials, the Joint Center for Political Studies, the Eagleton Institute of Rutgers University, *The Book of the States, 1983–84* (Lexington, Kentucky: Council of State Governments, 1983), and United States Bureau of the Census, *Statistical Abstract of the United States: 1986* (Washington, D.C.: United States Government Printing Office, 1986), pp. 26, 32.

multimember districts (MMD) to single-member districts (SMD) for their assemblies, and Virginia made a similar change in 1984.[7] Florida, Hawaii, South Carolina, and South Dakota switched their Senates from MMD to SMD in 1982, with Virginia following suit in 1984. The remaining 15 multimember states are Alaska, Arizona, Georgia, Idaho, Indiana, Maryland, New Hampshire, New Jersey, North Carolina, North Dakota, South Dakota, Vermont, Washington, West Virginia, and Wyoming.

To determine important factors for women's and men's legislative recruitment, we used stepwise multiple regression. This statistical test indicates the predictive power of each variable entered into the equation, such as the electoral system, when the other political and socioeconomic factors are taken into consideration. Each variable may be regarded as a separate dimension. Highly intercorrelated variables are eliminated through the computer routine. This elimination provides a parsimonious list of explanatory variables while obviating statistical complications—that is, multicollinearity—which could confound the results. For reliability and for comparison with others' research, blacks' tests were limited to 27 states. Hispanics' included 18 states, and Anglo women's used the 50 states.

Research Expectations

Previous research leads one to expect the following results:

1. Multimember legislative districts are favorable for black, Hispanic, and Anglo women but unfavorable for minority men. When voters have several candidates to choose for the legislature, they are more likely to give one of their votes to a woman. However, when choice is limited to one person, voters are more likely to choose a male candidate.[8]

2. No primary runoff and larger legislatures are favorable for minorities and Anglo women. When less than a majority vote will nominate a candidate in the primary election, more minorities are nominated and elected to state legislatures. Larger legislatures provide more minority districts and seats, and hence greater legislative opportunity.

3. Anglo and black women will do best in Republican and competitive states, black men and Hispanics in Democratic states.

4. Blacks, Anglo women, and Hispanics have greater legislative opportunity in metropolitan and large population states and in those states with more educational opportunity, higher men's income, greater aid to dependent children, a larger women's movement, and no dominant religious group. Legislative turnover also is expected to be favorable to minorities and women.

PREDICTORS OF BLACKS' PROPORTIONS IN STATE LEGISLATURES

Table 5.2 displays the most powerful predictors of greater proportions of African-Americans in state legislatures. The data set includes 22 single-member district states and five with multimember districts.

The most powerful predictors are listed at the top of table 5.2 followed by ones contributing less to explaining the variation in blacks' proportions in state legislatures. At the bottom of table 5.2, the multiple correlation (R) is squared (R^2). The R^2 informs us of the total percent of the variation in blacks' percentages in state legislatures explained by the above set of variables. For black women, the total R^2 is 64 percent, and for black men, it is 75 percent.

Table 5.2
Most Powerful Predictors of Larger Proportions of Black Women and Men in State Legislatures, 1985 (in States with 5 Percent or More Black Population) (Multiple Stepwise Regression) (N = 27)

VARIABLES CORRELATING WITH BLACK WOMEN LEGISLATORS	MULTIPLE CORRELATION COEFFICIENT (R)	VARIABLES CORRELATING WITH BLACK MEN LEGISLATORS	MULTIPLE CORRELATION COEFFICIENT (R)
1. More black women college graduates in states	.64	1. More black men in population	.80
2. More black women professionals	.74	2. Less metropolitan population	.83
3. More state population (logged)	.76	3. Single member legislative districts	.84
4. Multi-member legislative districts	.77	4. Lower aid to families with dependent children	.85
5. More aid to families of dependent children	.78	5. Less black men in labor force	.86
6. No Democratic party dominance of legislature	.79	6. Less black income	.863
7. More Catholic population	.80	7. More assembly seats per population	.867
Percent of Variance Explained	R^2 = 64%	Percent of Variance Explained	R^2 = 75%

Note: The F ratio for each variable in the analysis of variance was significant at the .007 level or less. The adjusted R^2 for black women and men is 50 percent and 66 percent, respectively.

Table 5.2 indicates that states with multimember legislative districts have greater percentages of black women legislators. The opposite is the case for black men. Since electoral arrangements are part of a state's political system, they offer recruitment opportunity only when other political and socioeconomic conditions in a state are favorable. Thus, highly populated northern states with more black women college graduates and professionals, with welfare orientations, with either a competitive party situation or Republican dominance, and with some Catholic population and multimember districts are ideal environments for higher percentages of black women legislators.

States that favor black men legislators in greater proportions are southern and northern ones with large African-American populations. Black male legislators' highest percentages are in southern states where the population is about 19 percent black. Most of these states are rural, have less black men in the labor force, less black income per capita, and lower expenditures for aid to dependent children. There are only two multimember states—Georgia and North Carolina— among the 11 former Confederate states. In general, the deep South is an environment where black men have much greater chances for election than do black women. States with larger legislatures—such as New York, Michigan, and Maryland—also promote greater percentages of African-American men legislators.

Political party dominance of state legislatures is not a major predictor of black men's legislative strength in table 5.2. But Democratic party control of state legislatures correlates independently with higher percentages of African-American men legislators ($r = .45$, significant at the .05 level).

Where Blacks Have Proportionate Representation

What state political and socioeconomic factors are associated with greater black legislative representation relative to each state's black population? Table 5.3 shows that single-member districts are favorable to black men while multimember legislative districts offer black women greater legislative opportunity. The variance explained is 80 percent for black women but only about half as much (44 percent) for black men.

Except for the electoral system variable, the remainder of table 5.3 shows results different from those in table 5.2 because the questions answered are different. In table 5.3, we see that the preponderance of socioeconomic and political conditions associated with greater black men's representation/population ratios are characteristics of the northern states. The factors promoting more black women legislators relative to their population are also found mostly in the northern states, including higher black income and more black women in the labor force. There is no political party association with black women's representation/ population ratios in state legislatures.

Table 5.3 indicates that black men and women generally are underrepresented legislatively in southern states where blacks have the greatest numbers. Conversely, in the 16 northern states that have fewer blacks, blacks' legislative representation is closer to their population strength, especially for black men legislators. In Ohio, Nevada, Pennsylvania, Missouri, Michigan, Connecticut, Illinois, and Oklahoma, black men's proportional representation is especially high. A few southern states also have high black men's representation/population ratios, including Tennessee, Alabama, and Texas. Black women's legislative recruitment is greater in several northern states—California, Illinois, Indiana, Michigan, and New York.

Table 5.3
Most Powerful Predictors of High Representation/Population Ratios of Black
Women and Men in State Legislatures, 1985 (in States with 5 Percent or More
Black Population) (Multiple Stepwise Regression) (N = 27)

VARIABLES CORRELATING WITH BLACK WOMEN LEGISLATORS	MULTIPLE CORRELATION COEFFICIENT (R)	VARIABLES CORRELATING WITH BLACK MEN LEGISLATORS	MULTIPLE CORRELATION COEFFICIENT (R)
1. More assembly seats per population	.79	1. More metro- politan population	.45
2. More black income	.83	2. Single member legislative districts	.52
3. More black women in labor force	.85	3. More black men college graduates	.57
4. No runoff primary	.87	4. More state population (logged)	.61
5. More chapters of National Organization of Women per population	.88	5. More aid to families with dependent children	.62
6. More legisla- tive turnover	.889	6. More black income	.65
7. Multi-member legislative districts	.892	7. No runoff primary election	.66
Percent of variance explained	R^2 = 80%	Percent of Variance explained	R^2 = 44%

Note: The F ratio for each variable in the analysis of variance was significant at less than .00 for
black women; for black men it was less than .05 until the sixth variable (.07) and seventh
(.08). The adjusted R^2 for black women and men is 72 percent and 24 percent, respectively.

LATINOS' OPPORTUNITY FOR RECRUITMENT
TO STATE LEGISLATURES

There were 100 Hispanic men legislators but only seven Hispanic women
legislators in 1984. Therefore, our attention turns primarily to explaining the
impact of electoral systems and other state contextual factors on Hispanic men.
In the analysis of 18 states contained in table 5.4, the Hispanic population
minimum was set at about 3 percent. This percentage provided for a data set
large enough for statistical analysis.

Table 5.4
**Most Powerful Predictors of Larger Proportions and Higher Representation/
Population Ratios of Hispanic Men in State Legislatures, 1984 (Multiple Stepwise
Regressions) (N = 18)**

VARIABLES CORRELATING WITH HISPANIC MEN LEGISLATORS' PROPORTIONS	MULTIPLE CORRELATION COEFFICIENT (R)	VARIABLES CORRELATING WITH HISPANIC MEN LEGISLATORS' REPRESENTATION/ POPULATION RATIOS	MULTIPLE CORRELATION COEFFICIENT (R)
1. More Hispanic men in population	.94	1. More Hispanic men in population	.75
2. More assembly seats per population	.983	2. More assembly seats per population	.78
3. More state population (logged)	.989	3. More state population (logged)	.84
4. Runoff primary	.991	4. Democratic Party dominance of legislature	.87
5. More Catholic population	.993	5. More metropolitan population	.88
6. Less metropolitan population	.994	6. More Hispanic men college graduates	.887
7. Democratic Party dominance of legislature	.995	7. No runoff primary	.889
8. Single member legislative districts	.996	8. Single member legislative districts	.894
Percent of variance explained	R^2 = 99%	Precent of variance explained	R^2 = 80%

Note: The F ratio for each variable in the analysis of variance was significant at less than .000 for
column 1; for column 2, it was .01 except for variable eight, which was .02. The column 1
adjusted R^2 is 98 percent and the column 2 adjusted R^2 is 62 percent.

States with larger Latino populations include the single-member district states
of California, Colorado, Connecticut, Florida, Hawaii, Illinois, Kansas, Nevada,
New Mexico, New York, Oregon, Texas, and Utah. The set also includes five
states with multimember legislative districts—Arizona, Idaho, New Jersey,
Washington, and Wyoming.

The left-hand column of table 5.4 sets forth the contextual variables that
correlate with higher proportions of Hispanic men legislators. The right-hand
column lists political and social conditions associated with Latino representation
in terms of their population proportions in the 18 states.

Single-member districts are favorable for Hispanic men's legislative recruitment, as expected. In states where the ratio of assembly seats to population is greater, more Latino men are elected. Larger percentages of Hispanic men legislators are associated with no runoff primary. Similarly, Latino men legislators are more proportional to their population in states with no runoff primary.

Higher proportions of Hispanic men in state legislatures are found in rural states with larger Roman Catholic populations, such as New Mexico. Other characteristics are a large state population and a Democratic party–dominated state legislature, as in Texas. Their representation also is greater in more metropolitan states and ones with more Hispanic men college graduates. The variance explained in table 5.4 in the proportion of Latino men legislators is 99 percent, while 80 percent of their higher representation/population ratios is explained.

Hispanic women legislators numbered only 16 in 1989, and their largest percentage is in New Mexico, which is a single-member legislative district state. Hispanics were nearly 40 percent of the population in that state in 1985. The four Latino women legislators compose about 5 percent of the state legislature while Hispanic men were 32 percent. The remaining 12 women are found in ones or twos in other states, including the multimember district states of Alaska, Arizona, and Washington, and the single-member district states of California, Colorado, Connecticut, New York, and Texas. There is no discernible pattern in 1989 as to whether multimember or single-member legislative districts offer Latino women more or less recruitment opportunity. However, as the numbers of Hispanic women legislators increase, it is reasonable to expect that their greater opportunity will be in multimember legislative states, as is the case for black and Anglo women.

ANGLO WOMEN'S LEGISLATIVE OPPORTUNITY

All states were used in the analysis of Anglo women's legislative opportunity. Table 5.5 is divided into two sections. The left side of the table contains the variables that are the most powerful predictors of greater proportions of Anglo women in state legislatures. The right-hand side contains the analysis of those factors highly correlated with greater representation in terms of Anglo women's population.

Multimember legislative districts have considerable impact on Anglo women's legislative opportunity, as table 5.5 shows. Democratic party dominance of state legislatures is a negative factor while states divided among the parties or Republican-dominated states provide the best political climate for Anglo women. The National Organization for Women (NOW), which has a positive correlation with non-Democratic party states, is favorable for women's recruitment. NOW chapters in states are indicative of strong women's movements encouraging Anglo and black women's legislative election.[9] Past or present women members of Congress also are favorable for Anglo women's recruitment to state legislatures.

Characteristics of most northern states—more women college graduates, more women professionals and women in the work force, and higher men's income—

Table 5.5
**Most Powerful Predictors of Larger Proportions and Higher Representation/
Population Ratios of Anglo Women in State Legislatures, 1984 (Multiple Stepwise
Regression) (N = 50)**

VARIABLES CORRELATING WITH ANGLO WOMEN PROPORTIONS	MULTIPLE CORRELATION COEFFICIENT (R)	VARIABLES CORRELATING WITH ANGLO WOMEN LEGISLATORS' REPRESENTATION/POPU- LATION RATIOS	MULTIPLE CORRELATION COEFFICIENT (R)
1. More women in labor force	.52	1. National Organ- ization of Women chapters per population	.49
2. More Anglo women in population	.69	2. More women professionals	.63
3. More women in Congress 1973–83	.72	3. More women in labor force	.68
4. National Organi- zation of Women chapters per population	.74	4. More women in Congress 1973–83	.71
5. Greater men's income	.77	5. Multi-member legis- lative districts	.74
6. More women pro- fessionals	.78	6. Greater men's income	.75
7. Competitive or Republican Party dominance of legislature	.79	7. More Anglo women in population	.768
8. Multi-member legis- lative districts	.80	8. More women college graduates	.773
$R^2 = 64\%$		$R^2 = 60\%$	

Note: The F ratio for each variable in the analysis of variance was significant at less than the .000
level. The column 1 adjusted R^2 is 60 percent, and the column 2 adjusted R^2 is 52 percent.

are favorable for Anglo as well as black women's nomination and election to
state legislatures. The average variation in Anglo women's representation explained by table 5.5 is 62 percent.

One of our expectations was that the single primary would be a benefit and
the runoff primary a bane for women's recruitment. Yet the single primary did
not appear as one of the most powerful predictors because it intercorrelates
highly with NOW chapters and other variables in table 5.5. Nevertheless, it is
a significant barrier for Anglo women and blacks. The direct Pearsonian correlation between Anglo women's representation and no runoff primary is .36
(significant at the .05 level).

ANGLO MEN'S LEGISLATIVE OPPORTUNITY

Compared with Anglo and black women, Anglo men do best in single-member districts. Yet compared with black and Hispanic men, Anglo men generally are better off in multimember districts. However, in terms of sheer numbers, Anglo men—who were 78 percent of state legislators in 1989—are receiving most of their challenges from Anglo women.

In several multimember district states, women's legislative proportions are growing rapidly. For example, in 1989, Vermont had 33 percent women legislators, New Hampshire 33 percent, Arizona 29 percent, Idaho 25 percent, Maryland 23 percent, and West Virginia 19 percent. Of course, some exceptional single-member district states with favorable political and socioeconomic contexts also have high women's proportions while some multimember states have low ones.[10]

Single-member district states are safer than multimember districts for Anglo as well as minority men legislators, since men have a greater probability of being reelected. Our correlation test of legislative incumbency and single-member legislative districts in the 50 states showed a coefficient of .35, significant at the .01 level. This test was for the nonreapportionment year of 1986. Consequently, if the objective is maximizing Anglo men's legislative recruitment, single-member state legislative districts are generally best.[11]

SUMMARY AND CONCLUSIONS

The effects of state legislative electoral systems are summarized in table 5.6. By disaggregating black men and women, we discovered that the effect of the legislative system in states has different impacts on each gender's recruitment opportunity. By analyzing Anglo and black women separately, we learned that multimember districts are best for both groups of women. However, for black, Hispanic, and Anglo men, single-member districts are most favorable. These results indicate that in future studies of the impact of electoral systems on ethnic groups, gender is a significant factor that must be included for accuracy as well as understanding.

Our results agree with previous research on women's legislative recruitment by Carroll, by Darcy, Welch and Clark, and by Rule.[12] They found that multimember legislative electoral systems are most favorable. In contrast, Welch and Studlar concluded that multimember districts make only a small difference in women's legislative recruitment. Their research does not appear comparable to the research of the others. Welch and Studlar compared two states while Darcy, Welch, and Clark covered 18 states, and Carroll's and Rule's studies were of all 50 states. Welch and Studlar's unit of analysis also differed from that of the other researchers. Welch and Studlar studied districts with varying numbers of representatives within states, that is, district magnitude. The other

Table 5.6
Summary of Most Favorable and Unfavorable Legislative Electoral Systems for Blacks', Hispanic Men's, and Anglos' Recruitment Opportunity

	SINGLE MEMBER LEGISLATIVE DISTRICTS	MULTI-MEMBER LEGISLATIVE DISTRICTS
Black women	–	+
Black men	+	–
Hispanic men	+	–
Anglo women	–	+
Anglo men	+	–

Note: The black legislative recruitment summary is based on analyses of 27 states with 5 percent or more black population. Hispanic women legislators are not included because they were too few and too dispersed to establish any pattern. Hispanic men's summary is based on analysis of 18 states with about 3 percent or more Latino population. Anglos' recruitment is based on analyses of 50 states.

researchers focused on women's legislative recruitment opportunity across many states with different electoral systems.[13]

In addition, our findings do not accord with Grofman, Migalski, and Noviello's study on blacks' election to state legislatures.[14] They found that single-member districts are best for blacks' recruitment. However, our study finds that this generalization applies to black men and not to black women. This difference may be attributable to their grouping black men and black women legislators together. Their sample also included 11 states with 15 percent or more blacks, whereas our sample included 27 states with 5 percent or more black population.

The research by Welch and Herrick on women's election to city councils (presented later in this volume) is also pertinent for comparison with this study. Both black women and black men did well in those few cities with black multimember districts where more than one person was elected by the voters. This finding appears to agree with our state legislative study results, which show that Anglo and black women's chances are improved considerably in states where there are districts with two or more representatives.

Contextual Analyses Expectations and Outcomes

Most of our research expectations regarding the impact of state legislative electoral systems and arrangements on minority men and Anglo women were confirmed in this study. The single primary, which does not require a runoff election, is favorable for African-Americans', Hispanic men's, and Anglo women's higher legislative proportions in terms of their population strength. In addition, larger legislatures per population were found to be of importance, for they ordinarily provide more minority districts and more election opportunity.

We hypothesized that minority men would have greater legislative representation in Democratic-dominated states and that this finding would not hold for black and Anglo women. Our hypotheses were only partially confirmed. As expected, Democratic party dominance is associated with higher percentages of minority men legislators whose numbers are greater in the South and Southwest. Also, as expected, a competitive or Republican party context is best for larger proportions of black and Anglo women, whose opportunity is mainly in the northern states.

However, when we turn to the relationship between parties and larger ratios of representation to population, we find several significant differences between Latinos and others. Since the Hispanic population is concentrated largely in the Southwest and since their proportions in state legislatures approximate their population, we again find that Democratic dominance offers the best political environment for them. However, African-American men have greater equity in Northern non-Democratic-dominated states. For African-American women and Anglo women's legislative representation in terms of population, either party in the northern states is favorable. This finding is characteristic of the "new wave" in women's recruitment, which began in the 1980s and promises to continue into the 1990s.[15]

In the northern highly populated and metropolitan states, more black and Anglo women college graduates and professionals, plus women's groups that promote their election, add to the probability of greater legislative recruitment when electoral arrangements are favorable.

IMPLICATIONS FOR ELECTORAL SYSTEM CHANGES

Since the findings indicate that single-member legislative district states disadvantage Anglo and black women, it is probable that men's legislative recruitment—particularly in the southern states—is benefiting from them at women's expense. Because minority men are disadvantaged in multimember districts and black women and Anglo women are advantaged by them, these differences lead to a dilemma if the objective is equal political opportunity for women and men.

The findings also indicate legislative underrepresentation for blacks and Hispanics in terms of their population. This underrepresentation is partially due to the dispersement—lack of segregation—of African-Americans as well as Latinos in many states.[16] This dispersement often prevents the creation of majority single-member legislative districts for minorities. An alternative to the resulting underrepresentation is to adopt another type of electoral system, one that will provide recruitment opportunity where there is desegregation and one that has been proven effective and understandable elsewhere. This strategy also could provide opportunity for women, whose legislative recruitment is ordinarily hampered by the single-member district system.

One such alternative electoral system is the cumulative vote.[17] It would be appropriate in states with existing multimember districts or in single-member district states desiring more equitable legislative representation. The cumulative vote was used in Illinois between 1870 and 1980. This system provides voters with several votes that can be given to one candidate or divided among two or more candidates in multimember districts. It thus gives minorities and women a legislative opportunity for representation approximately equal to their voting strength, provided they vote as blocs.

Another possibility is the single-transferable vote of proportional representation, which is used in the Republic of Ireland, where women have greater parliamentary representation than in the United States.[18] In this system the voter expresses first, second, third, etc., preferences for legislative candidates in a multimember district, as the chapter by Zimmerman explains in greater detail. This system gives minorities and women the opportunity for legislative recruitment commensurate with their population proportions.

Multimember districts with two or more legislators chosen within Anglo, African-American, or Latino majority areas is another alternative, as Welch and Herrick suggest in this volume. Such multimember districts were created and exist in the states of Maryland and Arizona, according to Conway's and Saint-Germain's chapters. This alternative is perhaps the simplest solution for majority black or Anglo districts. However, if applied where minority populations are dispersed, it may result in just another unfavorable multimember district where minority men are denied legislative recruitment opportunity. In that case, the cumulative and the single-transferable vote systems are the best electoral system alternatives for greater legislative opportunity for each gender and ethnic group.

Another possible reform is a term limitation for state legislators, such as the one adopted by initiative and referendum in California in 1990.[19] Persons elected to the lower house and the senate may serve for a maximum of 12 years. Opponents of legislative term limits argue that the loss of experienced legislators strengthens the positions of the governor and legislative staff. But proponents hold that fresh perspectives will be gained by removing long-term incumbents and that the influence of interest groups will be lessened. One study of twenty-one states indicates that the beneficiaries of term limitations would be women and recently elected Republican incumbents in southern States.[20] And as our data suggest, a number of Anglo and minority women legislators probably would be elected to take the place of male incumbents. This development will be most likely if term limitations are adopted in states with multimember legislative districts.

NOTES

The author thanks Robert Darcy, Georgia Persons, and Anthony DeSales Affigne for helpful comments on this chapter and Patrick Ament and Mary Herzik for research assistance.

1. Joseph A. Schlesinger, "The New American Political Party," *American Political Science Review*, December 1985, pp. 1153–54.

2. For a summary, see Richard L. Engstrom and Michael D. McDonald, "The Effect of At-Large versus District Elections on Racial Representation," in Bernard Grofman and Arend Lijphart, eds., *Electoral Laws and Their Political Consequences* (New York: Agathon Press, 1986). Exceptions include Albert Karnig and Susan Welch, *Black Representation and Urban Policy* (Chicago: University of Chicago Press, 1980), and Robert R. Brischetto, "Electoral Empowerment: The Case for Tejanos," in Roberto E. Villarreal, Norma C. Hernandez, and Howard E. Neighbor, eds., *Latino Empowerment* (Westport, Conn.: Greenwood Press, 1988).

3. See Malcolm Jewell, "The Consequences of Single- and Multi-Member Districting," in Bernard Grofman, Arend Lijphart, Robert McKay, and Howard Scarrow, eds., *Representation and Redistricting Issues* (Lexington, Mass.: Lexington Books, 1982), pp. 129–35, and Bernard Grofman, Michael Migalski, and Nicholas Noviello, "Effects of Multi-member Districts on Black Representation in State Legislatures," *Review of Black Political Economy*, Spring 1986, pp. 65–78.

4. Susan J. Carroll, *Women as Candidates in American Politics* (Bloomington: Indiana University Press, 1985); Robert Darcy, Susan Welch, and Janet Clark, *Women, Elections, and Representation* (New York: Longman, 1987); Pippa Norris, "Women's Legislative Participation in Western Europe," *West European Politics*, October 1985, pp. 90–101; Wilma Rule, "Electoral Systems, Contextual Factors, and Women's Opportunity for Election to Parliament in Twenty-Three Democracies," *Western Political Quarterly*, September 1987, pp. 477–98; and Wilma Rule, "Why More Women Are State Legislators," *Western Political Quarterly*, June 1990, pp. 437–48. See also Susan Welch and Donley Studlar, "Multimember Districts and the Representation of Women: Evidence from Britain and the United States," *Journal of Politics*, May 1990, pp. 391–412.

5. United States Bureau of the Census, *Statistical Abstract of the United States: 1986* (Washington, D.C.: United States Government Printing Office, 1987), p. 25.

6. There was only a 1.2 percent difference in women's legislative recruitment in 1984 and 1985.

7. Six of the multimember district states (Georgia, Indiana, New Hampshire, North Carolina, West Virginia, and Wyoming) also have single-member districts within them. These multimember/single-member states were included in the multimember set on the theory that women's success in multimember districts would be a boost to those in single-member districts within the state. It also was expected that in those few favorable single-member states, women of all ethnic backgrounds would benefit. These notions appear to be substantiated by the positive correlation of .25 ($p = .04$) between black women's and Anglo women's legislative representation/population ratios. There are near zero correlations between black men's and black women's legislative representation/population ratios, whereas the correlation between Anglo men's and Anglo women's is $-.53$ ($p =$ less than .01). Refer to *Redistricting Provisions: 50 State Profiles* (Denver: National Conference of State Legislatures, 1989), and Richard G. Niemi, Jeffrey S. Hill, and Bernard Grofman, "The Impact of Multi-Member Districts on Party Representation in U.S. State Legislatures," *Legislative Studies Quarterly*, Autumn 1985, pp. 441–55.

8. See e.g. Carroll, *Women as Candidates*.

9. T. J. Volgy, J. E. Schwartz, and H. Gottlieb, "Female Representation and the

Quest for Resources: Feminist Activism and Electoral Success," *Social Science Quarterly*, Winter 1986, pp. 156–68, and Rule, "Why More Women are State Legislators."

10. The correlation in 1989 between Anglo women's legislative representation and multimember district states was .37, significant at the .009 level. The beta was 6.46 with a T value of 2.73.

11. The direct correlation of Anglo men's legislative representation with single-member legislative district states was an insignificant .18 in 1989. However, more robust regression analysis of the relationship shows a T value greater than 2 and equal to that of black men legislators when other factors are controlled. Legislative incumbency is also positive with a T value over 4.

12. Refer to note 4 for references.

13. Refer to note 4 for references.

14. Grofman, Migalski and Noviello, "Effects of Multi-member Districts on Black Representation in State Legislatures."

15. Rule, "Why More Women Are State Legislators."

16. Refer to Grofman and Handley's chapter in this volume.

17. Richard L. Engstrom, Delbert A. Taebel, and Richard L. Cole, "Cumulative Voting as a Remedy for Minority Vote Dilution: The Case of Alamogordo, New Mexico," *Journal of Law and Politics*, Spring 1989, pp. 469–97. Also see Still's chapter in this volume.

18. Peter Mair, "Districting Choices under the Single Transferable Vote," in Grofman and Lijphart, eds., *Electoral Laws*, pp. 289–307.

19. *Legislature of the State of California et al. v. March Fong Eu, as Secretary of State, et al.*, 91 *Daily Journal* D.A.R. 12510 (legislative term and spending limits).

20. Gary S. Moncrief and Joel A. Thompson, "The Move to Limit Terms of Office: Assessing the Consequences for Female State Legislators." A paper presented at the annual meeting of the Western Political Science Association, Seattle, Washington, March 1991.

6

Barriers to Representing Women and Blacks in Pennsylvania: The Impacts of Demography, Culture, and Structure

Sandra A. Featherman

Pennsylvania ranks 46th in terms of the percent of its state legislature's seats held by women—7 percent in the House and 4 percent in the Senate—although women constitute more than 52 percent of the commonwealth's population.[1] Pennsylvania also has the lowest percent of women state legislators in the northern states.

The representation of blacks is not proportionate to their population share but is far less out of line than is the case for women. While almost 9 percent of the population is black, 7 percent of the state House members and 6 percent of the state senators are black. Pennsylvania ranks 16th among the states in the overall percent of its legislators who are black. One member of the state House is Hispanic.

Pennsylvania politicians often claim that there are few women or blacks in the state legislature because the state is rural and politically conservative. Although the state's nonmetropolitan population is the eighth largest in the nation, Pennsylvania is the ninth most metropolitan state.[2] It also is politically moderate.

PENNSYLVANIA GOVERNMENT: WOMEN AND BLACKS

Pennsylvania has 203 seats in its House of Representatives and 50 seats in its Senate, the second largest state legislature in the nation. There are no women and only one black among Pennsylvania's congressional delegates. No woman or black has been a United States senator, governor, lieutenant governor, or attorney general of the state. Two women were elected in 1988 to the statewide positions of auditor general and treasurer.

In 1990, there were 15 women representatives in the Pennsylvania House and two women members of the state Senate. The House membership included 15 blacks and one Hispanic, and there were three black senators.

Only four states—Alabama, Kentucky, Louisiana, and Mississippi—in the nation had lower percentages of women in their state legislatures than Pennsylvania, which ranks 46th among the states with an overall 6.7 percent women in both houses. Nationally, the median percentage of women in state legislatures is 17.1; Pennsylvania has less than half that percentage.

Women hold no leadership positions in the Pennsylvania House or Senate, hold no committee chairs in the Senate, and hold only one of 24 chairs in the House. Only Georgia, Louisiana, and Tennessee have worse records in terms of women holding key legislative positions.[3]

Judges in Pennsylvania are elected, and the record for women and blacks in the courthouse is dismal. The Pennsylvania Supreme Court has one black, the chief justice, but no women among its seven members. The superior and commonwealth courts—intermediate courts of appeal with 15 and nine members, respectively—include one black and two women. In the court of common pleas, 10.8 percent of the judges are black and 6.7 percent are female.[4]

Among Pennsylvania's 53 cities, only three had women mayors in 1987. Subsequently, Pittsburgh elected Sophie Masloff, who became mayor when her predecessor died in office. Masloff subsequently won a full-term election in 1989.[5]

Of 40 boroughs of 10,000 or more residents, four have women mayors. Of the 112 townships with a population of 10,000 or more, only seven have women presidents or township chairs.[6]

METHODOLOGY AND RESULTS

To examine the effect of the various explanatory factors on electing women and blacks to the state legislature, we made comparisons between Pennsylvania and the other 49 states, or between Pennsylvania and states appropriate for comparison. Variables tested are demographic, cultural, and structural. Demographic variables include population size, percent urban, personal income, state aid to families with dependent children (AFDC), and percent black. Cultural variables include percent of eligible members of the group, conservatism or liberalism of the state's voters, party competitiveness, and political culture. Structural variables are size of the legislature, number of legislative seats per 100,000 persons, competitiveness as evidenced by higher legislative salary, and electoral system.

Pennsylvania is a large state with an individualistic political culture, highly competitive elections, high legislative salaries, and single-seat legislative districts, which should mitigate against the election of women.[7] At the same time, the state has the second-largest legislature in the nation, state personal income and AFDC levels are above the median, and many national women's organization

Table 6.1
Percent Women State Legislators, 10 Largest States, 1990

STATE	POPULATION RANK	PERCENT WOMEN LEGISLATORS	STATE RANK
California	1	14.2	30
New York	2	10.4	36
Texas	3	9.4	39
Florida	4	20.6	13
Pennsylvania	5	6.7	45
Illinois	6	18.1	19
Ohio	7	11.4	34
Michigan	8	14.9	28
New Jersey	9	9.2	40
North Carolina	10	14.1	31

Mean Rank: 31.5

Source: "Women in State Legislatures 1990," a fact sheet issued by the Center for the American Woman and Politics, Rutgers University, 1990.

leaders come from Pennsylvania. These factors should be positive indicators for women's legislative recruitment in Pennsylvania.[8]

The state's lower-than-average percentage of population that is black, along with single-seat districts and competitive elections, should work against black legislative recruitment, whereas urbanization and large chambers are positive indicators. Furthermore, as Rule has shown, what helps to recruit black men or white women may not help to recruit black women.[9]

If these factors affect recruitment of women and blacks in the ways suggested, we would expect Pennsylvania, with its mixed indicators, to place somewhere in the middle among the states.

Demographic Variables

Pennsylvania is the fourth-largest state in the nation in population with nearly 12 million residents, but its one-half of 1 percent growth rate between 1970 and 1980 was the third lowest in the country. The state has two large cities, Philadelphia (1,688,210 residents) and Pittsburgh (423,938). No other city in the state has more than 125,000 residents.[10]

Pennsylvania's large population size should—and does—mitigate against women winning legislative seats. Table 6.1 reveals that of the 10 largest states, eight rank in the bottom half in terms of the percent of their legislative seats held by women, with a mean rank of 31.5. However, Pennsylvania ranks lowest on the list, with only 6.7 percent women legislators. Obviously, population size alone can not explain Pennsylvania's poor showing.

With respect to blacks, Pennsylvania is an urban state with a smaller proportion of nonwhite residents than the country as a whole. Only 8.8 percent of the people

Sandra A. Featherman

Table 6.2
Percent Black Elected Officials, 10 Largest States, 1984 and 1988

State	Percent Black Legis- lators, 1988	State Rank Percent Black Legis- lators, 1988	State Rank Ratio of Black Legis- lators to Black Popula- lation, 1988	Total Percent Black Elected Officials, 1984	State Rank Percent Black Officials, 1984
California	6.7	17.5	8	1.4	16
New York	9.5	11.0	23	1.0	18
Texas	8.3	13.0	18	0.9	20
Florida	7.5	15.0	24	2.7	11
Pennsylvania	7.1	16.0	12	0.5	31
Illinois	11.9	4.5	10	0.9	20
Ohio	9.8	9.9	7	1.0	18
Michigan	10.8	8.0	13	1.5	15
New Jersey	6.7	17.5	27	2.1	13
North Carolina	9.4	12.0	31	5.5	6
Mean Rank		12.4	17.3		16.8

Note: The highest rank is 1.

Sources: Harold W. Stanley and Richard G. Niemi, eds., *Vital Statistics in American Politics*, 2d
  ed. (Washington, D.C.: CQ Press, 1990), pp. 368–69, and *National Journal*, June 30, 1984,
  pp. 1272–73.

are black, compared with a national average of 11.7 percent. Hispanics are only
1.3 percent of Pennsylvania's residents, compared with 6.4 percent nationally,
while 0.6 percent of the state's populace is Asian, Pacific Islander, and Native
American, compared with 2.2 percent nationally.[11]

Seventy-one percent of the black population lives in the two largest cities,
with Philadelphia accounting for more than 61 percent of the state's black residents. Only six of the 67 counties have populations that are more than 5 percent
black. Philadelphia is the only county in which blacks have a substantial proportion of elected representatives.

Population size does not adequately explain black representation in the state
legislature. The 10 largest states are well above the national median in the
proportions of their legislators who are black, with a mean state ranking of 12.4
(see table 6.2). Pennsylvania ranks 16th. However, since the black percentage
of the population in Pennsylvania is smaller than the mean for the states, it is
more appropriate to measure Pennsylvania's performance in terms of the ratio
of the black voting-age population. That ratio is .827 for Pennsylvania, the 12th-
best record in the country.[12] Pennsylvania has not done nearly as well in its

black share of total elected officials, ranking only 31st in the country, although the mean rank for the 10 largest states is 16.8.[13]

Urbanization also cannot explain Pennsylvania's poor showing with regard to women legislators. Pennsylvania is the ninth most metropolitan state, but there presently appears to be no relationship between metropolitanization and the percent of women in a state legislature.

For blacks, on the other hand, there is a .426 correlation relationship between the percent of a state's population that is metropolitan and the percent of its legislature that is black. This relationship is significant at the .002 level. However, since many of the highly metropolitan states have larger proportions of their populations that are black than do less metropolitan states and since blacks in the North overwhelmingly live in metropolitan areas, this finding is not unexpected.

The percent of black legislators is highly related to the percent of the state population that is black. The correlation of .909 is significant at the .0000 level and means that we could expect such a result to occur by chance less than one out of ten thousand times. In fact, the slope of .4939 indicates that there is almost a linear relation in which an increase of 1 percent in the black proportion of the population is accompanied by a one-half percent increase in the proportion of black seats in a state legislature.

In Pennsylvania, there is an interesting byplay on race and political outcomes. There are only three blacks in the Senate, and they are from Philadelphia, where blacks are 38 percent of the population. In the House, 12 of the 15 black members are from Philadelphia, two are from Pittsburgh, which is 24 percent black, and one is from the city of Chester, which is 57 percent black. The one Hispanic member is from Philadelphia.

The women legislators, on the other hand, come from across the state. Of the two women state senators, one is from Philadelphia and one is from the Easton area. Four of the 15 women state representatives are from Philadelphia, one is from Pittsburgh, and the other 10 are from other sections of the state.

Pennsylvania ranks 19th in both AFDC level and disposable personal income per capita. Neither appears to bear a relationship to the percent of either women or blacks elected to the state legislature.

Cultural Variables

Cultural variables appear to be more significant than demographic ones in explaining state differences in women's share and, to a lesser extent, black's share of seats in state legislatures. Elazar's assessments of the political cultures of the states must be used cautiously, since two important changes have influenced the political culture of states in recent years.[14] First, the enormous shifts of population from northern states to Sunbelt states has affected the dominant political cultures of population-receiving states. Even more important, the federal Voting Rights Act of 1965 has altered the political strength of blacks, especially

Table 6.3
Percent Women in Legislature by Political Culture, 1989

STATES	MEAN RANK
9 Moralistic Culture States	34.28
9 Individualistic Culture States	24.39
8 Traditionalistic Culture States	6.44
24 Other States	28.98

STATES	CHI-SQUARE	SIGNIFICANCE
50	18.36	.0004

Note: The highest rank is 50 for this and other state culture tables.

in the South, in terms of the numbers of blacks being elected in the South. Nonetheless, political culture still has some explanatory power.

We would expect the moralistic states, which view politics as the means to achieve the "good community," to have the best showing in terms of electing women and blacks to office. The traditional states, which see politics as a means of preserving the existing order, should have the worst record. The individualistic states, which see politics as a dirty business in a competitive marketplace, should place somewhere between the other two cultures in terms of legislative success for women and blacks.

Elazar described nine states as predominantly moralistic: Colorado, Maine, Michigan, Minnesota, North Dakota, Oregon, Utah, Vermont, and Wisconsin. As can be seen in table 6.3, these states have a mean proportion of 22.0 percent women elected to their state legislature and a mean rank of 34.3. (For the political culture tests only for statistical ease, the ranks are ordered from 50 downward, with 50 being the top-performing state rank.) The nine individualistic states— Alaska, Delaware, Illinois, Indiana, Maryland, Nevada, New Jersey, Ohio, and Pennsylvania—have a mean proportion of 16.0 percent women and a mean rank of 24.4. In the traditional states, the outcome for women is truly dismal. Alabama, Arkansas, Georgia, Mississippi, South Carolina, Tennessee, and Virginia have a mean proportion of only 7.6 percent women and a mean rank of 6.4. Virginia, the highest ranking of the eight traditional states, ranks only 11th from the bottom of the list.

Comparing the proportion of women legislators by political culture, the nonparametric Kruskal-Wallis test yields a chi-square of 18.36, significant at the .0004 confidence level. This finding suggests that political culture bears a significant relationship to recruitment of women legislators. The variance of means is attributable largely to the traditional states category, indicating that the tra-

Table 6.4
Percent Black Legislative Success by Political Culture, 1989

States	Mean Rank
9 moralistic culture states	27.61
9 individualistic culture states	29.89
8 traditionalistic culture states	20.19
24 other states	24.83

STATES	CHI-SQUARE	SIGNIFICANCE
50	2.12	.5484

ditional states maintain vestiges of the previous privileged order, even in the face of large-scale changes in their political environments.

The traditional states have large black populations. Hence, it is no great surprise that, with the growth of black voting in the last decade and a half, the traditional states have the best records in both numbers and proportions of their legislators who are black. In fact, five of the traditional states are among the seven with the largest proportions of black legislators. However, if we assess black political success by comparing the ratio of the percent of blacks in the state legislature to the percent black population, we find the traditional states once more with the lowest ranking among the three political culture groupings, 20.2, as indicated in table 6.4.

It is difficult to interpret the outcome for blacks in moralistic and individualistic states. Many moralistic states have very small black populations. Half rank in the lowest quintile in percent of population that is black, four are less than 1 percent black, and three of these four states have no blacks in the state legislatures. However, the moralistic states overall have higher proportions of blacks in their legislatures than in their population. The mean rank was 27.6.

Black candidates in the individualistic states have been relatively successful, compared with the other categories, and the mean rank was 29.9. These rankings are close, and the variation within groups is substantial. The Kruskal-Wallis analyses reveal no significant effect for political culture on black political success.

Stanley and Niemi show a mean ratio of 48 percent for all the states in the nation, indicating that the black share of legislative seats was slightly less than half the black share of the voting-age population.[15] Parity would require a doubling of the number of seats held by blacks.

One would expect Pennsylvania, *ceteris parabis*, to place somewhere near the mean rankings for individualistic states. As table 6.5 indicates, Pennsylvania is by far the worst of the individualistic states with respect to recruiting women legislators and is better than most in terms of black recruitment.

Party competitiveness is another possible explanatory variable. In states where

Table 6.5
Rankings for States with Individualistic Political Cultures

State	Rank, Percent Women in Legislature	Rank, Percent Blacks in Legislature	Rank, Black Representation/ Population Ratio
Alaska	16.5	35.0	28
Delaware	26.0	22.5	39
Illinois	20.0	4.6	10
Indiana	33.0	20.5	20
Maryland	12.2	2.0	
Nevada	13.0	22.5	14
New Jersey	38.0	17.5	27
Ohio	35.9	9.5	
Pennsylvania	46.0	16.0	12
Mean Rank:	26.7	16.7	21.4

Sources: Ranks based on data from "Women in State Legislatures 1990," a fact sheet issued by
the Center for the American Woman and Politics, Rutgers University, 1990, and Harold W.
Stanley and Richard G. Niemi, eds., *Vital Statistics on American Politics*, 2d ed. (Washington,
D.C.: CQ Presss, 1990), pp. 368–69.

party control of legislative houses is held only narrowly, both parties may pressure
party officials in local districts to run candidates perceived as able to win in
contests expected to be close. This strategy could militate against women if they
are perceived to be weaker candidates than men or against black candidates
running in other than predominantly black districts.

Pennsylvania is a very competitive state. Control of the Senate and of the
House has turned over often since 1950. From 1955 to 1990, the House and
Senate have been controlled by opposite parties for 21 years, or 60 percent of
the time. From 1981 to 1990, Republicans maintained control of the Senate by
two to five seats. Democrats controlled the House from 1984 to 1990, by one
to four seats out of 203. The governorship shifts regularly between Democrats
and Republicans.

Another indication of competitiveness is the proclivity of voters to ticket split,
electing governors of one party at the same time that they elect senators of the
opposite party. For example, Democrat Robert Casey was elected governor
during the 1986 state election while Republican Arlen Specter was reelected to
the United States Senate. Furthermore, Pennsylvania is one of only six states in
which the vote in presidential elections from 1968 through 1988 has been Republican from 40 to 60 percent of the time.

Party competitiveness does not adequately explain the poor showing of women
in Pennsylvania, since the 10 other most competitive states in terms of party
control of state legislatures vary widely, from each other as well as from Pennsylvania, in their performance in electing women and blacks to their state legislatures. As table 6.6 indicates, the mean proportion of women in state

Table 6.6
Party Competitiveness and Women and Black Legislators, 1989

STATE	PERCENT SENATE REPUBLICANS	PERCENT HOUSE REPUBLICANS	PERCENT WOMEN LEGISLATORS	PERCENT BLACK LEGISLATORS
Connecticut	50		29.0	4.0
Illinois	47		18.6	11.9
Indiana	52	50	14.0	5.3
Kansas	55		25.5	2.4
Michigan	53		14.9	10.8
Montana	54	48	18.0	0.0
New Jersey		52	10.8	6.7
Oregon		47	20.0	3.3
Pennsylvania	54	49	6.7	7.1
Vermont	47	51	33.3	0.1
Washington	51		29.3	2.0
Mean Rank:			20.0	4.9

legislatures in these 11 states in 1989 was 20.0 percent, and the mean proportion of blacks elected was 4.9 percent. Considerable deviation occurred around both means. Again, Pennsylvania was by far the worst for women and among the better states for blacks.

With regard to political parties and recruitment, both of the women state senators are Democrats. In the state House, nine of the 15 women members are Republicans. All black members of the Senate are Democrats, as are all but one of the black House members. The one Hispanic male representative is also a Democrat.

Although conservatism often is suggested as a reason women are underrepresented in the Pennsylvania State Legislature, the commonwealth is not very conservative. Neither party dominates the state, and officials elected statewide tend to be moderate Republicans or moderate-to-liberal Democrats.

The state's congressional delegation is moderate as well. Not a single Pennsylvanian was among those selected as the 21 most liberal and 21 most conservative United States Senators or 21 most liberal and 21 most conservative members of the United States House of Representatives. The Pennsylvania House delegation Democrats were ranked almost exactly at the center of all House Democrats on a liberal-to-conservative scale while the state's Republican members ranked 31st in conservatism. Pennsylvania House and Senate delegations are clearly moderate.[16]

The lack of women in leadership positions from which candidates might be elected sometimes is cited as a possible reason for the dearth of women in elected office. An adequate pool of women, who have demonstrated leadership in the business or civic world, is presumed a precursor to full representational equality. Yet, Pennsylvania has produced a number of statewide and national women leaders in recent years. In addition to women bank presidents, college presidents, and well-known women school superintendents, Pennsylvania has a number of national women organization presidents, including Mollie Yard and Eleanor Smeal (National Organization for Women), Mary Purcell (American Association for University Women), Nancy Neuman (League of Women Voters), and Ernesta Ballard (National Abortion Rights Action League).

Structural Variables

The large number of House seats in Pennsylvania translates into just 59,246 persons per seat. The seven other largest states, by comparison, all include far more persons in each legislative district (from 84,545 to 352,100). Pennsylvania House districts, however, are the 10th largest in the nation.

Where there are fewer voters in a district, as in New Hampshire (with 2,743 persons per House seat), it may be easier for a woman to win, since women may be able to use volunteer organizational support effectively in a small district race. As Carroll noted, "The support of women and women's groups can help women run competitively and contribute to a victory."[17]

Some of the reasons that Carroll and others have found to inhibit women as campaigners are minimized by smaller districts. There is less travel and time away from family expended in campaigning, there is apt to be more confidence when one knows most of the potential voters, and there may be less aggressive competition when seats are not perceived as obvious stepping-stones to higher office. Nonetheless, there does not appear to be a significant relationship between persons per seat and percent of women House members, although the correlation, − 17.7 percent, is in the right direction.

When high salaries are paid to legislators, the seats are more apt to be sought. Conversely, when the salary is very low, many people cannot afford to give time to serve in their state legislatures. If the salary is high enough to support members as full-time legislators, such positions may be fought for quite aggressively.

Pennsylvania presently pays the second-highest legislative salary—$47,000— of all the states.[18] Per diem allocations, travel allotments, and other allowances bring the compensation up to more than $70,000 per year for the average member. Many members serve as full-time legislators. Since the positions are well compensated, they are seen as quite desirable by many lawyers and political activists. The high level of competition for these well-paid positions may well be a major reason why so few women are represented in the Pennsylvania State Legislature.

New York, which pays the highest base salary to its legislators ($57,500), and Michigan, which ranks just below Pennsylvania in compensation ($45,500), also rank low in proportion of women in their legislatures (36th and 28th, respectively).

Pennsylvania legislative elections are based on single-member districts. Rule has shown that women's representation cross-culturally is closely related to electoral system design.[19] While there is no proportional representation in Pennsylvania, there are other electoral systems with which the single-member district can be compared to possibly shed light on the question of whether structure is a major reason for women's poor legislative representation in the state. Comparisons can be made with respect to the election of black representatives as well.

Interestingly, Pennsylvania counties elect their commissioners by limited voting. Under this system, political parties normally nominate a fixed number of candidates, somewhat less than the number to be elected, and each voter may cast votes only for the same fixed number in an at-large election. For example, each party might be able to nominate only six candidates for a nine-seat body, and each voter might be able to cast only six votes. Because this system guarantees seats to the minority political party, it is often alluded to as a semiproportional system, although it is not proportional because the minimum number of seats is guaranteed to the minority party no matter how small or how large its share of votes.

Pennsylvania counties have three-seat county commissions. Each party nominates two candidates, and three candidates are elected. It has been found that the minority party candidates within a county, while formally running against the majority party candidates, often actually run against each other, since only one of the minority party candidates can realistically be expected to win.[20]

In Pennsylvania, 62 of the 67 counties are governed by these county commissions and have a total of 186 commissioners. In 1989, no commissioner was black, and only 20 (11 percent) were women.[21] These dismal results occurred even though each party runs two candidates for county commissioner in each county and either a majority or a minority party could nominate a woman or a black as a candidate, as well as a white male candidate, if it wished. Of the four counties with larger councils in place of commissions, only one had women serving on it.

White women's proportions under the limited vote are greater at the county level than at the legislative level, but the opposite is the case for black men and women. The reasons for white women's underrepresentation at the county level may be the very low number of commissioners elected per district and the parties' failure to nominate women.[22] For blacks, this difference may reflect the low black population dispersal throughout the state and the parties' practice of nominating only white males.

In Pennsylvania in 1989, there were only two black women in the state House of Representatives and one black woman in the state Senate. All three came from Philadelphia. No black women held any congressional, statewide, or countywide elective office. Black women held 1.2 percent of the seats in the Pennsylvania State Legislature, which is exactly the same percent they held nationally. It is probable that the single most significant factor explaining political recruitment of black women and men in Pennsylvania is the percent of the population that is black.

Philadelphia, the county with the greatest proportion of black residents, accounts not only for the three black women state legislators but also for two black women city council members and most of the black women elected judges in the state. However, with respect to representation in the state legislature, black women lag far behind men.

SUMMARY AND CONCLUSIONS

Population size, political culture, and legislative salary level appear to be related to the proportion of women elected to a state legislature. In the case of Pennsylvania, at least two of these factors appear to best explain the poor performance of the state in electing women to the state legislature. Pennsylvania is a large, highly competitive state where election to the state legislature is eagerly sought by individuals because of the high level of compensation, the possibility of upward political mobility, and the rewards available from the party structure to party loyalists through the slim majorities and the seesawing of the legislative control of the state House and Senate.[23]

For blacks, the metropolitan and the black percentages appear to be closely related to the proportion of blacks elected. In Pennsylvania, only districts in metropolitan areas and districts with large black populations elect blacks to the state legislature. Competitiveness and high salaries may negatively affect black recruitment from districts with low proportions of black residents, just as these factors negatively affect the recruitment of women.

NOTES

1. United States Bureau of the Census, *1980 Census of Population: General Population Characteristics, Pennsylvania* (Washington, D.C.: United States Government Printing Office, 1982), pp. 40–84.

2. *Statistical Abstract of the United States* (Washington, D.C.: United States Government Printing Office, 1989), p. 28.

3. "Women State Legislators: Leadership Positions and Committee Chairs 1989," a fact sheet issued by the Center for the American Woman and Politics, Rutgers University, 1990.

4. *The Pennsylvania Manual* (Harrisburg: Pennsylvania Department of General Services, 1987), pp. 430–38, 443–79, and "Black Elected Officials in the United States," in the Political Trend Letter section of *Focus* (Joint Center for Political Studies), January 1989, p. 3.

5. *The Pennsylvania Manual*, pp. 557–69.

6. Ibid., 569–603.

7. Irene Diamond, *Sex Roles in the State House* (New Haven: Yale University Press, 1977), pp. 8–24, 166; Robert A. Bernstein, "Why Are There So Few Women in the House?" *Western Political Quarterly*, March 1986, pp. 155–64; and Susan J. Carroll, *Women as Candidates in American Politics* (Bloomington: Indiana University Press, 1985), pp. 124–31.

8. Wilma Rule, "Why Women Don't Run: The Critical Contextual Factors in Women's Legislative Recruitment," *Western Political Quarterly*, March 1981, pp. 60–77.

9. Wilma Rule, "Multimember Districts, Contextual Factors, and Black and Anglo Women's Recruitment to State Legislatures," paper presented at the 1990 annual meeting of the American Political Science Association, San Francisco, California.

10. *1980 Census of Population: General Population Characteristics, Pennsylvania*, pp. 40–8 to 40–18.

11. United States Bureau of the Census, *State and Metropolitan Area Data Book, 1982* (Washington, D.C.: United States Government Printing Office, 1982), p. 451.

12. Harold W. Stanley and Richard G. Niemi, eds., *Vital Statistics on American Politics*, 2d ed. (Washington, D.C.: CQ Press, 1990), pp. 368–69.

13. *National Journal*, June 30, 1984, pp. 1272–73.

14. Daniel J. Elazar, *American Federalism: A View from the States*, 3d ed. (New York: Thomas Y. Crowell Company, 1984), pp. 110–49.

15. Stanley and Niemi, *Vital Statistics*, pp. 368–69.

16. Richard E. Cohen and William Schneider, "The More Things Change . . . ," *National Journal*, January 27, 1990, pp. 196, 198.

17. Carroll, *Women as Candidates*, p. 163.

18. Information provided by the National Conference of State Legislatures, Denver, Colorado.

19. Wilma Rule, "Electoral Systems, Contextual Factors, and Women's Opportunity for Election in Twenty-Three Democracies," *Western Political Quarterly*, September 1987, pp. 477–98.

20. Sandra Featherman, "Limited Voting: A View from the Politician's Seat," paper presented at the annual meeting of the American Political Science Association, Washington, D.C., August 1980.

21. *Focus*, p. 3, and *The Pennsylvania Manual*, pp. 522–55.

22. This situation may be similar to that in Japan and Greece, where the electoral system for the lower house of the Parliament should be favorable to women. But the small number of representatives elected per district—the low district magnitude—discourages parties from nominating women. See Rule, "Electoral Systems, Contextual Factors, and Women's Opportunity for Election to Parliament in Twenty-Three Democracies."

23. Pennsylvania may be changing as of the 1990 elections. Women's political organizations helped to elect seven additional women to the Pennsylvania State Legislature in 1990. See, e.g., *National NOW Times*, November/December 1990, p. 4.

7

Florida: The Big Electoral Shakeup of 1982

Anita Pritchard

The 1982 Florida State Legislature changed from multi- to single-member districts and reapportioned legislative districts. In addition, all Florida Senate seats, rather than the usual one-half, were contested. The effect was dramatic.

In the following election, the proportion of Anglo women serving in the Florida House of Representatives increased from 10 percent to 14 percent of the membership, and the proportion of women senators increased from 10 percent to 20 percent. Black representation increased from five to 10 members in the House and from none to two in the Senate, a total of 7.5 percent of the membership of the state legislature. The number of Hispanic legislators increased from one to four. The Latino legislative representation was 2.5 percent in 1982 but climbed to almost 7 percent in 1988.

This chapter focuses on how the changes in electoral structures affected the subsequent election of Anglo women, black, and Hispanic legislatures.

REAPPORTIONMENT AND SINGLE-MEMBER DISTRICTS

The reapportionment of 1982 was accompanied by a major structural change—the Florida State Legislature adopted single-member districts. Before 1982, 21 representatives and five senators were elected in single-member districts; the remainder were elected in districts that varied in size from two to six representatives and two to three senators. Nearly all the legislators elected in single-member districts represented rural areas with low population density. The 99 representatives and 35 senators serving in multimember districts were elected at large, but they ran for a specific seat or district.

The legislature changed to single-member districts in response to legal and political pressures. The legal pressures included state and federal court suits involving claims that multimember districts discriminated against racial minorities, and the political pressures were evident at public hearings held across the state by the House Select Reapportionment Committee in 1982. The same four or five organizations appeared at each hearing to argue the virtues of single-member districts: Common Cause, National Association for the Advancement of Colored People (NAACP), the League of Women Voters, and the local political party committees. Few supporters of multimember districts appeared at these public hearings, and the chair of the House Select Committee was convinced that the people of Florida wanted single-member districts.[1]

Because of the change to single-member districts and a rapidly growing population, the reapportionment process created dramatically changed districts. For example, before the reapportionment in 1982, there were two multimember districts in Broward County—one five-member district and one six-member district. Following redistricting, Broward County was represented by 14 single-member districts. The effects of these two structural changes—the change in districting systems and the reapportionment—are intertwined and cannot be analyzed separately. A third change required all Senate seats (40), rather than the usual one-half, to be contested. Because of the drastic changes in districts, many citizens would have been represented by senators who had not contested in their districts if the usual schedule was followed.

MINORITY REPRESENTATION IN THE FLORIDA LEGISLATURE

Since the 1982 structural changes included adoption of single-member legislative districts in majority black and Hispanic areas, representation of these groups in the state legislature should have increased with the changes.[2] The only other minority group in Florida, Native Americans, constitutes only 1.2 percent of the population and is concentrated in a few parts of the state. However, no district was created for Native Americans in the redistricting process.

The most persistent argument for single-member districts is that multimember districts result in discrimination against racial and other minorities. For example, Grofman, Migalski, and Noviello maintain that multimember districts dilute minority representation at the state level.[3] Racially polarized voting in multi-member districts with plurality elections allows the majority to elect all representatives. Therefore, it is argued that a geographically concentrated minority might be able to elect some representatives if the multimember district is divided into several single-member districts.

Black Representation

The number of black legislators increased after the adoption of black majority single-member districts. Before 1982 there were five black representatives, including one woman, and no black senators in the Florida State Legislature (see

Table 7.1
Black Women's and Men's Election to the Florida House of Representatives and Senate, 1980–88

HOUSE OF REPRESENTATIVES

ELECTION YEAR	BLACK WOMEN		BLACK MEN	
	NUMBER	PERCENT	NUMBER	PERCENT
1980	1	.8	4	3.3
1982*	1	.8	9	7.5
1984	1	.8	9	7.5
1986	1	.8	9	7.5
1988	2	1.7	8	6.7

SENATE

ELECTION YEAR	BLACK WOMEN		BLACK MEN	
	NUMBER	PERCENT	NUMBER	PERCENT
1980	0	0.0	0	0.0
1982*	1	2.5	1	2.5
1984	1	2.5	1	2.5
1986	1	2.5	1	2.5
1988	1	2.5	1	2.5

Total percent blacks in the 1988 Legislature = 7.5 percent
Ratio black men to women in 1988   = 3:1

*In 1982, the change from multimember to single-member districts was effective, boundaries were altered, and elections were held for all legislative seats.

Source: John Phelps, *The Clerk's Manual: [Florida] House of Representatives and the Senate, 1980–82, 1982–84, 1984–86, 1986–88.*

Table 7.1). Ten black representatives and two black senators were elected in 1982; their number and the districts they represent have remained the same. One of the newly elected black representatives and one of the senators were women, and both are still serving in their respective chambers. Another black woman was elected to the House in 1988. Black women's representation is about one-third of black men's in the Florida State Legislature (see table 7.1). Hispanic women have not fared as well, as noted in the next section. Blacks constitute 11.8 percent of the Florida population and hold 7.5 percent of the seats in the state legislature.

An examination of the "black" districts suggests that the legislators who drew the district boundaries in 1982 were committed to creating several minority districts. Of the 10 black representatives currently serving, five represent two counties—Duval and Dade—which also elected five black legislators under the multimember district system. The remaining five members are from counties with no black representation before the adoption of single-member districts, and they are the only blacks in their county delegations. Broward County has one black in an 11-member delegation, Orange County has one in a six-member delegation, Hillsborough County (Tampa area) has one in an eight-member delegation, and the Tallahassee area has one in a three-member delegation. In each of the counties, with the exception of the Tallahassee area, the "black" district is a relatively small, compact district. The two black senators are from Duval and Dade counties.

These patterns suggest that the number of black legislators increased because of the change to single-member districts with substantial black populations or majorities. For example, there is one black district among the eight House districts in Hillsborough County. The state legislature could have created single-member districts that would have divided the black population among several districts. Therefore, the legislature's responsiveness to concerns about minority representation was a crucial factor in determining the political consequences of the electoral system. In this respect, the experience with single-member districts in the Florida State Legislature reflects the experience with single-member districts in urban politics, where research indicates that the use of single-member districts with a commitment to minority interests when drawing district lines has benefited minorities in urban elections.[4]

Hispanic Representation

An evaluation of the structural changes' effect on representation of Hispanics (defined as someone with a Spanish surname and/or born in Cuba) is complicated by population changes in Florida. In 1980–82, the only Hispanic in the House of Representatives represented a Tampa district (see table 7.2). In 1982 three Hispanics were elected to the House from Dade County, which brought the total up to four. After the 1984 election there were seven Hispanic representatives, six from Dade County and one from Hillsborough County. In the 1986 election, one more Hispanic was elected to the House in Dade County, bringing the total number of Hispanic representatives to eight. The number remained stable following the 1988 election. One Hispanic was elected to the Senate in Dade County in 1986, and two more were elected in 1988. One Hispanic woman was elected in 1982 to the House, where she served until her election to the Senate in 1986. A second Hispanic woman was elected to the House in 1984 but did not seek reelection in 1988. Hence, there were 10 Hispanic men in the Florida State Legislature in 1988 and only one Hispanic woman legislator. Hispanics constitute 9.5 percent of the Florida population and 6.9 percent of the state legislature.

If structural changes alone were responsible, the increase in Hispanic legislators would have occurred in 1982 rather than over four elections. A second variable, changes in population distribution, also must have had an effect. The

Table 7.2
Hispanic Women's and Men's Election to the Florida House of Representatives and Senate, 1980–88

HOUSE OF REPRESENTATIVES

ELECTION	HISPANIC WOMEN		HISPANIC MEN	
YEAR	NUMBER	PERCENT	NUMBER	PERCENT
1980	0	0.0	1	0.8
1982*	1	0.8	3	2.5
1984	2	1.7	5	4.2
1986	1	0.8	7	5.8
1988	0	0.0	8	6.7

SENATE

ELECTION	HISPANIC WOMEN		HISPANIC MEN	
YEAR	NUMBER	PERCENT	NUMBER	PERCENT
1980	0	0.0	0	0.0
1982*	0	0.0	0	0.0
1984	0	0.0	0	0.0
1986	1	2.5	0	0.0
1988	1	2.5	2	5.0

```
Total percent of Hispanics in the 1988 legislature = 6.9 percent
Ratio of Hispanic men to women in 1988              = 10:1
```

*In 1982, the change from multimember to single-member districts was effective, boundaries were altered, and elections were held for all legislative seats.

Source: John Phelps, *The Clerk's Manual: [Florida] House of Representatives and the Senate, 1980–82, 1982–84, 1984–86, 1986–88.*

Hispanic population in Florida is concentrated in Dade County, which experienced considerable population changes in the 1980s. The white population declined while the Hispanic population increased. These population changes were reflected in the election of Hispanic legislators; their numbers increased as the proportion of Hispanic population in Dade County increased. In this situation, it is difficult to evaluate the relationship between single-member districts and Hispanic representation. Eight of the 21 House districts in Dade County currently are represented by Hispanics. In a multimember districting system, however, Hispanics might be a majority in one or two large multimember districts and might elect a larger proportion of the representatives.

Table 7.3
Anglo Women's and Men's Election to the Florida House of Representatives and Senate, 1980–88

HOUSE OF REPRESENTATIVES

ELECTION	ANGLO WOMEN		ANGLO MEN	
YEAR	NUMBER	PERCENT	NUMBER	PERCENT
1980	12	.10	102	.85
1982*	17	.14	89	.74
1984	19	.16	84	.70
1986	17	.14	85	.71
1988	14	.12	88	.73

SENATE

ELECTION	ANGLO WOMEN		ANGLO MEN	
YEAR	NUMBER	PERCENT	NUMBER	PERCENT
1980	4	.10	36	.90
1982*	8	.20	30	.75
1984	8	.20	30	.75
1986	8	.20	29	.73
1988	9	.23	26	.65

Total percent of Anglos in the 1988 Legislature = 86 percent
Ratio of Anglo men to women in 1988   = 5:1

*In 1982, the change from multimember to single-member districts was effective, boundaries were altered, and elections were held for all legislative seats.

Source: John Phelps, *The Clerk's Manual: [Florida] House of Representatives and the Senate, 1980–82, 1982–84, 1984–86, 1986–88.*

ANGLO WOMEN IN THE FLORIDA LEGISLATURE

The potential effects of structural changes on the election of Anglo women legislators received little attention in either the legal or the political movements preceding the adoption of single-member districts.[5] Despite this lack of interest, it is clear that 1982 was an unusual election for Anglo women candidates. This conclusion is supported by data on women elected to the Florida State Legislature during the 1980–88 elections (see Table 7.3). First, the increase in the proportion of Anglo women legislators—from 10 percent to 14 percent in the House and 10 percent to 20 percent in the Senate—was higher in 1982 than in following elections, and the substantial increases occurred in both chambers. Second, the proportion of women (including Anglos and minorities) serving in the Florida

State Legislature was similar to the national average during 1975–81 but exceeded this average after the 1982 election. The average national percentage of women legislators in 1981 was 12 percent; in Florida, 11 percent. In 1982, the corresponding numbers were 13 percent and 20 percent.

And finally, as a result of the 1982 election, the proportion of Anglo women serving in the Senate exceeded the proportion in the House. This distribution is unexpected for two reasons. First, Senate seats are more competitive. There are 40 Senate seats, compared with 120 in the House, and only one-half are contested each election year except for the reapportionment elections. Second, most senators serve in the "recruitment hierarchy," and representatives generally do not. For example, among members of the Florida House of Representatives serving in 1982–84, 16 percent of the women and 17 percent of the men previously held elective office, whereas comparative figures for senators were 100 percent (women) and 70 percent (men).

Explaining the Changes

It is not immediately obvious why the structural changes were followed by increases in the proportion of Anglo women legislators. Women are not geographically concentrated, and the preponderance of evidence suggests that women benefit from multimember rather than single-member districts.[6] However, previous research identified two processes that limit the number of women elected to public office: the opportunities to gain office and the decisions by nonincumbents to contest for office. We analyze the effects of the structural changes on each process and examine the reasons underlying the unusual distribution of Anglo women legislators in the Senate and House. Given that incumbency is a well-documented barrier to increased representation of an "outgroup,"[7] the number of open-seat races basically defines the opportunities to gain office. The number of open-seat races for each of the election years is displayed in table 7.4. To provide a broader base of comparison, this table includes data on the 1972 through the 1986 elections. The districting changes in 1972 were not as extensive as in 1982 because the state legislature continued to use multimember districts. The elections between the reapportionment elections are referred to as "mid-cycle" elections.

Since all 40 Senate seats were contested following reapportionment in both 1972 and 1982, rather than the usual 20 seats, the number of open-seat races should be double the mid-cycle average if retirement decisions remain stable. The number of open-seat Senate races was 17 in 1972 and 13 in 1982, whereas the mid-cycle average for 1974–80 was six and for 1984–86 was three and one-half. Since the 17 open-seat races in 1972 are more than double the 1974–80 average, reapportionment apparently encouraged higher retirement rates. The number of open-seat contests in 1982 is double the 1974–80 average of six seats but is notably higher than the 1984–86 average of

Table 7.4
Women Nonincumbent Candidates and Open Seats in the Florida House of Representatives and Senate,* 1972–86

HOUSE OF REPRESENTATIVES

YEAR	WOMEN NON-INCUMBENT CANDIDATES	PERCENT OF CANDIDATES	OPEN SEAT RACES IN HOUSE	PERCENT OF HOUSE SEATS
1972**	24	14	47	39
1974	29	13	35	29
1976	31	14	30	25
1978	28	12	40	33
1980	17	12	17	14
1982**	53	20	40	33
1984	22	17	7	6
1986	32	16	20	17

SENATE

YEAR	WOMEN NON-INCUMBENT CANDIDATES	PERCENT OF CANDIDATES	OPEN SEAT RACES IN HOUSE	PERCENT OF HOUSE SEATS
1972**	5	7	17	43
1974	4	11	6	15
1976	2	6	5	13
1978	8	15	8	20
1980	3	7	6	15
1982**	17	23	13	33
1984	2	10	2	5
1986	7	21	5	13

*This table includes all women candidates, both Anglo and minorities, because the data on candidates do not provide information on the race of candidates. However, very few minorities contested for or were elected to the Florida State Legislature before 1982.

**In 1972, legislative districts were redrawn. In 1982, the change from multimember to single-member districts was effective, and legislative districts were redrawn.

three and one-half. Because of the short time-frame following the 1982 election, we rely primarily on the comparison with the 1974–80 elections and conclude that the increase in open-seat races in 1982 is due primarily to the doubling of contested seats.

The number of open-seat races also increased in the House. There were 40 open-seat House races in 1982 and 47 in 1972, compared with the 1974–80 mid-cycle average of 30.5 and the 1984–86 average of 13.5. Since the number of contested House seats remained stable, the increase in open-seat races is due to higher rates of retirements. The drop in open-seat races both preceding and

Table 7.5
Nonincumbent Candidates for the Florida House of Representatives and Senate, 1982

HOUSE OF REPRESENTATIVES

	NUMBER OF CANDIDATES	NUMBER NOMINATED	PERCENT NOMINATED	NUMBER GAIN OFFICE	PERCENT GAIN OFFICE
Women	53	28	53	10	19
Men	213	87	41	37	17

SENATE

	NUMBER OF CANDIDATES	NUMBER NOMINATED	PERCENT NOMINATED	NUMBER GAIN OFFICE	PERCENT GAIN OFFICE
Women	17	11	65	5	29
Men	56	23	41	9	16

following the 1982 election suggests that incumbents considering retirement chose to do so when their districts were redrawn.

The second process, decisions by nonincumbents to contest for office, also is apt to affect the number of Anglo women legislators because women candidates in Florida, as elsewhere, usually are elected at the same rate as men candidates. Since there were more opportunities to gain office in 1982, the number of nonincumbent women candidates should and does increase (see table 7.4). However, the notable development is the increase in the proportion of women candidates. The proportion of women candidates for House seats is .20, compared with the 1974–80 average of .13; in Senate races, the proportion of women candidates is .23, and the 1974–80 average is .10. The same pattern does not appear in the 1972 election, when few women in Florida or anywhere else were competing for public office. In 1982, the women House candidates gained office at the same rate as men candidates, but women Senate candidates gained office at higher rates than their male counterparts (see table. 7.5). Nineteen percent of all nonincumbent women candidates and 17 percent of nonincumbent men candidates for House seats gained office; in the Senate, the percentages are 29 and 16.

In summary, the higher-than-average increase in Anglo women representatives in 1982 was aided by an increase in retirements and a higher proportion of women candidates who gained office at the same rate as men candidates. In the Senate, there were more open-seat races primarily because all Senate seats were contested in 1982, and a higher proportion of women candidates gained office at higher rates than their male counterparts. The Anglo women legislators elected in 1982 benefited from two conditions—more opportunities to gain office and a higher proportion of women candidates.

The question is: Why did the proportion of women candidates increase in 1982? One plausible explanation is that potential women candidates perceived unusual opportunities to gain office. There were more open-seat races, and many incumbents contested for reelection in redrawn districts. However, a recruitment effort by activists in the women's movement may also have been partially responsible. Following the defeat of the Equal Rights Amendment (ERA) in the Florida State Legislature in 1981, activists and officers in state and national women's organizations, particularly the National Organization for Women (NOW), led a drive to recruit more women candidates for legislative seats. The action teams for the ERA, which had been organized in nearly every county, were utilized in the campaigns of several women candidates.[8] In any case, it is clear that an increase in women candidates is not necessarily sufficient; it was the increase in the proportion of women candidates in 1982 that contributed to the unusual increase in women legislators. If an increase in women candidates is accompanied by a similar increase in men candidates and if there are few sex differences in success rates, it is difficult to see how the proportion of women in state legislatures can increase substantially.

The remaining task is to evaluate the reasons for the higher proportion of Anglo women legislators serving in the more competitive chamber—the state Senate—following the 1982 election. A plausible explanation for the unusual pattern includes consideration of the differences between Senate and House seats. First, Senate seats are more competitive—there are 40 Senate seats compared with 120 in the House. This barrier was reduced in 1982 because all seats were contested, and as a result, the number of open-seat races doubled to 13 from a mid-cycle average of six. Also by 1982, the effects of the second barrier— serving in the recruitment hierarchy—were reduced. The number of women holding elective office in Florida slowly increased during the 1970s, and we believe these women were as apt to contest for a Senate seat as men in similar situations in 1982.

However, it was the substantial increase in open-seat races in 1982 that permitted the above factors to exert more than a slow, steady effect. The number of Anglo women in the Senate increased from four to eight, or 20 percent of that chamber. These observations also apply to representation of black and Latino women, which also showed increases. For the first time, a black woman was elected to the Florida Senate and a Hispanic woman was elected to the House. The proportion of black women was 2.5 percent in the Senate in 1982. There were no Latino women in that chamber in 1982, and the proportion of Latinos in the House was only 1 percent.

CONCLUSION

The changes in electoral structures in Florida did influence the representation of the three groups—blacks, Hispanics, and Anglo women. The number of black and Hispanic legislators increased, although minority representation in the state legislature remains below representation in the population. Furthermore, minority women, particularly Hispanic women, did not benefit as much as minority men. Only three black women and one Hispanic woman currently serve in the Florida State Legislature. The effects of the structural changes on minority representation were not simple or straightforward. The number of black legislators apparently increased because of the legislature's commitment to create single-member districts with substantial black populations or majorities. The increase in Hispanic legislators followed the change to single-member districts and the large increase in the Latino population in Dade County. The effects of these changes are confounded and prevent a clear assessment of the relationships between the change to single-member districts and greater Hispanic representation.

The effects of the structural changes on the representation of Anglo women were even more complex. A change in the electoral system and the doubling of open Senate seats contributed to the unusual increase in women in that chamber. Beyond this consequence, the structural changes apparently contributed indirectly to the election of women legislators by influencing two sets of decisions. More House incumbents retired, thereby creating more opportunities to gain office, and the proportion of women candidates increased. However, the structural changes were accompanied by an unusual effort by women's organizations to recruit women candidates. Therefore, the effects of these two forces—structural changes and the recruitment drive—cannot be analyzed separately.

The long-term effects of the 1982 structural changes in the Florida State Legislature on women's and minority representation are problematic. Although the proportion of women candidates in the 1984–86 elections generally remained higher than the 1974–80 average, the number of open-seat races declined notably. Given the high reelection rates of Florida state legislators (only 6 percent were defeated in the period 1974–80), the decline in open seats does not bode well for future substantial increases in the number of minority and women legislators.

NOTES

1. Carla Coleman and Nancy Leikauf, ''1982 Reapportionment: A View from the House Rafters,'' unpublished paper, p.18, available from Anita Pritchard.

2. See Timothy Lenz and Anita Pritchard, ''Electoral Laws and the 'Vicious Art' of Politics in Florida,'' paper presented at the 1988 annual meeting of the Southern Political Science Association, Atlanta, Georgia.

3. See Bernard Grofman, Michael Migalski, and Nicholas Noviello, ''Effects of Mul-

timember Districts on Black Representation in State Legislatures," *Review of Black Political Economy*, Spring 1986, pp. 65–78.

4. See W. E. Lyons, and Malcolm E. Jewell. "Minority Representation and the Drawing of City Council Districts." *Urban Affairs Quarterly*, March 1988, pp. 432–47.

5. This portion of the discussion is from an earlier paper—"The Effects of Change in Electoral Structures upon the Election of Women Officeholders: The Case of Florida"— which was presented at the annual meeting of the American Political Science Association in Atlanta, Georgia, September 1989.

6. Susan J. Carroll, *Women as Candidates in American Politics* (Bloomington: Indiana University Press, 1985), p. 110; Robert Darcy, Susan Welch, and Janet Clark, *Women, Elections, and Representation* (New York: Longman, 1987); Wilma Rule, "Electoral Systems, Contextual Factors, and Women's Opportunity for Election to Parliament in Twenty-Three Democracies," *Western Political Quarterly*, September 1987, pp. 477–98; Wilma Rule, "Why More Women Are State Legislators," *Western Political Quarterly*, June 1990, pp. 437–48; and Susan Welch and Donley Studlar, "Multimember Districts and the Representation of Women: Evidence from Britain and the United States," *Journal of Politics*, May 1990, pp. 391–412.

7. For example, see Kristi Andersen and Stuart Thorson, "Congressional Turnover and the Election of Women," *Western Political Quarterly*, March 1984, pp. 143–56; Robert Darcy and Sarah S. Schramm, "When Women Run against Men," *Public Opinion Quarterly*, Spring 1977, pp. 1–12; Albert Karnig and B. Oliver Walter, "Elections of Women to City Council," *Social Science Quarterly*, March 1976, pp. 605–13; and Susan Welch, Margery Ambrosius, Janet Clark, and Robert Darcy, "The Effects of Candidate Gender on Electoral Outcomes in State Legislative Races," *Western Political Quarterly*, September 1985, pp. 464–74.

8. This information was provided by present and past state officers of the Florida chapter of the National Organization for Women. For a discussion of the role of women's organizations in the recruitment of women candidates, see Rule, "Why More Women Are State Legislators."

8

Creative Multimember Redistricting and Representation of Women and Minorities in the Maryland Legislature

M. Margaret Conway

Maryland is rare among the states in the proportion of its elected and high-level appointed officials who are women or blacks. As table 8.1 indicates, office holding by women and minorities extends from city and county councils to the state legislature, the governor's cabinet, and the United States Congress. Women and minorities are particularly successful in being elected to legislative offices. The proportion of legislative members who are women or minorities increased substantially between 1959 and 1989 (see table 8.2).[1] How can the electoral success of women and minorities be explained?

Attaining elected public office requires successful passage through a four-stage process—eligibility, selection, nomination, and election[2]—but research differs on the probability of women and minorities being nominated and elected.[3] Crucial to their success, however, are the criteria used to determine eligibility to run for office, the characteristics of those defining the eligibility criteria, and the informal selection process. Eligibility may involve self-selection criteria such as educational attainment, relevant experience, and family income levels sufficient to support a family member serving as a relatively low-paid state legislator, or the criteria may include extensive prior political party work and/or membership in a particular party club or faction.

Selection criteria vary not only between states but also within a state. This research examines some of the factors that result in the election of women and minorities from several Maryland legislative districts but not from others.

The use of multimember districts for Maryland House of Delegates elections clearly provides an increased opportunity for women and minority candidates to be elected. However, specific characteristics of Maryland's various jurisdictions and their political cultures, as well as elements of the 1982 redistricting plan, contribute to the varying electability of women and minorities in different local

Table 8.1
Women and Minorities in Selected Maryland Public Offices, 1989 (in Percent)

OFFICE	WHITE WOMEN	BLACK WOMEN	BLACK MEN
State Senate	12.8	0	12.8
State House of Delegates	21.3	4.3	10.6
Governor's Cabinet	20.0	13.3	6.7
County councils and Baltimore City Council	16.8	4.5	5.3
State Court of Appeals	0.0	0.0	14.3
State Court of Special Appeals	7.6	0.0	7.6

Table 8.2
Maryland General Assembly, Representation of Women and Minorities, 1959–89

YEAR	WHITE WOMEN	BLACK WOMEN	BLACK MEN
1959	1	1	0
1969	13	1	5
1979	21	4	14
1989	36	6	21

jurisdictions. Social, economic, and political changes in society in general also are important in explaining increased representation of women and minorities in Maryland.

Some background information on Maryland and its legislature clarifies how changes in society have influenced Maryland politics, facilitating the election of women and minorities. The Maryland State Legislature consists of a 47-member Senate and a 141-member House of Delegates; all members are elected for four-year terms in the same midterm election (e.g., 1986, 1990). Each senatorial district elects one senator and three delegates.[4] By 1982, 80 percent of the population of Maryland lived in the Interstate 95 corridor stretching from north of Baltimore to Washington, D.C. Most of the Interstate 95 corridor's population resided in five local jurisdictions—Baltimore City, Baltimore County, the two suburban counties adjacent to Washington (Prince George's and Montgomery), and Anne Arundel County, which contains the state capital of Annapolis and which has developed as a suburb of the metropolitan Baltimore area at the county's northern end and of the Washington area in its central section. Other counties in the outer suburban fringes around Baltimore and Washington have experienced rapid population growth. The more populous jurisdictions differ in sociodemographic patterns, political histories, and political cultures, and thus some are more supportive of the candidacies of women and minorities than are others.

THE CHANGING ENVIRONMENT

Several environmental factors resulting from Maryland's location adjacent to the nation's capital significantly affect its politics. One is the extensive political coverage by the Washington-based national news media and Baltimore and Washington local media, with television emphasizing highly visible political events and social problems. In addition, Washington, D.C., and Baltimore are blessed with very good newspapers.

Another consequence of Maryland's proximity to the nation's capital is the extensive opportunities for participation in the growing number of interest groups and political movements operating in Washington.[5] These opportunities provide socialization to the realities of politics and training in political skills. Thus, Washington, D.C., stimulates political activism, which has spillover effects on Maryland politics.

An important characteristic of the Washington, D.C., area and to a lesser extent the Baltimore area is the significant proportion of the voting age population prohibited from engaging in partisan political activities because they are federal government employees.[6] Their spouses, however, may seek partisan elective office. In Montgomery County, for example, when the political machine that had previously dominated the county lost power in the 1950s, a strong precinct-based Democratic party organization developed. Many of the women initially elected to public office in that county began their political careers in precinct work.

Several other factors also have contributed to the political system's openness to the election of minorities and women to public office. The shift to a technical and service economy has occurred at a higher rate in the Washington, D.C., area than in most other metropolitan areas. Furthermore, more women are employed outside the home in the Washington, D.C., metropolitan area than anywhere else in the country, and that employment is largely in white-collar jobs.[7] Lastly, in recent elections 60 percent of primary election voters in the suburban jurisdictions have been women, and women are slightly more apt to support women for elective office than are men.[8]

Very visible female role models were important in bringing women into politics in several jurisdictions. Those role models included Gladys Spellman, Prince George's County Council member and later a United States representative, and Verda Welcome of Baltimore, one of the first black members of the House of Delegates and subsequently a member of the state Senate. During the early years of women's success in attaining elected office, career paths to political office varied (Parent-Teacher Association, the civil rights movement, League of Women Voters), but many initially came to politics through nonparty recruitment paths. A person who had not been active in party politics would be much less likely to gain access to a dominant party slate, although nonparty organizations provide an important source of support for women and minority candidates.

Maryland is largely a one-party Democratic state; after the 1986 election, only 18 of 141 members of the House of Delegates and 7 of 47 senators were Republicans.[9] Many issues emphasized by the Democratic party are ones on which the electorate perceives women as more competent than men.[10] Many of those policy areas are also primarily the responsibility of state governments.

The national Democratic party's increased openness and accessibility are fully reflected in the Maryland Democratic party's rules and in the extensive representation of women and minorities on the more populous jurisdictions' central committees and on the state committee. The party central committees in the counties and in Baltimore City nominate candidates to replace legislators from their party and jurisdiction who resign or die in office. Although a number of factors influence who is nominated, jurisdictions with more women and minorities on the party central committee are more likely to support the appointment of women and minorities to legislative vacancies.

POLITICAL ENVIRONMENT, ELIGIBILITY, AND SELECTION

A number of factors affect the ability of women and minorities to win nomination and election to legislative office in Maryland. First, individuals must be able to devote the time that legislative careers demand yet must be sufficiently affluent that they can afford to work at a relatively low-paying job (in 1990 a legislator's salary was $25,000 a year). Traditionally, state legislative service was low paying as well as part-time, and that restricted the recruitment pool to those employed in occupations flexible in time demands and financially rewarding, such as law or real estate. Interestingly, only three women and three blacks serving in the 1989 legislature were attorneys, and only one woman and no blacks were employed in real estate. For many Maryland legislators, their salary is their family's second income, with the spouse providing the principal income. However, several women and minority men were employed in jobs from which they received released time to serve in the state legislature. (e.g., teacher, education system administrator, labor union officer).[11]

Second, successful legislators must have the education or experience necessary to deal with the complicated issues considered by the legislature. Maryland's more populous jurisdictions have a much higher than average proportion of women and minorities with high levels of education.[12]

Although Maryland has a higher proportion of women legislators (22 percent in 1990) than most other states, these legislators tend to come from a few jurisdictions. A similar pattern exists in minority representation (see table 8.3).

Table 8.3
Maryland General Assembly, Percent of Delegation from Various Jurisdictions Who Are Women or Minorities, 1987–88

JURISDICTIONS	WOMEN		BLACKS	
	SENATE	HOUSE	SENATE	HOUSE
Baltimore City	11	19	44	52
Baltimore County	14	21	0	0
Ann Arundel County	0	17	0	0
Montgomery County	50	50	0	0
Prince George's County	0	38	0	0
All Others*	10	13	0	2

*This category includes all districts that contain part of one of the four large suburban counties and part of an adjacent smaller county.

What are the characteristics of those jurisdictions that are more apt to nominate and elect women minorities? How can the ability of women and minorities to contest successfully for legislative office be explained?

POLITICAL ENVIRONMENT AND SELECTION, NOMINATION AND ELECTION

The historian George Callcott argues that between 1940 and 1980, four distinct political cultures existed in Maryland.[13] Baltimore City had its own distinct political culture, as did western Maryland, the Tidewater counties on the eastern shore and the lower western shore of the Chesapeake Bay, and the suburban counties around Baltimore and Washington, D.C. Eligibility and selection-nomination processes would be expected to differ among these four political cultures, with consequences for the inclusion of women and minorities in the political process. Furthermore, the five most populous jurisdictions have different political histories. During the twentieth century each experienced political control by a political machine or by political clubs. This pattern of political control ended or at least declined significantly between the beginning of the 1950s and the middle of the 1970s; the timing of the entry of women and minorities into legislative office is partly a function of when the machines or clubs declined in influence in each jurisdiction.

Examining first the representation of women, we see that all but one of the 10 women nominated for the Senate in 1986 and all but eight of the women nominated for the House of Delegates resided in one of the five most populous jurisdictions (see table 8.4). In 1986, half the women nominated for legislative office lived in two Washington, D.C., suburban jurisdictions, and 45 percent of

Table 8.4
Women's Success Rates by Jurisdictions, Maryland General Assembly 1986 Elections

House	Number Running	Nominated Number	Nominated Percent	Elected Number	Elected Percent
Ann Arundel	5	2	40	2	100
Baltimore County	17	6	35	4	67
Montgomery	20	12	60	8	67
Prince George's	15	8	53	8	100
Baltimore City	16	5	31	5	100
Other*	9	8	89	6	75
SENATE					
Ann Arundel	0	0	0	0	0
Baltimore County	3	2	67	1	50
Montgomery	7	5	71	3	60
Prince George's	2	0	0	0	0
Baltimore City	4	2	50	1	50
Other*	1	1	100	1	100

*These numbers include all districts that contain part of one of the four large suburban counties and part of an adjacent smaller county.

those elected resided in those two suburban counties. In contrast, Anne Arundel County, the least supportive of women candidates among the five most populous jurisdictions, elected only two women from districts wholly within that county.

The reasons that some jurisdictions are more likely than others to elect women to the state legislature can be summarized. Women are more apt to be elected from areas that have a more affluent, well-educated population. Those districts are largely in longer-established suburban jurisdictions and in the Washington, D.C., area. In addition, areas with more traditional political cultures, such as rural districts or areas with a higher proportion of first- and second-generation immigrants, tend to nominate and elect few women to the state legislature.

The willingness of political leaders to include women and minorities in their political coalitions is also important in opening opportunities to gain public office. For example, the political organization led by Peter O'Malley and Steny Hoyer, influential in Prince George's County beginning in the 1960s, worked to build an inclusive rather than exclusive political coalition.

Table 8.5
Maryland State Legislative Contests, Political Success Rates, 1986

House	Number Running	Nominated Number	Nominated Percent	Elected Number	Elected Percent
Men	229	178	78	108	61
Women	82	41	50	33	80
Difference of Proportions Test		Z=4.51	p .0001	Z=3.84	p .0001
SENATE					
Men	111	60	54	41	68
Women	17	10	59	6	60
Difference of Proportions Test		Z=.816	ns	Z=.873	ns

The practice of slating is also significant in determining who is elected to legislative office (and to other offices at the state and local levels). Candidates for various offices join slates, and being on the "best" slate enhances a candidate's chances for electoral success. The dominant party's legislative district slate usually would be assembled or greatly influenced by the district's state senator, although other party influentials, a district's party club, or a countywide organization may influence the slate's composition.[14] The dominant slate benefits from the greater name recognition of at least some of its members and its greater ability to raise necessary campaign funds and to acquire other resources, such as campaign workers.

When multimember districts are used for legislative elections, the political risks arising from including women or minority race members on the slate are minimized. Furthermore, substantial political benefits in terms of a broader base of political support can be achieved.

The probability that women and minority candidates will be elected is to a significant degree dependent on getting on the preferred slate of their district's dominant party. As table 8.5 indicates, in 1986 women were less successful in gaining nominations for the House of Delegates than men, but if nominated, they were more likely to be elected. Much of this variation in success rates is attributable to whether the candidates were on the dominant slate in the primary election and were members of the district's majority party.

Minorities' representation in the Maryland State Legislature occurs primarily through the election of blacks from two jurisdictions—Baltimore City and Prince George's County. Beginning in the 1960s, Baltimore's black community gained increasing legislative representation. Verda Welcome, a civil rights movement leader, was elected to the state legislature before Maryland's reapportionment revolution. As the black population of Baltimore increased and dispersed into more areas of the city, increased representation of blacks occurred. In the 1982 redistricting, four of the nine districts in Baltimore City were created with a black majority population and one with an almost even split between blacks and whites. To maintain representation of various ethnic and minority groups and to avoid having districts that extended beyond the city's boundaries, eight of the nine General Assembly districts within the city were drawn with a population average ranging a few percentage points (but in no case as much as 5 percent) below the 89,723 that a strict population apportionment would have mandated.

A different pattern of minority representation occurred in the Washington suburbs. Between mid–1970 and 1990, approximately 100,000 blacks moved from Washington, D.C., into suburban Prince George's County, and approximately the same number of whites moved out. A significant proportion of the black citizens moving into the county were predisposed to be politically active. In the 1982 redistricting, one of the seven districts in the county was crafted to have a black majority population and two to have an even split between whites and blacks. In the 1982 election two districts and in 1986 all three districts elected blacks to the legislature. By 1990, minority race members comprised 50 percent of the county's population, and the election of blacks to the legislature would increase as a consequence of the 1990 elections and the redistricting of Maryland General Assembly districts before the 1994 elections.

OTHER DISTRICT CHARACTERISTICS AND WOMEN'S ELECTORAL SUCCESS

Legislative districts may be subdivided into three single-member House of Delegates districts or into a one-member and a two-member district. For example, after the 1982 redistricting, District 1, located in the state's two western-most counties, elected one senator from the entire district but was divided into two districts for electing members of the House of Delegates. Subdistrict 1A (most of Garrett County and part of Allegheny County) elected one member of the House of Delegates, and 1B (part of Allegheny County) elected two members. In the 1982 redistricting, jurisdiction or incumbency concerns resulted in 10 of the 47 legislative districts being split into subdistricts for elections to the House of Delegates.

After the 1986 election, of the 30 members of the House of Delegates elected from subdivided senatorial districts, only four were women (two elected from single-member districts and two from two-member districts). Three of the four women resided in outlying suburban counties experiencing rapid population growth and attracting affluent, well-educated professionals. The fourth was elected from a district in the western part of the state; she had previously been active in a number of voluntary, professional, and party organizations.

Why are so few women elected from these subdivided districts? Is it the size of the district (one or two elected rather than three), or is it the nature of the political and social environment in which these types of districts are found? Women constitute 25 percent of those elected to the House of Delegates from three-member districts, but only 13 percent of those elected from two-member districts and 17 percent of those sent to the legislature from single-member districts. Women are less likely to be elected from rural jurisdictions and most likely to be elected from suburban areas. The divided districts tend to occur in rural areas or in formerly rural areas undergoing transformation into suburbs.

In districts containing more than two counties or parts of counties and in which delegates are elected at large by the voters of the entire district, the 1982 redistricting law stipulates that no county or part of a county may have more than one resident delegate. Three of the 47 General Assembly districts elected delegates under this rule. In 1986, no woman was elected from a district to which this requirement applied.

THE NONELECTORAL AVENUE TO THE LEGISLATURE

Approximately one-fourth of the members of the Maryland General Assembly first gain legislative office by appointment to replace a member who dies or resigns. When a vacancy occurs, three candidates may be nominated by the departed legislator's party committee in the local jurisdiction. The governor appoints the replacement legislator from among the three persons nominated. Since the 1970s, however, the practice has been to send the governor only one name for appointment. Although a number of factors determine who is appointed to fill a vacant legislative office, the willingness of the jurisdiction's relevant party central committee to support women candidates, and of the governor to appoint a woman, is influential. Incumbents, including those who first gain office through appointment, are usually victorious when seeking reelection to the legislature. Between 1983 and 1986, one woman member of the House of Delegates was appointed to the state Senate and two women were appointed to the House of Delegates. All three ran for election in 1986, and two were successful (the senator and one delegate). Three women were appointed to the House of Delegates during the 1987–90 period, increasing the number of women legislators from 39 to 42 and the proportion of women in the state legislature to 22.3 percent.

CONCLUSION

As this case study of Maryland demonstrates, the election of women and minorities to the legislature within a state using multimember districts varies greatly with the political, social, and economic characteristics of the local jurisdictions. The demographic representation of women and minorities is also a function of legislative district and subdistrict boundaries and of the number of legislators elected per district. Drawing district boundaries is a creative act that can have a significant impact on the numbers of women and minorities elected to the legislature.

NOTES

This research has benefited substantially from discussions with Sue Dowden, Greg Lebel, Charles (Buzz) Ryan, and Georgia Sorenson. Karl Aro of the Legislative Reference Service, Maryland General Assembly, supplied a copy of the 1982 redistricting plan and the State Court of Appeals decision on the cases challenging the 1982 state legislative redistricting. Data on women and minority elected and appointed officials were obtained from various volumes of the *Maryland Manual*, published by the Division of State Archives, State of Maryland. Steve Shandy of the Institute for Governmental Service, University of Maryland, also provided valuable assistance in data collection.

1. In 1989, Maryland ranked 12th in the number of women serving in the state legislature.

2. See, for example, Wilma Rule, "Why Women Don't Run: The Critical Contextual Factors in Women's Legislative Recruitment," *Western Political Quarterly*, March 1981, pp. 60–77; Moshe M. Czudnowski, "Political Recruitment," in Fred I. Greenstein and Nelson W. Polsby, eds., *Handbook of Political Science* (Reading, Mass.: Addison-Wesley, 1975), pp. 155–242; Susan Welch, "Recruitment of Women to Public Office," *Western Political Quarterly*, September 1978, pp. 372–80; Robert Darcy, Susan Welch, and Janet Clark, *Women, Elections, and Representation* (New York: Longman, 1987); and Paula Dubeck, "Women and Access to Political Office: A Comparison of Female and Male Legislators," *Sociological Quarterly*, Winter 1976, pp. 42–52.

3. Jeane Kirkpatrick, *Political Women* (New York: Basic Books, 1974); R. Darcy and Sarah Slavin Schramm, "When Women Run against Men: The Electorate's Response to Congressional Contests," *Public Opinion Quarterly*, Spring 1977, pp. 1–12; and A. Karnig and O. Walter, "Elections of Women to City Councils," *Social Science Quarterly*, March 1976, pp. 605–13.

4. Before the United States Supreme Court decisions on reapportionment in the early 1960s, each of the 23 counties in Maryland had one state senator and up to six delegates, depending on the county's population. Baltimore was assigned six districts, each with one senator and six delegates. Beginning with the 1966 election, Maryland's legislative districts were apportioned on the basis of population. The number of districts (47) was last altered by law in 1972.

5. See, for example, Kay Lehman Schlozman and John T. Tierney, *Organized Interests and American Democracy* (New York: Harper and Row Publishers, 1986), and Jack L. Walker, "The Origin and Maintenance of Interest Groups in America," *American Political Science Review*, June 1983, pp. 390–406.

6. United States Bureau of the Census, *Census of Population: General Social and Economic Characteristics, Maryland, 1980* (Washington, D.C.: United States Government Printing Office, 1981), pp. 22–487 to 22–494.

7. In 1980, about one-quarter of employed women in the suburban counties worked in professional or managerial jobs and approximately 55 percent in technical, sales, and administrative support jobs.

8. This information was provided by Sue Dowden and is based on the Maryland Poll conducted semiannually by the Survey Research Center, University of Maryland.

9. Data on party identification of those elected were obtained from the *Maryland Manual, 1987–1988* (Annapolis: Maryland State Archives, 1987).

10. According to "The New American Women Survey" conducted by Hickman-Maslin and American Viewpoint for the National Women's Political Caucus, significant pluralities of the national electorate believe that women do a better job than men on domestic policy issues such as health care cost, education, civil rights, drug abuse, environmental issues, poverty, day care, and government spending. See "The New American Woman Survey," August 1987, p. 13.

11. *Maryland Manual, 1989–1990* (Annapolis: Maryland State Archives, 1989).

12. *Census of Population . . . Maryland*, Table 182.

13. George Callcott, *Maryland and America, 1940–1980* (Baltimore: Johns Hopkins University Press, 1985).

14. Two research projects on recruitment processes to the Maryland State Legislature are currently in progress, one by Pamela Edwards of Wittenberg University and the other by Gregory Lebel of the University of Maryland. The projects include an examination of slating of candidates by a political leader, faction, or party organization of an endorsed and supported ticket.

9

The Effect of the "Cutback" on the Representation of Women and Minorities in the Illinois General Assembly

David H. Everson

The 1870 Illinois Constitution adopted the method of cumulative voting for choosing members of the House of Representatives. Proposed by Joseph Medill, one of the founders of the Republican party and owner-editor of the *Chicago Tribune*, cumulative voting was intended to reduce the twin effects of partisan and sectional divisiveness in Illinois by virtually guaranteeing minority party representation from districts where there was a strong partisan majority.[1]

Severe partisan and sectional splits in Illinois had deep historical roots. The southern part of the state had been settled largely from Kentucky, Tennessee, and Virginia, whereas the northern section had settlers from New England, New York, and Pennsylvania. The Civil War had heightened sectional divisions and given them a clear national partisan cast: the Republican North versus the Democratic South.[2]

At the 1870 convention, Medill argued that cumulative voting would "secure representation for our long enduring Republican friends in democratic Egypt [southern Illinois] and give the swallowed-up and buried under democrats of northern Illinois a chance, also, of being heard in our legislative halls by men of their own selection."[3]

The new system allocated three representatives to each house district and allowed each voter three votes. A voter could choose to cast three votes for one candidate (often called a "bullet"), one and one-half votes for each of two candidates, or one vote for each of three candidates.[4] The judicious use of the "bullet" would normally guarantee minority party representation. It should be noted that *minority*—as used in 1870—referred only to partisan minorities.

When cumulative voting was adopted in Illinois, there was a sense that the experiment might spread to other states, but it never did. It is somewhat ironic that after Illinois abandoned the practice, cumulative voting emerged as a remedy in voting rights cases where there are at-large elections and a dispersed minority.[5]

In time, one of the problems with the new system of cumulative voting in Illinois emerged—the two parties limited total nominations to three (two for the majority party, one for the minority) for three offices, thereby depriving voters of any choice in the general election. From 1922 to 1970, the two parties limited the nominations to three in about one-half of the districts.[6]

Several attempts were made to remove cumulative voting in Illinois. One effort was made in the proposed new 1920 state constitution; however, the charter was rejected five-to-one by the voters. In 1925, a constitutional amendment on reapportionment, eliminating cumulative voting, was introduced in the general assembly but was tabled.[7]

Although controversial over its entire 110-year lifetime, cumulative voting did work remarkably well in achieving its goal of minority party representation.[8] In fact, one could conclude that it virtually achieved proportional representation for two parties.[9] From 1920 to 1968, the Republican percentage of seats in the Illinois House almost faithfully reflected the Republican percentage of the presidential vote in the state, suggesting that basic party splits were represented accurately in the House.[10] In 1970, when a new constitution was approved, Illinois voters opted to retain cumulative voting by a healthy margin. The issue was deemed sufficiently controversial that it was one of three items voted on separately by the electorate.[11] However, the new constitution contained a ticking time bomb—a limited initiative provision—restricted to changes in structural and procedural subjects of the legislative article. That act of intentional foresight by the framers of the new constitution paved the way for the eventual demise of the grand experiment.[12]

THE CUTBACK

In 1980, after an ill-timed legislative pay increase, an initiative campaign was launched to reduce the size of the House from 177 to 118 members and to eliminate cumulative voting. As might be expected, legislators and lobbyists led the opposition while a cluster of reform groups, including the League of Women Voters, supported the change.[13] Much of the debate by the proponents of the "cutback," as it came to be known, centered on the benefits to be gained from a reduction in the size of the house, for example, reducing legislative inefficiency and costs. Proponents claimed that the amount of legislation introduced would be trimmed. Additional arguments for the cutback included the contention that one-on-one legislative elections would be more competitive and therefore would increase legislator accountability. Moreover, it was argued that the reduction in the size of the House would "streamline the legislative process" and "bring government closer to the people by cutting the size of the House districts in half."[14]

Opponents of the change countered that the cutback would not achieve what its supporters claimed, such as a reduction in legislative costs. They pointed to the example of Massachusetts, which had recently reduced the size of its House and had seen legislative costs rise.[15] Moreover, the opponents contended that the change would deny representation to "independents, to Democrats in Republican areas, and to Republicans in Democratic areas."[16] Perhaps the most persistent argument of the opponents was that the cutback would cause a reduction in minority representation. However, minority representation no longer meant precisely what it had in 1870. The term *minority* had been expanded to cover three separate groups: partisan, demographic, and philosophic minorities, with the latter often called "independents." In this context, *independent* meant someone who deviated from the norm within a party, for example, an independent Republican or Democrat. Representatives elected from minority parties in strong partisan majority districts—suburban Democrats or Chicago Republicans are examples—often were labeled "independents." It was argued, with some justification, that such representatives were among the most innovative in the House, and opponents of the cutback argued that they would become extinct.

Illinois is a large state with competitive political parties and a diverse population, including significant racial and ethnic minorities. For example, Illinois has a black population of about 14.0 percent (compared with the nation's 11.2 percent) and a Hispanic population of almost 7.0 percent (compared with the nation's 7.1 percent). Illinois faithfully reflects national trends in presidential voting. Indeed, Illinois often is called a political and social microcosm of the nation.[17]

With the substantial minority population of Illinois, it was probably inevitable that minority representation in a demographic sense would arise as an issue with respect to the effects of the cutback. It was argued that the ranks of demographic minorities—women and blacks—in the House would be reduced by the cutback.[18] Specifically, it was contended that "the value of cumulative voting as an aid to electing women legislators" could "hardly be doubted."[19] The argument rested on the assumption that women and minorities had targeted the "bullet" (three votes) to elect members of their respective minority groups to the House.

The cutback campaign was intense for the affected parties, especially incumbent legislators. However, the general public did not appear highly moved by the issue. Only 63 percent of the voters in the 1980 election registered an opinion on the cutback. Nevertheless, in the wake of the pay-raise controversy, the cutback passed with a 69 percent vote in favor. Although it cannot be proved, it is probable the electorate was less concerned with the issue of cumulative voting and more concerned with the opportunity to lop off one-third of the legislature in a single stroke.

The first House elections under the new single-member districts would take place in 1982. Would the benefits of the proponents or the horrors of the opponents result?

In a piece written shortly after the abolition of cumulative voting, it was argued that the percentage of black representatives would probably not decline because blacks tended to be elected from overwhelmingly black urban districts, with almost all such districts in Chicago. In other words, the nature of the district, not the bullet, was probably responsible for the election of black representatives. An earlier study had reached the same conclusion.[20] All but two of the blacks ever elected to the General Assembly had come from Chicago. The only exceptions were elected from the heavily black-populated East St. Louis. Put another way, aside from St. Clair (East St. Louis) and Cook counties, no counties had ever elected blacks to the General Assembly. The bullet did not serve to help elect downstate blacks in cities with more modest minority populations, such as Rockford or the Quad Cities.

It also was noted that the percentage of blacks in the Illinois House was higher than the national average but was similar to the percentage of blacks in the Illinois Senate, which elected members from the conventional single-member districts.[21] Consequently, it was inferred that cumulative voting was probably not the reason that blacks had been chosen in the numbers they had been in the House.

Cumulative voting may aid the election for "dispersed minorities" via the judicious use of the bullet—at least, that is the theory. However, for whatever reason, that does not seem to have happened in downstate Illinois.

This conclusion was less certain concerning the representation of women; their percentage in the House was about twice as high as that in the Senate and was above the national average, lending more credibility to the argument that cumulative voting aided their election.[22] Moreover, women were elected from Chicago and downstate, suggesting that women may have been using the bullet to select and retain representatives.

CUTBACK EFFECTS

There is now a decade of experience with the electoral effects of the cutback, so that the arguments concerning its effect on the representation of blacks and women can be assessed. The worst fears of the opponents of the cutback have not been realized.

The first experiment on the effect of the cutback on minority representation would come in 1982. However, the 1982 elections would be complicated by the twin effects of the cutback and redistricting. The elimination of 59 legislators at one stroke and the redrawing of district boundaries often pitted incumbent against incumbent (15 races in all). Moreover, the Democratic party had controlled the drawing of the 1981 legislative district map by the state legislature. The 1970 Illinois Constitution has a procedure wherein if the General Assembly is unable to enact a redistricting statute, an eight-member, bipartisan commission is created. If the commission deadlocks, a ninth member is chosen by lot. By the luck of the draw, the Democrats won the lottery and crafted the new legislative lines, leading to a decade of dominance in the General Assembly, particularly the House.[23] Therefore, it is difficult to determine where the cutback ends and redistricting kicks in as far as electoral effects are concerned.

For example, incumbency became an increasingly potent factor in Illinois legislative elections in the decade of the 1980s. In 1984, for example, 102 of 106 House incumbents were reelected.[24] This fact has undoubtedly aided the reelection of women and black incumbents, but it may also have served to limit a greater representation of the same groups by discouraging challengers.

In percentage terms, the ranks of both women and blacks were increased slightly in the House in the 1982 elections.[25] The absolute numbers, of course, were reduced. However, total minority representation of women and blacks in the general assembly was about the same because of increases in minority representation in the Senate, which was independent of cutback effects.

Opponents of the cutback often had tried to personalize the issue by pointing out particular minority members likely to lose their seats under the new system. Five women and two black men were among the partisan minorities represented in the "Class of 1980," the first chosen under cumulative voting. An examination of the fate of five minority party women elected to the House in 1980, but not in 1982, found two reelected and suggested that two may have been direct victims of the cutback and one an indirect victim.[26] The lone black Republican lost in the 1982 primary election, but Taylor Pouncey—who had been elected in 1980 as an independent—was reelected in 1982 as a Democrat. However, such particularized losses would be a one-time effect. The more critical issue was what would happen to the representation of women and blacks generally.

What has happened since 1982? Let us first consider the representation of blacks. One might expect that the absolute number of blacks in the Illinois Legislature, as a whole, and in the House in particular, would have declined markedly in the post cutback era, given the fact that one-third of the House membership had been chopped off. However, with blacks, this decline did not occur. In the decade of the 1970s (1973 through 1980), before the cutback, the total number of blacks elected to a given session of the legislature varied between 19 and 21. In the 1980s (1982 through 1988), the comparable numbers ranged between 20 and 22.

Total legislative representation, of course, is made up of House and Senate members. Black representation in the Senate as an absolute number and percentage has increased after the cutback, albeit marginally. In the 1970s in the House, the numbers of blacks were either 14 or 15. In the 1980s, after the cutback, the numbers have been a constant 14.[27] Hence, the proportion of blacks in the Illinois House has not declined—in fact, it has increased from about 8 percent to about 12 percent, more than double the national average (see table 9.1).

Could it be that the cutback and the elimination of cumulative voting had the effect of increasing black representation? This conclusion is doubtful. The more probable answer is that the 1981 reapportionment—followed by subsequent court action—is the cause. In 1981, the United States District Court—in response to

Table 9.1
Black Members in the Illinois House, 1972–82

ELECTION YEAR	NUMBER	PERCENTAGE
1972	14	8
1974	15	8
1976	14	8
1978	15	8
1980	15	8
---cutback		
1982	14	12
1984	14	12
1986	14	12
1988	14	12

Source: Illinois Legislative Research Unit.

a suit brought by blacks, Hispanics, and Republicans—altered part of the new districting map to increase black and Hispanic representation.[28] It is worth noting that it was only after this court decision that the first Hispanics were elected to the General Assembly. In other words, cumulative voting had not served to elect a Hispanic to the House.

What about the fate of women in the decade of the 1980s? In the last legislature before the cutback, the number of women in the 1980 House was 25, or 14 percent.[29] The Illinois proportion of women in 1980 was 40 percent higher than the national average of 10 percent. The number of women in the House since 1980 has ranged from a low of 19 in 1982 and 1984 to a high of 21 in 1988, or 18 percent (see table 9.2). Unlike the number of blacks, the absolute number of women in the legislature is considerably lower than it was before the cutback. And women's proportions now are only slightly above the national average of 17 percent.

CONCLUSIONS

It is impossible to determine what the representation of women or blacks would have been in the House if the cutback had not happened. It is, however, of some interest that women constituted 18 percent of the House seats and 20 percent of the Senate seats and blacks constituted 12 percent of the membership in each house.

The conclusion is obvious. Predictions about the consequences of the cutback from both sides were erroneous. The cutback failed to achieve most of its positive

Table 9.2
Women Members in the Illinois House, 1978–88

ELECTION YEAR	NUMBER	PERCENTAGE
1978	23	13
1980	25	14
--cutback		
1982	19	16
1984	19	16
1986	20	17
1988	21	18

Source: Illinois Legislative Research Unit.

objectives. It did not reduce legislative costs or the number of bills introduced. In 1980, 3,644 bills were introduced, and in 1988, 4,311 bills were introduced. It did not make legislative elections more competitive. It does appear to be true that the House is more efficient than before the cutback, but most observers credit that change to the strong hand of the speaker of the house.

Nevertheless, the worst fears were not realized either. The cutback did not produce a drastic reduction in the representation of women and blacks, as its opponents had feared. Why did the reduction not occur?

In the case of blacks, the answer apparently lies in the fact that blacks were never elected as minority members in majority white districts. Their election was due to the high concentration of black votes in particular urban districts, mostly in Chicago.

In the case of women, it may be that cumulative voting had something to do with the election of women to the Illinois House before the cutback. However, since the cutback, about one-fifth of the women who have ever served in the General Assembly have been reelected.[30] And the percentages of women selected to the state Senate also have risen. Illinois is in step with national trends toward electing more women legislators, although it has fallen in women's proportions relative to the national average.

Despite the fact that the chapter on cumulative voting in Illinois and its effects is closed, the story of its use as a minority protection device is not over. It would appear that cumulative voting may be more effective as a device for ensuring minority representation where it is currently being employed—in local at-large elections with dispersed minorities.

NOTES

1. David H. Everson et al., *The Cutback Amendment* (Springfield, Ill.: Sangamon State University, 1982), pp. 1–2.

2. David Kenney, *Basic Illinois Government* (Carbondale: Southern Illinois University Press, 1974), p. 92.

3. Quoted in Everson et al., *Cutback Amendment*, p. 6.

4. Ibid., p. 11.

5. Richard L. Engstrom, Delbert A. Taebel, and Richard L. Cole, "Cumulative Voting as a Remedy for Minority Vote Dilution: The Case of Alamogordo, New Mexico," *Journal of Law and Politics*, Spring 1989, pp. 469–97.

6. Everson et al., *Cutback Amendment*, p. 6.

7. Ibid., pp. 6–7.

8. Ibid., p. 7.

9. James Kuklinski, "Cumulative and Plurality Voting: An Analysis of Illinois' Unique Electoral System," *Western Political Quarterly*, December 1973, p. 736.

10. Everson et al., *Cutback Amendment*, p. 7.

11. Ibid., p. 12.

12. Ibid., pp. 12–13.

13. Ibid., pp. 23–26.

14. Ibid., p. 23.

15. Ibid., p. 25.

16. Ibid.

17. David H. Everson, "Illinois as a Bellwether," *Comparative State Politics*, February 1990, pp. 16–20.

18. Everson et al., *Cutback Amendment*, pp. 31–32.

19. Ibid., p. 32.

20. Illinois Legislative Council File 7–583, 1970.

21. Everson et al., *Cutback Amendment*, p. 32.

22. Ibid., p. 33.

23. Paul Green, "Legislative Redistricting in Illinois, 1871–1982: A Study of Geo-Political Survival," in Anna J. Merritt, ed., *Redistricting: An Exercise in Prophency* (Jacksonville: Illinois University, 1982), p. 33.

24. David H. Everson, "Illinois 1984, Legislative Elections," in *Illinois Elections* (Springfield: Illinois Issues, 1986), p. 87.

25. David H. Everson and Joan A. Parker, "Legislative Elections: Reviving an Old Partnership," in *Illinois Elections*, p. 96.

26. Everson, "Illinois 1984, Legislative Elections," p. 24.

27. Illinois Legislative Research Unit, *Black Legislators in Illinois, 1876–1989* (Springfield: Illinois General Assembly, 1989), p. 6.

28. *Chester J. Rybicki v. State Board of Elections of Illinois*, memorandum opinion, January 12, 1986. See also Green, "Legislative Redistricting in Illinois," pp. 35–38.

29. Everson et al., *Cutback Amendment*, pp. 32–33.

30. Illinois Legislative Research Unit, *Illinois Women in Congress and the General Assembly* (Springfield: Illinois General Assembly, 1989), p. 1.

10

Patterns of Legislative Opportunity in Arizona: Sex, Race, and Ethnicity

Michelle A. Saint-Germain

Women and minorities have slowly increased their presence in state legislatures over the past 20 years, but few studies until recently considered how structural arrangements affect their recruitment and election.[1] Darcy found that women candidates fared better in multimember districts than in single-member districts.[2] Darcy, Welch, and Clark concluded that whereas multimember districts are more advantageous to the election of Anglo women candidates, single-member districts may favor male candidates of certain groups, such as blacks, who are more geographically concentrated than other minorities.[3] For less-segregated Hispanics, the effects of at-large or multimember districts are not so clear. Minority women candidates, however, "are exceptions to [both] the generally favorable effect of multimember districts on the election of women and to the generally favorable effect of single-member districts on the election of minorities."[4]

This chapter examines the impact of electoral arrangements for the Arizona State Legislature on the election of women and minority candidates. Arizona, which achieved statehood in 1912, is the sixth-largest state in the continental United States. Arizona has grown rapidly as its economy has shifted from that of a regional service center for citrus, copper, and cotton to high-technology manufacturing, service, and tourism.[5] Its population has increased by more than 50 percent each decade since 1950, and the percent urban has increased from 55.5 percent in 1950 to 83.8 percent in 1980. But even with 2.6 million inhabitants in 1980 (the latest year for which census figures are available), Arizona still had a relatively low population density of 23.9 persons per square mile. Women made up just over half (50.8 percent) the population in 1980, with variations within different ethnic groups.[6]

Sharing a border with the Mexican state of Sonora and forming part of the Sonoran desert, Arizona has a long-established Hispanic tradition. This influence is reflected in the large proportion of the Arizona population that is Hispanic (16 percent), one of the largest concentrations in the United States. Arizona also has the second-largest number of American Indians, including the Navaho, Tohono O'odham, and Apache tribes. American Indians and blacks represent about 5.6 percent and about 2.8 percent of the population, respectively.

The Arizona State Legislature has two chambers: a Senate with 30 seats and a House with 60 seats. The state has been divided into 30 consecutively numbered electoral districts since 1970. Elections are held for the state legislature every two years, and most other statewide posts, such as governor or secretary of state, are elected for four-year terms. The boundaries of Senate and House districts exactly coincide with one senator and two representatives elected from each district.[7]

With a sizable population of Hispanics, American Indians, and blacks, Arizona offers the opportunity to contrast the effects of the single-member Senate district elections and the effects of the multimember House district elections on the candidacies of women and minorities who run for the state legislature.

The data for this research consist of information on each candidate (N = 1594) for a seat in the Arizona State Legislature in the 10 biennial elections held between 1970 and 1988.[8] This information includes the name and political affiliation of each person running for a House or Senate seat in each electoral district for each election, plus sex, ethnicity, incumbency, opposition, and election results.[9] The following questions were addressed: What is the proportion of women and minority candidates elected to the Arizona State Legislature? How does this proportion compare with the proportion of the state's population represented by these groups and with election results in other states? Are there differences for Senate and House elections? If so, are these differences related only to electoral arrangements or to other factors as well? What is the effect of turnover rates on the election of women and minority candidates to the Arizona State Legislature? What are the trends for the future?

FINDINGS

During the elections studied, there were 1,594 candidates for the state legislature: 520 for the Senate and 1,074 for the House. The distribution of candidates by ethnicity and sex is shown in table 10.1. The majority of candidates have been Anglo (86.7 percent). The other candidates have been distributed among Hispanics (9.5 percent), American Indians (2.1 percent), and blacks (1.7 percent).

Election Rates by Ethnicity and Sex

Despite the fact that there are fewer minority than Anglo candidates, the election rate for minority candidates is higher than for Anglo candidates. About three-quarters of all Hispanic (73.7 percent) and American Indian (78.8 percent)

Table 10.1
Arizona Legislative Election Outcome by Ethnicity and Sex, 1970–88

ETHNICITY AND SEX	PERCENT OF STATE POPULATION	NUMBER OF CANDIDATES	PERCENT OF CANDIDATES	SEATS WON	PERCENT OF ALL SEATS WON	PERCENT WON BY GROUP	PROPOR-TIONATE RATIO
HISPANIC	16.0	152	9.5	112	12.4	73.7	0.78
Female	8.0	19	1.2	9	1.0	47.4	0.13
Male	8.0	133	8.3	103	11.4	77.4	1.43
AMERICAN INDIAN	5.6	33	2.1	26	2.9	78.8	0.52
Female	2.9	2	0.2	0	0.0	0.0	0.00
Male	2.7	31	1.9	26	2.9	83.9	1.07
BLACK	2.8	27	1.7	23	2.6	85.2	0.93
Female	1.3	6	0.4	6	0.7	100.0	0.54
Male	1.5	21	1.3	17	1.9	80.9	1.27
WHITE	75.6	1382	86.7	739	82.1	53.5	1.09
Female	38.5	333	20.9	163	18.1	48.9	0.47
Male	37.1	1049	65.8	576	64.0	54.9	1.73
TOTAL	100.0	1594	100.0	900	100.0	56.5	——

candidates, four-fifths of black (85.2 percent) candidates, and one-half of Anglo (53.5 percent) candidates won their elections.

For three out of these four groups, males had higher rates of election than females. Nearly 55 percent of Anglo male candidates won their elections, compared with almost 49 percent of Anglo female candidates. The corresponding figures for Hispanics were 77.4 percent of males and 47.4 percent of females. The other two groups present a stark contrast. No American Indian woman candidate won an election during the period studied, yet 83.9 percent of American Indian male candidates won. The high rate of election for black males (80.9 percent) is surpassed by the 100 percent election rate for black females, but this result is due entirely to the repeated reelection of one black woman over the time period studied.

RATIO OF REPRESENTATION TO POPULATION

Examining only candidates who were elected, we find that Anglos are overrepresented with a representative-to-population ratio of 1.09. All three minority groups are underrepresented, with ratios of .78 for Hispanics, .52 for American Indians, and .93 for blacks.

There are interesting differences, however, by sex. The males in each ethnic group are overrepresented compared with their proportion of the population, and the females are underrepresented. Anglo females have a representative-to-population ratio of .47 versus 1.73 for Anglo males. Black women have a slightly higher ratio of .54, but the rate for black men is 1.27. Hispanic women have a ratio of only .13, compared with 1.43 for Hispanic men. No American Indian women served in the Arizona State Legislature over the time period studied (a ratio of zero), compared with a ratio of 1.07 for American Indian men.

Comparison with Other States

Compared with women in other states, black and Anglo women in Arizona have achieved a relatively high rate of representation.[10] Wyoming had the highest representative-to-population ratio for black women in 1985 at 2.75, followed by Oregon at 1.37, and Colorado at 1.00. All other states fell below parity; Arizona ranked fifth (based on a single black legislator). Arizona ranked 14th in 1985 for Anglo women but would fall into the top five or 10 states today. With regard to the representative-to-population ratio for black men, Arizona ranked 29th in 1985. Over the years studied, however, the ratio has increased, and today the state would probably rank somewhat higher. No comparable figures were available for Hispanics or American Indians.

Sex Differences by Geographic District

There was considerable variation by geographic district. In some districts nearly half the candidates over this time period were female, but in other districts there were no female candidates. Some of this difference is due to the party identification of the district, since more women run as Democrats (50 percent) than Republicans (40 percent) or Independents (10 percent) despite the fact that Republicans dominated the state legislature during this time period and 76 percent of Republican candidates won, compared with 49 percent of Democratic candidates. No women (or men) who ran as Independents or write-in candidates won.

Electoral success varies by geographic district as well. Of the 30 electoral districts in Arizona, 17 districts since 1970 have elected only male candidates to the Senate, and nine districts have elected only male candidates to the House. In contrast, just one district has elected only female candidates to the Senate, and no district has elected only women to the House.

Sex Differences by Electoral Arrangements

When we examined the data for differences in sex and ethnicity by electoral arrangements, we found greater differences for women than for minorities. As predicted by Darcy, more of the candidates for the House (24 percent) are women—running in multimember districts—than for the Senate (20 percent), which employs single-member districts.[11] This difference is reflected in the larger proportions of women candidates elected to the House (21.8 percent), compared with the Senate candidates (15.7 percent).

Another accounting for these results may be differences in incumbency. Over the years studied, the proportion of candidates running as incumbents has varied from a low of 39 percent to a high of 58 percent. The odds are clearly in favor of incumbents. Of those who ran as incumbents, 95 percent were reelected. Because fewer women have been elected, fewer women (40 percent) have run as incumbents than men (50 percent). However, about equal numbers of House and Senate candidates run as incumbents.

The power of incumbency also is shown by the much larger proportion of incumbents (27 percent) who have run unopposed, compared with nonincumbents (2 percent). It is not so much incumbency per se as running unopposed that has favored male candidates over female candidates. The proportion running unopposed has varied widely, from 6 to 24 percent. However, twice as many candidates for the Senate (20 percent) as for the House (10 percent) run unopposed. Although the length of terms of office and the salaries are identical, there is more competition for the 60-member House than for the 30-member Senate, presumably because fewer votes are needed to win a seat in a two-person (multimember) House election than in a one person (single-member) Senate election.

Nearly all women run in contested elections (92 percent) compared with most men (85 percent). That is, twice as many men have run unopposed (15 percent) as women (8 percent). Even longtime incumbent women usually face opposition from one or more challengers. Most women run in urban, Republican districts that are highly competitive (with an average of two or more candidates for each seat), rather than in districts with lower rates of competition.[12]

As expected, candidates running in districts with low levels of competition were more apt to win their electoral contests (71 percent) than those running in districts with moderate (59 percent) or high (48 percent) levels of competitiveness. This finding is partly due to the fact that there is less turnover in districts with low levels of competition, where more candidates run as incumbents (52 percent) than in districts with moderate (48 percent) or high levels of competition (39 percent).

Ethnic Differences by Geographic District

Over the time period studied, the legislature was dominated by the Republican party except for 1974 to 1978, when the Senate went narrowly Democratic. Recruitment of minority candidates, however, varies widely by party. Republican candidates have been overwhelmingly Anglo (96 percent), with 2.0 percent Hispanic, 1.5 percent American Indian, and less than 1.0 percent black. Democrats are also mostly Anglo (75 percent), but have somewhat larger minority representation, with 18 percent Hispanic, 3 percent American Indian, and 3 percent black.

Arizona tends to be not only ethnically but also geographically polarized by political party. The majority of the 30 electoral districts fall solidly into either the Republican ($N = 14$) or the Democratic ($N = 10$) camp, with the remaining ($N = 6$) districts leaning or mixed. Solid districts are defined as those where between 80 percent and 100 percent of all legislators have been elected from only one party. Leaning districts have elected from 60 to 80 percent of all legislators from the same party. Mixed districts have elected from 40 to 60 percent of all legislators from one party. Over the time period studied, seven districts elected only Republicans, and two districts elected only Democrats. The remaining 21 districts sent candidates from both parties to the legislature. In any district, House and Senate members may be elected from different parties, or the two representatives to the House may be split between different parties. In all, there were 17 Republican or leaning Republican districts, 11 Democratic or leaning Democratic districts, and two mixed districts. Most rural districts were Democratic or mixed, whereas urban districts tended to be Republican (in Phoenix) or mixed (in Tucson).

To an even greater extent than women, minority legislators have been concentrated in only a few districts. All American Indian candidates have run in only one district in the northern part of the state—District Three—which is populated heavily by tribal groups. Two districts in each of the major urban population centers, Tucson and Phoenix, have seen as many Hispanic candidates as Anglos, or more Hispanics, but few Hispanics have run in other districts. The same two urban districts in Phoenix also have had more black candidates than Anglo candidates over the past 20 years.

Elections show a similar pattern. For example, 13 of the 30 districts since 1970 have never elected a minority candidate. Another nine districts have elected mostly Anglo candidates (25 or more out of a possible 30). Of the remaining eight districts, one has been dominated by American Indians, four by Hispanics (with two of these also seeing some participation by blacks), and three have been relatively mixed.

Ethnicity and Electoral Arrangements

In contrast to the case for women candidates examined above, there was no statistically significant difference in the numbers of minority candidates by chamber. Candidates for the Senate have been mostly Anglo (86 percent), with about 11 percent Hispanic, 2 percent American Indian, and 1 percent black. Candidates for the House show a similar pattern, with 87 percent Anglo, about 9 percent Hispanic, 2 percent American Indian, and 2 percent black.

The pattern for electoral success also varied little by chamber for ethnic minorities. Eighty percent of those elected to the House were Anglo, with 16 percent Hispanic, 1 percent black, and 3 percent American Indian. For the Senate, 83 percent were Anglo, 11 percent Hispanic, 3 percent black, and 3 percent American Indian.

Unlike the (mostly Anglo) women candidates, minority candidates tend to run in less competitive districts. Highly competitive districts have more Anglo candidates (98 percent), whereas less-competitive districts have fewer Anglo candidates (67 percent). In districts with moderate competition, 83 percent of the candidates are Anglo.

Significantly higher proportions of Hispanics (24 percent), blacks (22 percent), and American Indians (49 percent) have run unopposed than Anglo candidates (11 percent). Minority candidates also have had higher rates of winning elections. Eighty-five percent of blacks, 79 percent of American Indians, and 74 percent of Hispanics won their electoral contests, compared with 54 percent of Anglos, although there are large differences by sex within ethnic groups.

More minority (male) candidates run as incumbents. Seventy percent of blacks and American Indians and 61 percent of Hispanics run as incumbents, compared with 43 percent of Anglos.

In summary, the picture that emerges is one of a small number of "safe" seats for members of particular ethnic groups in districts that emerged after the 1970 census. There is one rural district in which American Indians are elected regularly, and four urban districts (two in each large city) in which more Hispanics and more blacks are routinely elected than Anglos. A small number of candidates from different minority groups essentially are ensured seats in the legislature, and some minority incumbents run virtually unopposed to be reelected again and again from the same district. Few Anglo challengers run in these districts. The flip side of this scenario is that there is only limited participation by minority candidates in other districts in which Anglo candidates are virtually ensured seats. Competition for seats in the Arizona legislature is ethnically homogeneous in most districts.

Minority Women Candidates

The proportion of female candidates and their success rate vary by ethnicity. About one-quarter of Anglo (24 percent) and black (22 percent) candidates were female, with about half that number of Hispanic candidates being female (12.5 percent). Only two of the American Indian candidates were women (6 percent). The ratio of male to female candidates for Anglos and blacks is approximately three-to-one. For Hispanics, the ratio is closer to six-to-one and is about seventeen-to-one for American Indians. Since these computations are based on a small number of cases, the ratios may not be reliable indicators.

In terms of absolute numbers, there have been relatively few minority women candidates (N = 27). Of these, there were 19 Hispanics, six blacks, and two American Indians. A total of 15 won seats for a success rate of 57.7 percent.

The interaction of party and ethnicity is particularly evident for minority women, who generally run as Democrats rather than Republicans. No minority women who ran as Republicans were elected. Over 95 percent of the women elected to the Senate have been Anglo, as were 90 percent of the women elected to the House. All Republican women elected to the Arizona State Legislature have been Anglo, compared with 80 percent of all the Democratic women.

All districts with more minority than Anglo representation have been solidly or mostly Democratic. The one district sending a majority of American Indian candidates to the state legislature also has elected mostly Democrats but has never elected a woman candidate. In the four districts with more Hispanic and black than Anglo representation, a mix of about 75 percent male and 25 percent female candidates has been elected.

In summary, women candidates, who are mostly Anglo, do better in urban, Republican districts and in multimember House districts. Black and Hispanic candidates, who are mostly male, do better in urban, Democratic districts. American Indians have one "safe" rural district. There is no difference for the mostly male minority candidates in terms of single-member Senate races or multimember House races. There are so few cases of minority women candidates that no general conclusions are possible at this time. However, the trends support the findings in other studies that minority women candidates fare less well than male minority candidates.

CONCLUSIONS

The proportion of female candidates for the Arizona State Legislature doubled from 15 percent in 1970 to over 32 percent in 1988. During this period, an average of one-quarter of all candidates were women. The proportion of candidates with minority racial or ethnic backgrounds has fluctuated over the past

20 years from a low of 7.5 percent in 1970 to a high of 16.3 percent in 1984. The overall average has been about 13.3 percent.

Despite changes in recent years, minority men, women in general, and ethnic minority women in particular tend to be underrepresented as candidates for the Arizona State Legislature compared with their numbers in the population. Half the population of Arizona is female, but just one-quarter of the candidates for the state legislature have been female. The number of candidates who are Hispanic, American Indian, or black also has been about half as high as their proportion in the population would suggest. The level of direct representation for women, and especially ethnic women, is lower than their numbers would suggest if all other things were equal. Nevertheless, Arizona, with 30 percent women in its state legislature, has one of the highest rates of female representation in the United States.

There is no one simple explanation for these observed effects. For ethnic minority candidates, their traditional affiliation with the Democratic party has limited their chances of election in a Republican-dominated state. Also, the relatively small size of and/or the pattern of distribution of the minority population in relation to the boundaries of electoral districts leave them with few areas in which they have the number of votes required to carry an election. Though not identified as an ethnic group, Mormons are also a considerable presence in Arizona and tend to dominate politically in some electoral districts.

For urban women, the picture looks somewhat brighter. There has been substantial progress over the past 20 years as women have nearly tripled their representation in the state legislature, from 11 percent in 1970 to 30 percent in 1990. Arizona's first female speaker of the house, Jane D. Hull, was elected in 1988. As long as women keep increasing their numbers as candidates and keep winning half of their races, we can expect to see more women in the Arizona legislature in the future. Those women, however, will not be from all parts of the state unless districts traditionally resistant to women candidates change.

NOTES

This research was supported in part by grants from the Social and Behavioral Sciences Research Institute and the Office of the Vice President for Research of the University of Arizona. Sarah Kelsik provided invaluable research assistance.

1. However, see Susan J. Carroll, *Women as Candidates in American Politics* (Bloomington: Indiana University Press, 1985); Robert Darcy and Charles D. Hadley, "Black Women in Politics: The Puzzle of Success," *Social Science Quarterly*, September 1988, pp. 629–45; and Wilma Rule, "Why More Women Are State Legislators," *Western Political Quarterly*, June 1990, pp. 437–48.

2. Robert Darcy, "Women Candidates in Single- and Multi-Member Districts," *Social Science Quarterly*, December 1985, pp. 945–53.

3. Robert Darcy, Susan Welch, and Janet Clark, *Women, Elections, and Representation* (New York: Longman, 1987).

4. Ibid., p. 126.

5. *Arizona Statistical Abstract: A 1989 Data Handbook* (Tucson: Division of Economic and Business Research, College of Business and Public Administration, University of Arizona, 1989).

6. Sallie A. Marston and Michelle A. Saint-Germain, ''Urban Restructuring and the Emergence of New Political Groupings: Women and Neighborhood Activism in Tucson, Arizona, USA,'' *Geoforum*, forthcoming.

7. Bruce B. Mason and Heinz R. Hink, *Constitutional Government in Arizona*, 4th rev. ed. (Tempe: Arizona State University, 1972).

8. *Official Canvass: General Election* (Phoenix: Office of the Secretary of State, 1970–88).

9. Sex and ethnicity of winning candidates also were determined by visual inspection of photographs in a voter's guide published by U.S. West Communications. Corroborating documentation was available from the State Legislative Library, the *Arizona Republic*, and a veteran member of the House, Tom Goodwin.

10. Data are from Wilma Rule, ''Electoral Systems and Recruitment to State Legislatures: Different Impacts for Anglo and Black Women?'' paper presented at the Annual Meeting of the Western Political Science Association, Newport Beach, California, March 22–24, 1990.

11. Darcy, ''Women Candidates in Single- and Multi-Member Districts.''

12. For this analysis, we classified as more competitive those districts that averaged two or more candidates running for each seat.

11

Alternative Judicial Election Systems: Solving the Minority Vote Dilution Problem

Richard L. Engstrom

One of the latest controversies concerning election systems in the United States involves the manner in which state and local judges are elected. The entire judiciary is elected in 20 states, and part of the judiciary is elected in another 14 states.[1] The fairness of the election systems used to select judges, however, has been questioned in many jurisdictions with substantial black and/or Hispanic populations. Minority voters complain that these systems structure electoral competition in a manner that systematically dilutes the impact of their votes, severely impeding their ability to elect blacks and Hispanics to the bench. These discriminatory systems are cited as one reason that, as of 1985, only 3.8 percent and 0.5 percent of the full-time state and local judgeships in the United States were held by blacks and Hispanics, respectively. The judiciary is predominantly male as well as Anglo, since women filled only 7.2 percent of these judgeships in 1985.[2]

Litigation seeking changes in the way in which judges are elected had been initiated, by 1990, in district courts in Alabama, Arkansas, Florida, Georgia, Illinois, Louisiana, Mississippi, North Carolina, Ohio, and Texas, and the initial decisions demonstrated that judicial election systems are vulnerable to invalidation on vote dilution grounds.[3] These cases raise not only interesting issues related to the discriminatory nature or potential of the existing election systems but also the equally important issue of how vote dilution should be remedied within the judicial election context. What election systems should replace those currently in use? This question may stimulate a wider debate about election arrangements than one typically hears in the United States.

THE DILUTION ISSUE

The central issue in almost all of the challenges to judicial election systems has been the submergence of minority voters in majority white or Anglo multimember districts. Judges usually are elected at large, and minority group voters therefore are unlikely to elect the candidates of their choice unless their candidate preferences are shared by nonminority voters. Evidence from numerous settings, however, documents that when minority voters prefer minority candidates for judges, that preference is rarely shared by white or Anglo voters.[4]

Racially divided voting in judicial elections should come as no surprise. Race is, after all, the most pronounced demographic division in American politics. Racial divisions in voting have been documented in setting after setting in vote dilution cases involving the election of legislators, and there is no reason to expect judicial elections to be unique in this dimension. Indeed, judicial elections are often low stimulus affairs in which the personal characteristics of candidates are apt to serve as important voting cues for the electorate. Ethical canons restrict judicial candidates from certain types of campaign activities, including expressing opinions on controversial issues that may require judicial resolution.[5] Media attention to these more subdued campaigns tends to be low, and voters usually have only minimal information about the candidates.[6] In this context, race is a personal characteristic that is likely to be salient to voters.[7]

A study of voting in judicial elections in Louisiana, for example, highlights the extent to which candidate preferences may differ by race in judicial elections. The study examined all 52 elections in that state from 1978 through March 6, 1988, in which the voters had a choice between or among black and white candidates for a judgeship. The results of the analysis for elections to the state district and appellate courts are reported in table 11.1. Table 11.2 contains the results for parish (county) and municipal courts. The correlation coefficients reveal that the relationship between the percentage of registered voters in the various precincts and the vote cast for the black candidates was almost invariably strong and statistically significant. The final two columns in each table contain the estimated percentage of the votes cast by blacks and whites, respectively, that were in favor of the black candidates. These percentages were derived by regressing the votes for the candidates in each election onto the racial composition of the relevant precincts. Comparisons of the black and white percentages reveal acute racial divisions in these elections. Black voters preferred a black candidate in 90.4 percent (47) of the elections. White voters, in contrast, did not cast a plurality, let alone a majority, of their votes for a black candidate in any election.[8]

When voting is polarized racially, at-large elections have a pronounced tendency to underrepresent minorities on governmental bodies.[9] The specific type of at-large elections typically used to elect judges is, in addition, among the most potentially dilutive. Minority voters in most at-large systems, if they are sufficiently organized, may attempt to elect a candidate of their choice through "single-shot" voting. The "pure" at-large system provides each voter with as

Table 11.1

Correlation Coefficients and Regression Estimates of Racial Divisions in the Vote for Black Candidates: District Courts and Court of Appeals

Date of election	District (Parishes)	District courts and court of appeals Black candidate	Correlation coefficient[2]	% of blacks' votes	% of whites' votes
9/16/78	1A-Caddo	Lynch[1]	.770	93.8	45.2
	9C-Rapides	Larvadain	.935	82.0	9.5
	9E-Rapides	Berry	.916	75.2	10.7
	19M-East Baton Rouge[4]	Jones	.943	68.8	10.9
	Orleans-Criminal Magistrate	Wilson	.883	32.0	2.0
3/3/79	Orleans-Civil H	Ortique	.829	96.7	13.8
4/7/79					
(Runoff)	Orleans-Civil H	Ortique[1]	.871	98.8	13.0
2/6/82	Orleans-Criminal I	Julien	.834	41.0[3]	5.0
		Wilson	.866	31.3	3.2
3/20/82					
(Runoff)	Orleans-Criminal I	Julien	.962	88.1	16.3
9/11/82	18D-Iberville, Pointe Coupee, West Baton Rouge	Richard	.786	36.2[3]	0.0
11/2/82	18A-Iberville, Pointe Coupee, West Baton Rouge	Richard	.731	56.6	0.0
6/18/83	Orleans-Civil D	Davis	.865	97.0	6.6
10/22/83	15K-Acadia, Lafayette, Vermilion	Cooks	.950	97.0	20.6
	14-Calcasieu	Gray	.994	91.6	4.3
	19A-East Baton Rouge	Rayford	.949	91.6	17.0
9/29/84	19C-East Baton Rouge	Nelson	.884	15.8	1.8
	Orleans-Civil F	Dorsey	.686	51.6	23.2
	Orleans-Civil I	Johnson[1]	.858	85.2	30.1
	Orleans-Criminal B	Douglas	.887	74.2	7.2
11/6/84					
(Runoff)	Orleans-Criminal B	Douglas	.959	88.3	10.9
3/30/85	1D-Caddo	Stewart[1]	.955	97.1	13.6
2/1/86	Orleans-Civil F	Magee	.930	75.3	9.3
		Wilkerson	-.534	21.8	34.6
	Orleans-Criminal J	Blanchard	.855	74.7	15.0
3/1/86					
(Runoff)	Orleans-Civil F	Magee[1]	.953	92.3	12.8
9/27/86	19H-East Baton Rouge	Clark	.662	11.8	3.2
10/24/87	15G-Acadia, Lafayette, Vermilion	Cooks	.934	82.2	14.9
	Fourth Circuit Court of Appeals, Orleans	Douglas	.672	54.0	22.2
11/21/87	19B-East Baton Rouge	Pitcher[1]	.795	100.0	36.9
11/21/87					
(Runoff)	15G-Acadia, Lafayette, Vermilion	Cooks	.851	93.8	14.7
3/8/88	21B-Livingston, St. Helena, Tangipahoa	Ramsey	.955	79.4	4.6
	Orleans-Civil G	Hughes	.875	36.0	3.5
4/6/88					
(Runoff)	Orleans-Civil G	Hughes	.888	87.5	9.9

1. The following candidates were elected, with the percentage of vote they received in parentheses; Lynch (56.1), Ortique (52.1), Stewart (50.7), Johnson (57.1), Magee (52.7) and Pitcher (52.7).

2. All correlation coefficients reflect a statistically significant relationship between the racial composition of precincts and the vote for the black candidate.

3. The black candidate received a plurality of the votes cast by black voters.

4. Registration data for this election allow comparisons between black Democrats and other voters only. Black Democrats, however, comprised 98.7 per cent of the black registered voters.

Source: Richard L. Engstrom, "When Blacks Run for Judge: Racial Divisions in the Candidate Preferences of Louisiana Voters," *Judicature* 73 (August–September 1989), p. 88.

Table 11.2

Correlation Coefficients and Regression Estimates of Racial Divisions in the Vote for Black Candidates: Parish and Municipal-Level Courts

		Parish and municipal-level courts			
Date of election	Court (Parishes)	Black candidate	Correlation coefficient[2]	% of blacks' votes	% of whites' votes
5/27/78	City Court B, Baton Rouge[4]	Rayford	.979	99.7	12.5
9/16/78	Juvenile Court B, Orleans Parish	Douglas	.911	57.1	3.0
		Young	.799	23.8	1.7
10/27/79	Juvenile Court E, Orleans Parish	Young	.933	64.7	4.5
	First City Court C, New Orleans	Pharr	.525	6.1	1.6
12/8/79 (Runoff)	Juvenile Court E, Orleans Parish	Young	.863	79.5	25.3
9/13/80	First City Court A, New Orleans	Young	.894	72.2	3.9
11/4/80 (Runoff)	First City Court A, New Orleans	Young	.974	91.7	15.1
10/17/81	First City Court C, New Orleans	Thomas	.823	93.5	16.8
11/2/82	City Court B, Shreveport	Huckaby	.966	99.2	14.0
12/11/82 (Runoff)	City Court B, Shreveport	Huckaby	.983	99.6	8.6
3/26/83	City Court B, Baton Rouge	Pitcher[1]	.959	99.0	15.9
9/29/84	City Court, Bastrop	Minniweather	.986	69.1	0.4
	City Court A, Monroe	Hunter	.989	89.8	5.9
	Juvenile Court A, Orleans Parish	Gray	.916	68.9	9.8
		Dannel	.052	19.7	18.7
	Juvenile Court C, Orleans Parish	Young	.884	46.2[3]	4.7
11/6/84 (Runoff)	Juvenile Court A, Orleans Parish	Gray[1]	.961	95.7	16.2
9/27/86	Juvenile Court D, Orleans Parish	Dannel	.831	84.1	21.0
	Municipal Court, New Orleans	McConduit	.859	71.2	11.9
11/4/86 (Runoff)	Municipal Court, New Orleans	McConduit[1]	.898	84.4 ·	26.5
8/29/87	Juvenile Court A, Jefferson Parish	Council	.914	80.8	3.1

1. The following candidates were elected, with the percentage of vote they received in parentheses; Pitcher (56.6), Gray (55.8) and McConduit (54.5).

2. All correlation coefficients reflect a statistically significant relationship between the racial composition of precincts and the vote for the black candidate except that for Dannel in the 1984 Juvenile Court, Division A election in Orleans Parish.

3. The black candidate received a plurality of the votes cast by black voters.

4. Registration data for this election allow comparisons between black Democrats and other voters only. Black Democrats, however, comprised 98.6 per cent of the black registered voters.

Source: Richard L. Engstrom, ''When Blacks Run for Judge: Racial Divisions in the Candidate Preferences of Louisiana Voters,'' *Judicature* 73 (August–September 1989), p. 89.

many votes as there are seats to be filled and allows voters to choose among all candidates. The winning candidates are determined by a simple plurality rule— the top N vote recipients fill the N available seats. Under this arrangements, minority voters may concentrate their support on a particular candidate and withhold their support from all other candidates; that is, minority voters may cast only a single vote for their preferred candidates and refrain from casting any of their other votes. By targeting their voting strength in this manner and withholding votes from candidates competing with their preferred choice, minority support may be sufficient (depending on its relative size and how the nonminority's votes are distributed across the candidates) to place their preferred candidate among the top N vote recipients.

The at-large election systems employed to elect judges almost invariably preclude the casting of single-shot votes. Judicial elections are usually conducted within a place or post system. Each judicial seat is contested as a separate and distinct at-large election. Candidates file for a particular seat on a multimember court, and all voters are restricted to choosing one from among the set of candidates for that seat. This separation precludes minority voters from employing the single-shot strategy as a way to elect a minority candidate. This type of anti-single-shot system has been found to make the election of minority candidates in the at-large context especially difficult.[10]

Dilutive electoral systems are vulnerable to invalidation. The major medium through which their legality is challenged is section 2 of the federal Voting Rights Act as amended in 1982. This provision prohibits the use of an electoral arrangement that *results* in vote dilution even if the reasons for which the arrangement is used are nonracial. This results test is considered violated if it is demonstrated, given "the totality of circumstances," that minority voters "have less opportunity than other members of the electorate to participate in the political process and to elect representatives of their choice."[11]

The applicability of this provision to judicial election systems has been contested on the grounds that judges are not "representatives" and therefore judicial election arrangements are not covered by the provision. The United States Supreme Court has rejected this argument, however. The Court held, in 1991, that Congress had not meant to exclude judges by employing the word *representatives* and that therefore judicial election arrangements are subject to the act's results-based dilution test.[12] Another argument sought to exempt the vast majority of judgeships from this provision. It was contended that regardless of how many trial court judges were elected to hear cases in any particular judicial district, each of these positions was a separate and distinct single-member office. As such, they could not be disaggregated for electoral purposes, and therefore there was no remedy for any dilution that might occur. This argument also was rejected by the Supreme Court.[13] If a state or locality chooses to elect its judges, the Court made clear, whether trial or appellate, the system employed for that purpose must comply with section 2 of the Voting Rights Act.

Many judicial election systems will be vulnerable to invalidation on minority vote dilution grounds. At-large elections and other types of multimember districts for electing state and local legislators have been found to be dilutive in numerous settings, and multimember place systems for the judiciary are not apt to present drastically different situations from those in the legislative context.[14] The most challenging issue presented by the judicial election cases may not be whether the systems are dilutive, but rather, what should replace them.

THE REMEDIAL ISSUE

When at-large or otherwise multimember district election arrangements for state or local legislative bodies are found to be dilutive, the remedy is almost invariably the adoption of single-member (or smaller multimember) districts. To date, "subdistricting" within a court's territorial jurisdiction also has been the basic medium for remedying dilution in the judicial election context. The United States District Court in Mississippi ordered single-member district elections in eight trial court jurisdictions that had been found to have dilutive systems, while the district court in Texas ordered an interim election plan based on single- and two-member districts in jurisdictions of that state's basic trial courts found to have dilutive arrangements.[15] The Louisiana State Legislature adopted a series of single- and multimember subdistricts for a number of the state's basic trial and appellate courts in response to a district court order invalidating the election systems for those jurisdictions.[16]

Although subdistricts will normally resolve the dilution problem, criticisms of this alternative have been raised. The basic complaint is that judges elected through subdistricts may demonstrate favoritism toward litigants to whom they are electorally accountable, resulting in "neighborhood justice" or "home cooking." No evidence has been marshaled to support this criticism despite the fact that judges commonly make rulings and decisions that directly affect litigants who reside outside a court's territorial (and electoral) jurisdiction. Still, the argument that judicial jurisdiction and electoral accountability should be coterminous has stimulated interest in alternative ways to conduct elections at large, ways that may cleanse the at-large format of its dilutive consequences. In particular, attention has been focused on alternative voting rules within the at-large context, specifically limited and cumulative voting.[17]

Both limited and cumulative voting rules provide minority voters with an opportunity, at least theoretically, to elect a candidate or candidates of their choice in an at-large election despite little or no crossover voting from nonminority voters. Under a limited voting arrangement, each voter is allocated a number of votes less than the number of seats to be filled. If four judges are to be elected from a particular geographical area, each voter may be allowed to cast only a single vote (or two or three). Under cumulative voting rules, voters are allowed to cumulate or aggregate the votes they are granted. In a four-vote, four-seat context, voters could cast all four of their votes for a particular candidate (a practice known as "plumping"), give one candidate three votes and another a single vote, or cast their four votes in any other combination. Cumulative voting allows voters to express their preferences with greater flexibility than the traditional one-vote-per-candidate format. Winning candidates are determined by a simple plurality rule.

The opportunity minorities have to elect candidates through limited or cumulative voting is demonstrated theoretically by a coefficient known as "the threshold of exclusion."[18] The value of this coefficient identifies the percentage or proportion of the electorate that a group must exceed in order for it to elect a candidate on its own. The coefficient is based on a set of worst-case assumptions (from the minority's perspective) concerning the voting behavior of the non-minority voters. These assumptions are (1) the nonminority voters cast all of the votes available to them, (2) none of their votes are cast for the minority voters' preferred candidates, (3) their votes are concentrated entirely on a number of candidates equal to the number of seats to be filled, and (4) their votes are divided evenly across candidates. Nonminority voters are assumed to cast a maximum vote with no crossover and no dispersion.

The value of the threshold of exclusion for a limited voting system, expressed as a percentage, may be determined through the following formula:

$$\frac{(\text{number of votes})}{(\text{number of votes}) + (\text{number of seats})} \times 100.$$

The value of this threshold depends not only on the number of seats but also on how limited the vote is. The less limited the vote, the higher the threshold value will be. For example, in the four-seat illustration, the threshold is 20.0 percent if only a single vote is allowed, 33.3 percent if two votes are allowed, and 42.9 percent if every voter has three votes (see table 11.3).

The value of the threshold of exclusion for a cumulative voting system, expressed as a percentage, may be determined through this formula:

$$\frac{1}{1 + (\text{number of seats})} \times 100.$$

This threshold is based on the assumption that all minority voters plump for their candidates, and it is equivalent to that for limited voting when each voter has only a single vote. Its value varies directly, and inversely, with the number of seats to be filled. If four seats are to be filled, the value is 20.0 percent, whereas if seven seats are to be filled, the value is 12.5 percent (see table 11.3).

The threshold of exclusion illustrates that with cumulative or limited voting, a relatively small (and even residentially dispersed) minority group has the potential, provided the group members are politically cohesive, to elect candidates of their choice in a multiseat judicial election. Single- or multisubdistricts, in short, are not the only democratic alternative to the present at-large systems. This threshold, it must also be remembered, is the point beyond which a cohesive

Table 11.3
Threshold of Exclusion Values

THRESHOLD VALUES

NUMBER OF SEATS	CUMULATIVE VOTING	LIMITED VOTING		
		1 VOTE	2 VOTES	3 VOTES
2	33.3	33.3	--	--
3	25.0	25.0	40.0	--
4	20.0	20.0	33.3	42.9
5	16.7	16.7	28.6	37.5
6	14.3	14.3	25.0	33.3
7	12.5	12.5	22.2	30.0
8	11.1	11.1	20.0	27.3
9	10.0	10.0	18.2	25.0

minority can elect a candidate *regardless of how other voters behave*. If the behavior of the other voters in any way deviates from the worst-case assumptions, the minority group may be smaller and/or less cohesive and still have a realistic opportunity to elect a candidate or candidates of its choice through one of these voting systems.

This opportunity provided by limited or cumulative voting has been verified empirically on a number of occasions in recent years. Limited or cumulative voting has been the basis for the voluntary settlement of dilution lawsuits affecting about 30 local governmental units (municipalities, counties, and school districts) in the late 1980s, the elections under these alternative at-large arrangements have been held in most of these units. In almost all cases, minority candidates have been elected. Blacks in Alabama, for example, have used these systems with success, as have Hispanics in New Mexico and Native Americans in South Dakota.[19] These experiences demonstrate that both limited and cumulative voting rules are capable of cleansing the dilutive consequences of an otherwise at-large election arrangement.

CONCLUSION

At-large judicial election systems, especially those in which separate elections are held by places or posts, have become and can be expected to continue to be an important political and legal issue. Minority demands for changes in these systems are widespread. These demands have stimulated a wider examination of alternatives than normally considered in the legislative election context. Although subdistricts can be an effective cure for dilution, concerns that the electoral accountability of judges be coterminous with their territorial jurisdiction have stimulated interest in alternative ways to conduct at-large elections.

This interest in alternative at-large structures has placed limited and cumulative voting rules on the electoral reform agenda. These alterations in at-large systems have provided minority voters with a medium through which to elect minority candidates in nonjudicial elections, even when voting has been racially polarized. There is no reason to expect them to be less effective at cleansing dilution in the judicial election context. Minority voters should seriously consider these arrangements as well as subdistricts when considering remedies for dilutive systems. Proponents of at-large judicial elections should similarly consider these alternatives as a way of making that system more equitable. At a minimum, the debate over how to remedy dilutive judicial election systems should stimulate a broader examination of electoral systems than has been typical in the United States.

NOTES

1. In an additional six states, "retention" elections are held in which the only issue is the continued tenure of an incumbent judge. See Fund for Modern Courts, *The Success of Women and Minorities: The Selection Process* (New York: Fund for Modern Courts, 1985), pp. 5, 43.

2. Ibid., pp. 10, 13. See also Barbara Luck Graham, "Do Judicial Selection Systems Matter? A Study of Black Representation on State Courts," *American Political Quarterly*, July 1990, pp. 331, 333.

3. See *Martin v. Allain*, 658 F. Supp. 1183 (S.D. Miss. 1987); *Clark v. Edwards*, 725 F. Supp. 285 (M.D. La. 1988); *Rangel v. Mattox*, Civ. A. No. B–88–053 (S.D. Tex. 1989); and *League of United Latin American Citizens v. Mattox*, Civ. A. No. MO–88-CA–154 (W.D. Tex. 1989).

4. See the findings on polarized voting in the four cases cited above and in *Chisom v. Roemer*, Civ. A. No. 86–4057 (E.D. La. 1989). slip. op. at 35.

5. See James J. Alfini and Terrence J. Brooks, "Ethical Constraints on Judicial Election Campaigns: A Review and Critique of Canon 7," *Kentucky Law Journal* 77, no. 3 (1988–89): 671–722.

6. Charles A. Johnson, Roger G. Shaefer, and R. Neal McKnight, "The Salience of Judicial Candidates and Elections," *Social Science Quarterly*, September 1978, pp. 371–78; R. Neal McKnight, Roger Schaefer, and Charles A. Johnson, "Choosing Judges: Do the Voters Know What They're Doing?," *Judicature*, August 1978, pp. 94–98; Allen T. Klots, "The Selection of Judges and the Short Ballot," in Glenn R. Winters, ed., *Judicial Selection and Tenure* (Chicago: American Judicature Society, 1973), pp. 78–84; Jack Ladinsky and Allan Silver, "Popular Democracy and Judicial Independence: Electorate and Elite Reactions to Two Wisconsin Supreme Court Elections," *Wisconsin Law Review*, Winter 1967, pp. 128–69; and Herbert Jacobs, "Judicial Insulation—Elections, Direct Participation, and Public Attention to the Courts in Wisconsin," *Wisconsin Law Review*, Summer 1966, p. 818.

7. See two articles by Burton Atkins, Mathew R. DeZee, and William Eckert: "State Supreme Court Elections: The Significance of Race," *American Politics Quarterly*, April

1984, pp. 211–24, and "The Effect of a Black Candidate in Stimulating Voter Partici-
pation in Statewide Elections: A Note on a Quiet 'Revolution' in Southern Politics,"
Journal of Black Studies, December 1985, pp. 213–25; and Richard L. Engstrom and
Victoria M. Caridas, "Voting for Judges: Race and Roll-Off in Judicial Elections," in
William Crotty, ed., *Political Participation and American Democracy* (Westport, Conn.:
Greenwood Press, 1991), pp. 171–91.

8. For a more detailed explanation of the methodology on which these figures are
based, see Richard L. Engstrom, "When Blacks Run for Judge: Racial Divisions in the
Candidate Preferences of Louisiana Voters," *Judicature*, August-September 1989,
pp. 87–89.

9. See Richard L. Engstrom and Michael D. McDonald, "The Effect of At-Large
versus District Elections on Racial Representation in U.S. Municipalities," in Bernard
Grofman and Arend Lijphart, eds., *Electoral Laws and Their Political Consequences*
(New York: Agathon Press, 1986), pp. 203–25, and the studies referenced therein.

10. See Richard L. Engstrom and Michael D. McDonald, "The Election of Blacks
to Southern City Councils: The Dominant Impact of Electoral Arrangements," in Laurence
Moreland, Robert Steed, and Todd Baker, eds., *Blacks in Southern Politics* (New York:
Praeger, 1987), pp. 253–55, and Michael D. McDonald and Richard L. Engstrom, "Minority Representation and Councilmanic Election Systems: A Black and Hispanic Comparison, " in Anthony Messina, Laura Rhodebeck, Frederick Wright, and Luis Fraga,
eds., *Ethnic and Racial Minorities in Advanced Industrial Democracies: Social, Economic, and Political Incorporation* (Westport, Conn.: Greenwood Press, forthcoming).

11. *Voting Rights Act Amendments of 1982*, 96 Stat. 131, 42 U.S.C. § 1973. The
"equal protection" clause of the Fourteenth Amendment to the United States Constitution,
in contrast, requires a showing of discriminatory purpose before a dilutive arrangement
can be declared unconstitutional. See *City of Mobile vs. Bolden*, 446 U.S. 55 (1980).
Changes in judicial election systems by state or local governments covered by the "pre-
clearance" requirement contained in section 5 of the Voting Rights Act are subject to
approval by the attorney general of the United States or the issuance of a declaratory
judgment by the United States District Court for the District of Columbia. In this process,
the state or local government must demonstrate that there is neither a discriminatory intent
nor a discriminatory effect associated with the change in the system. See *Clark v. Roemer*,
111 S.Ct. 2096 (1991).

12. *Chisom v. Roemer*, 111 S.Ct 2354 (1991).

13. *Houston Lawyers' Association v. Attorney General of Texas*, 111 S.Ct. 2376
(1991).

14. The major precedent establishing the evidentiary requirements in these cases is
Thornburg v. Gingles, 478 U.S. 30 (1986).

15. *Martin v. Mabus*, Civ. A. No. J84–0708(B) (S.D. Miss. 1988), and *League of
United Latin American Citizens v. Mattox*, Civ. A. No. MO–88-CA–154 (W.D. Tex.
1990), *vacated by League of United Latin American Citizens v. Clements*, No. 90–8014
(5th Cir. 1990).

16. This arrangement was contingent on the ratification of a state constitutional amendment that was rejected by the voters in a racially divided vote. Estimates based on a
regression analysis employing precinct-based election-day sign-in data by race and the
votes cast on the proposed amendment (see note 8) reveal that 66.5 percent of the blacks
voting on the amendment were in favor of it, but only 17.2 percent of the nonblacks
supported the change.

17. See Robert McDuff, "The Voting Rights Act and Judicial Elections Litigation: The Plaintiffs' Perspective," *Judicature*, August-September 1989, pp. 82–85, and Samuel Issacharoff, *The Texas Judiciary and the Voting Rights Act: Background and Options* (Austin: Texas Policy Research Forum, 1989).

18. Douglas Rae, Victor Hanby, and John Loosemore, "Thresholds of Representation and Thresholds of Exclusion: An Analytic Note on Electoral Systems," *Comparative Political Studies*, January 1971, pp. 479–88.

19. See Edward Still, "Cumulative Voting and Limited Voting in Alabama," in this volume; Richard L. Engstrom, Delbert A. Taebel, and Richard L. Cole, "Cumulative Voting as a Remedy for Minority Vote Dilution: The Case of Alamogordo, New Mexico," *Journal of Law and Politics*, Spring 1989, pp. 469–97; Richard L. Cole, Richard L. Engstrom, and Delbert A. Taebel, "Cumulative Voting in a Municipal Election: A Note on Voter Reactions and Electoral Consequences," *Western Political Quarterly*, March 1990, pp. 191–99; and Richard L. Engstrom and Charles J. Barrilleaux, "Native Americans and Cumulative Voting: The Sisseton-Wahpeton Sioux," *Social Science Quarterly*, June 1991, pp. 387–93.

PART IV

ELECTING LOCAL LEADERS

12

Minority and Gender Representation in American County Legislatures: The Effect of Election Systems

Victor DeSantis and Tari Renner

No system of electing representatives to public office is politically "neutral." Any change in the electoral structure or rules of the game will benefit some coalition, faction, or party at the expense of others. Consequently, different interests have often clashed as intensely over these rules as they have over the substantive content of public policy. The structural reformers of the Progressive Era, for example, pushed for short ballots with nonpartisan and at-large elections because they perceived these changes would increase their influence by reducing the importance of urban machines and ethnic-based political power. Similarly, the modern civil rights movement advocates changing back to single-member district elections to maximize the probability that minorities will be elected to public office.

Recent empirical evidence indicates that the latter movement appears to be having substantial success. The proportion of American municipalities that report using at-large elections declined in all regions of the country from the early to latter 1980s.[1] Much of this success is a result of the federal Voting Rights Act of 1965 and its amendments.

LEGAL BACKGROUND

The 1982 amendments attempted to reverse the United States Supreme Court's 1980 narrow interpretation of congressional intent in *City of Mobile vs. Bolden* (446 U.S. 55). The Court held that in order to invalidate an election system, the Voting Rights Act required demonstration of a racially discriminatory intent and not just a discriminatory result. The 1982 amendments to the Voting Rights Act clarified that federal protection was warranted when an election system produced discriminatory consequences regardless of political intent. The United

States Supreme Court, in *Thornburgh v. Gingles* (106 S.Ct. 2752), in 1986 very broadly interpreted these amendments in striking down the contours of several North Carolina state legislative districts.

Since this latter shift in national policy, numerous lawsuits challenging local government election systems have been brought to the district courts. In *Dillard v. Crenshaw County* (C.D. Ala., 649 F. Supp. 289), the district court ordered several Alabama counties to elect all county commissioners from single-member districts. In *McNeal v. Springfield* (C.D. Ill., 658 F. Supp. 1015), the district court ruled in 1987 that Springfield must change its election system to a district plan and expand the size of the city council to create a black majority district in the city. Springfield is only 10 percent black, and it would have been virtually impossible to create a black majority constituency with only five districts. A similar decision was reached by the district court in 1987 in *Derrickson v. City of Danville* (C.D. Ill., 87–2007). In this case, Danville, Illinois, also was ordered to elect representatives by district and expand its legislative body.

RESEARCH ON ELECTORAL SYSTEMS

In light of the Voting Rights Act amendments, the *Thornburgh v. Gingles* decision, and subsequent challenges to municipal and county election processes, social science researchers have focused increased attention on the relationship between municipal election systems and representation on city councils and state legislatures. Although most of this literature analyzes minority representation, the number of studies examining female representation is increasing. The two types of studies are not, of course, mutually exclusive. In fact, some of the most recent research in the field has analyzed the impact of election systems on minority and nonminority women.

Overall, the existing literature suggests that district elections produce more equitable representation for minorities but less equitable representation for females. Specifically, it appears that black males benefit from district or single-member elections in city councils and state legislatures. Black females, on the other hand, are best represented in multimember state legislative systems. The latter is also the case for white females (see the chapter by Welch and Herrick and the legislative chapter by Rule). The spatial distribution of minorities is what makes smaller constituencies more conducive to their success at the polls. Women, on the other hand, are not concentrated geographically and could benefit from at-large constituencies or multimember districts, which might not cast the electoral contests as starkly in male-versus-female terms.

Research has analyzed primarily American municipalities and state legislatures. Consequently, there remains no empirical evidence for either minority or gender representation in American counties, which in many states have important policy-making authority. The geographic and political characteristics of counties, as well as the types of electoral systems, differ among cities, towns, and villages.

Furthermore, the number of Section 2 Voting Rights Act lawsuits against counties is increasing.

Even though the county has held a prominent position in the South since early colonial times, it has been only in the twentieth century that counties have become more important in many other areas of the country. The increased role of counties is evident in recent patterns of finances and functional responsibilities. The fiscal crisis that hit many cities during the 1970s and 1980s caused many municipal governments to look to the county to take over full or partial responsibility for many public services. This development is reflected in the increased number of intergovernmental contracts and joint service agreements and the dramatic increase in the amount of money raised and spent at the county level. Clearly, the county has become a more important aspect of daily life for a large portion of the American population.

HYPOTHESES

This research examines the impact of election processes on minority and gender representation for county legislative bodies and employs two hypotheses:

Hypothesis 1: District elections will produce *more* equitable black representation in county legislatures than do at-large election systems, independent of the effect of jurisdiction, population, per capita income, education level, black population, form of government, region, and urbanization.

Hypothesis 2: District elections will produce *less* equitable gender representation in county legislatures than do at-large election systems, independent of the effect of jurisdiction population, per capita income, education level, form of government, region, and urbanization.

The dependent variables that we seek to explain are black representation (in Hypothesis 1) and women's representation (in Hypothesis 2) on county councils. The primary causal or independent variable of interest in each hypothesis is type of election system. There are, however, other possible causes of minority and sexual representation that need to be accounted for in the analysis in order to increase our confidence in the findings. Suppose, for example, we find that counties with district election systems produce greater equity in minority representation than those with at-large systems. Hypothetically, this relationship might be apparent only because district systems are more prevalent in urban than in rural counties and because the former jurisdictions are more apt to elect proportionate numbers of minorities to their county legislatures. In this hypothetical scenario, urbanization would be the "true" cause of minority representation on county councils and not the type of election system. However, if we control for or "weed out" the effect of urbanization in our analysis and the relationship is still apparent, we will be much more confident that the type of election system has a direct impact on minority representation than if we failed to take urbanization into account.

This research controls for the impact of the following possible contaminating variables that might be correlated with the independent and dependent variables in our analysis: education level, form of government, income, minority population proportion, population size, region, and urbanization. In the analysis of gender representation, each variable is examined, with the exception of minority percentage. Although the latter is clearly a possible cause of minority representation, we had no reason to expect that it would have an impact on the proportion of females on the council.

DATA AND METHODS

The data used in this research are from the International City Management Association's (ICMA) 1988 county form of government survey. The questionnaire was mailed to the county clerks in all 3,044 American counties. A total of 1,295 jurisdictions (42.5%) responded to two requests (see table 12.1).

The dependent variable in the first hypothesis is degree of equity of minority representation. The survey questionnaire asked respondents to specify the number of black county legislators. The minority percentage on the council is simply divided by the minority percentage in the jurisdiction's population. When blacks are represented on the council in the exact proportion as in the population, the measure equals 1.00. Scores below this figure indicate underrepresentation and those above it indicate overrepresentation.

Unfortunately, there were too few Hispanics and black women to include in this analysis. Only about 1 percent of all county council members (105 out of 8,112) were reported to be Hispanic, and the number of black women councillors was negligible also. There were 325 black male (4 percent) and 850, mostly Anglo, female (10 percent) council members. The analysis of Hispanic representation from this particular data set is complicated further by the extremely low response rate (17.1 percent) of the East South Central region. The majority of this region's counties are in Texas (254 out of 362).

A comparison of the ICMA data and *The 1988 Roster of Black Elected Officials* indicated that less than 30 counties that responded to this survey had black women on their councils. These numbers proved to be too small to draw meaningful conclusions except that almost all were chosen through district elections.

Differences have arisen over the specific minority threshold required for jurisdictions to be included in empirical studies. Several researchers have argued that minority groups must constitute a specific percentage of the total population before they can expect any degree of direct representation. Whereas some studies do not rely on minority thresholds, others have thresholds of 5 percent, 10 percent, or 15 percent. Our research uses the 10 percent threshold as a reasonable compromise. Threshold is clearly not an issue, however, in the analysis of women's representation, in which all jurisdictions with valid responses are included.

The measurement of gender representation also is less complicated than mi-

Table 12.1
Survey Response

Classification	Number of Cities Surveyed	Number Responding	Percent Responding
Total, all cities............	3,044	1,295	42.5
Population Group			
Over 1,000,000............	22	13	59.1
500,000–1,000,000........	53	24	45.3
250,000–499,999..........	92	52	56.5
100,000–249,999..........	230	118	51.3
50,000–99,999...........	382	165	43.2
25,000–49,999...........	627	231	36.8
10,000–24,999...........	936	384	41.0
5,000–9,999.............	435	182	41.8
2,500–4,999.............	173	80	46.2
Under 2,500.............	94	46	48.9
Geographic Region			
Northeast...............	196	85	43.4
North Central...........	1,053	493	46.8
South...................	1,375	491	35.7
West....................	420	226	53.8
Geographic Division			
New England.............	52	14	26.9
Mid–Atlantic............	144	71	49.3
East North Central......	436	192	44.0
West North Central......	617	301	48.8
South Atlantic..........	546	265	48.5
East South Central......	362	62	17.1
West South Central	467	164	35.1
Mountain................	276	142	51.4
Pacific Coast...........	144	84	58.3
Metro Status			
Central.................	336	176	52.4
Suburban................	347	143	41.2
Independent.............	2,361	976	41.4

nority representation. In this research, women's representation is measured by the percentage of women serving in each county's legislative body.

The independent variable of primary interest is the form of election system. Respondents were asked the number of legislators who were elected using various electoral systems. For the purpose of this analysis, three different categories are used. If it was reported that all members were nominated and elected at large, they are included in the at-large category. If it was reported that all legislators were nominated and elected by ward or district, they are included in the district category. All other responses are considered to be a mixed system. This latter category includes cases in which some members are elected by district and others from the county at large, and systems where candidates are nominated by ward and elected at large. This measurement will permit an analysis of the representational consequences of district versus at-large systems and district versus mixed systems.

The control variables are measured in the following ways: proportion of a jurisdiction's population with 12 or more years of education (education level), presence or absence of an appointed county administrator (form of government), median per capita income (income level), black population percentage (minority population level), 1985 population in thousands (population size), whether the county is in the South or outside of the South (region), and whether the county is part of a metropolitan statistical area as defined by the United States Bureau of the Census (urbanization).

Multiple regression is a statistical procedure that removes the influence of these other possible causal variables. It provides the distinctive impact of each cause on the dependent variable, controlling for all of the other causes included in the analysis by the researcher. It permits the analyst to determine (1) which independent variables under examination had a significant effect on the dependent variable and (2) which independent variables had the strongest impact on the dependent variable.

DATA ANALYSIS: MINORITY REPRESENTATION

Table 12.2 displays the multiple regression data for minority representation, mainly black male county councillors. Consistent with our expectations, the difference between district and at-large systems produces a statistically significant decrease in black representation on county councils. The beta (or standardized regression coefficient) value of $-.258$ means that there is an average decrease of .258 standard deviations of our dependent variable for every one standard deviation change in this election system variable, controlling for all of the other causes included in the analysis. The t value of -4.160 and significance of .000 means that the probability that these results could have occurred by chance is less than .001.

The independent effect of district versus mixed electoral systems, however, is not statistically significant. The beta value of $-.080$ indicates that a shift toward mixed systems tends, on average, to reduce black representation, but this change is so small that its probability of chance occurrence is relatively high (.185). In other words, patterns in the data would occur about one-fifth of the time even if there was no relationship between this election system variable and minority representation in county legislatures. Social scientists typically use the .05 significance level; that is, they are willing to reject chance occurrence only when its probability falls below 5 percent.

Consistent with our expectations, education level and black population proportion have a statistically significant positive effect on the equity of black representation in county councils. The beta value of .267 for education indicates

Table 12.2
Regression Analysis Results with Minority (Black Men's) Representation/
Population Ratio in County Councils as the Dependent Variable

Multiple R	= .487
Multiple R Square	= .237
Standard Error	= .417
Number of Cases	= 284

Variable	BETA	t	SIGNIFICANCE
District vs. At-Large	-.258	-4.160	.000
District vs. Mixed	-.080	-1.330	.185
Black Population	.308	4.434	.000
Education	.267	2.610	.010
Appointed Administrator	-.028	-.495	.621
Income	-.100	-.981	.327
Population	.138	1.891	.064
Non-South vs. South	.197	2.98	.003
Urbanicity	.016	.202	.840

that a one standard deviation increase in education is associated with a .267 standard deviation increase in black council representation. The probability that these results would have occurred randomly is less than one percent. The data also indicate that increases in the percentage of blacks in American counties are associated with more proportionate representation in the local legislature (recall that the dependent variable is measured by the degree of equity of minority representation and not absolute numbers). The beta value for black population percent is .308, and the probability of chance occurrence is less than one in a thousand. In fact, this latter variable has the strongest independent impact on minority representation of any variable included in this analysis.

Region is the only other variable that appears to have a significant impact on the dependent variable. The beta value of .197 indicates that the equity of black council representation increases when one moves from the South to the non-South. The probability that this relationship would appear by chance is only .003.

Contrary to our expectations, form of government, income, population size, and urbanization do not have a significant effect on minority representation. The presence of an appointed county administrator and higher per capita income, however, appear to be associated with lower levels of racial equity on county councils. The beta values are −.028 and −.100 for form of government and income, respectively. The probability of chance occurrence, on the other hand, far exceeds .05 for each variable. Alternatively, population size and urbanization are positively correlated with minority representation. The beta values are .138 for the former and .016 for the latter. As with form of government and income, however, the correlations are more than 5 percent likely to have occurred by chance.

Although the equity of minority representation on American county councils was found to be significantly greater in district-election jurisdictions than in at-large systems, this conclusion should be tempered by several facts. First, the differences between mixed and at-large systems were not found to be statistically significant. Second, the impact of district versus at-large elections did not have the strongest impact on black representation among the variables analyzed. The absolute values of the standardized regression coefficients for both education level and black population were greater than that for district election systems. Finally, the R square value indicates that only about 24 percent of the total variation in minority representation in county legislatures can be explained by the entire set of independent variables included above. This finding suggests that other factors are important in explaining the dependent variables, factors that have not been accounted for in this analysis.

DATA ANALYSIS: FEMALE REPRESENTATION

The data to test our second hypothesis regarding the mostly white female representation in county legislatures are presented in table 12.3. Contrary to our expectations, types of election systems do not appear to have a significant impact on the number of women elected when controlling for the other variables. District systems appear to produce lower levels of female representation compared to at-large councils (beta = −.025) and mixed systems (beta = −.022). These negative relationships, however, are not statistically significant at the .05 level. The probability that these patterns in the data could have occurred by chance is very high (.374 for the district-at-large differences and .456 for the district-mixed system differences). Consequently, though we expected to find that women would be disadvantaged most by district elections and advantaged most by at-large elections, such a finding was not upheld by the data.

It is also clear that region is not associated significantly with female representation on county councils. Movement from the South to the non-South appears to produce slightly higher numbers of elected women (beta = .044). As with the election system differences, however, the chance probability of these results exceeds 5 percent (significance = .232).

On the other hand, the results for the other variables are consistent with our expectations. Education, the presence of an appointed county administrator (form of government), income, population, and urbanization have a statistically significant positive effect on female representation. Among these variables, education and population size appear to be having the strongest impact, with betas

Table 12.3
Regression Analysis Results with Percent of Mostly White Female Representation on County Councils as the Dependent Variable

Multiple R	=	.331
Multiple R Square	=	.110
Standard Error	=	.136
Number of Cases	=	1294

Variable	BETA	t	SIGNIFICANCE
District vs. At-Large	-.025	-.889	.374
District vs. Mixed	-.022	-.746	.456
Education	.123	3.035	.003
Appointed Administrator	.084	3.063	.002
Income	.076	2.120	.034
Population	.112	3.574	.000
Non-South vs. South	.044	1.195	.232
Urbanicity	.097	2.881	.004

of .123 and .112, respectively. The corresponding values for form of government, income, and urbanization are somewhat lower at .084, .076 and .097, respectively.

The Multiple R square statistic, however, indicates that we are explaining only 11 percent of the difference in the number of women on county councils using all of the variables in this research. These results are even lower than the Multiple R square for black men's representation. The combined impact of the variables is not a very good predictor of female representation.

CONCLUSION

This research, by studying American counties, has attempted to fill a gap in the empirical literature on the representational consequences of election systems. It was hypothesized that district elections produce more equitable representation for minorities but less equitable representation for females. The data provide modest support for the former and none for the latter. District systems resulted in more racial equity for black men than at-large systems. But the difference between district and mixed systems was statistically insignificant for them. On the other hand, none of the electoral systems had a statistically significant impact on the mostly white women's representation in city councils.

The results for minority representation in American counties are consistent with most of the research on other types of jurisdictions. The female representation data, however, are consistent with the findings of Karnig and Oliver[2]

(1976) and Welch and Karnig[3] (1979), who examined American municipalities. They are inconsistent with more recent studies examining the impact of multi-member and single-member districts. The Welch and Herrick chapter and the Rule chapter in this volume and Darcy, Welch, and Clark[4] have found that the proportion of female candidates and officeholders was greater in multimember than in single-member constituencies.

The scope of this research was limited by the inability to include Hispanics or to separately examine black females. The small number of cases in each instance prevented any meaningful analysis. Consequently, the findings pertain primarily to black men and white women. Black women, in fact, are proportionately more disadvantaged in county legislatures than either black males or white females. Black males and black females are each about 6 percent of the American population. Since the 4 percent of blacks on county councils are virtually all males, black males are moderately underrepresented while black females are grossly underrepresented. The situation of white females is between the two. They compose about 52 percent of the population and occupy 10 percent of the county council seats. Hispanics are over 10 percent of the population and no more than two percent of county council members.

New groups in the electoral process typically begin with small numbers and increase in an incremental fashion. Hispanics and black and Anglo females, however, appear to have an exceptionally long road to travel toward representational parity. Recent research suggests that candidate recruitment is one of the more important obstacles to this end. It may be that the most politically active and experienced members of these groups opt to run for those offices with greater visibility or those with a greater perception of power or those offering more chances for election.

Effective and equitable representation is clearly more complicated than the mere number-counting in this research. It is helpful, however, to identify the magnitude and causes of the numerical disparities that exist and to trace the extent to which they change over time.

NOTES

1. Tari Renner, "Municipal Election Processes: The Impact on Minority Representation," *The 1988 Municipal Yearbook* (Washington, D.C.: International City Management Association, 1988), pp. 13–21.

2. Albert K. Karnig and Walter Oliver, "Election of Women to City Councils," *Social Science Quarterly*, March 1976, pp. 605–13.

3. Susan Welch and Albert K. Karnig, "Correlates of Female Office-Holding in City Politics," *Journal of Politics*, May 1979, pp. 478–91.

4. Robert Darcy, Susan Welch, and Janet Clark, "Women Candidates in Single and Multi-Member Districts: American State Legislative Races," *Social Science Quarterly*, December 1985, pp. 945–63.

13

The Impact of At-Large Elections on the Representation of Minority Women

Susan Welch and Rebekah Herrick

Interest in electoral structures has grown in recent years. One focus of that interest is on the impact of local election structures on the representation of blacks, Hispanics, and women of all races. Though analysts are not unanimous, the preponderance of evidence indicates that at-large elections impede the representation of blacks.[1] Although the gap between the degree of black representation afforded by at-large elections and that offered by district elections has shrunk in the past decade, differences still exist.[2]

The findings concerning election structures and Hispanic representation, however, are less clear-cut.[3] Spatial segregation of Hispanic populations is not nearly as high as for blacks, and voting along the lines of Hispanic ethnicity is not as distinct (though little research on this topic exists).[4] Welch found significant regional differences in the relationship of election structure to Hispanic representation. In California, at-large systems yielded slightly better representation, but in Texas they had a significant negative effect.[5] These differences are also related to the degree of spatial segregation.

Do these patterns found for blacks and Hispanics also obtain for black and Hispanic women? Most research has indicated that women are somewhat better represented in multimember districts, including at-large seats, than in single-member districts.[6] The differences, though consistent in direction, have been quite small. Moreover, most studies have been of white officeholders. Left unanswered is whether electoral structures have the same impact on minority women as on white women. We explore the topic, using 1988 data from 314 United States cities of 50,000 or more population and a black or Hispanic population of at least 5 percent.

PREVIOUS RESEARCH

Single-member districts help ensure greater proportional representation of blacks than do at-large elections chiefly because blacks are segregated spatially in almost all communities. In at-large cities, black minorities usually cannot elect blacks without white support. Thus, to the extent that voting is along lines of race, black representation is facilitated in cities employing districts.

Black women, like black men, are highly spatially segregated compared with Hispanic women and Hispanic men, who are less spatially segregated. Neither group of women is spatially segregated with other women. Thus, women as women are not especially advantaged in district elections because district boundaries do not increase their chances of being extraordinarily large majorities in the same way that districts do for blacks. Moreover, voting on the basis of gender is not widespread. Thus, for women, as for Hispanics, district elections do not offer a potentially obvious advantage.

Indeed, rather than facilitating the representation of women, district elections might impede it.[7] Women may be more comfortable in running for office in multimember districts; voters may be more apt to vote for a woman as one of several candidates; or turnover (and the opportunity for new members to be elected) might be higher in multimember systems. Welch and Studlar tested these explanations and found that women are more likely to run in multimember districts and are slightly more likely to be elected there.[8]

Only two previous studies have examined the representation-structure link for black and white women separately, and only one has analyzed that link for Hispanic women. Karnig and Welch, based on 1978 data from United States cities of 25,000 and above, showed that council representation of black men was larger where district elections were employed.[9] The representation ratios of black women, Hispanic women, and Hispanic men were not affected by whether the city had district elections.

These findings were confirmed in a more recent study, which showed that political structure still had little effect on the representation of black women while it had a noticeable effect on the election of black men.[10] This analysis, however, did not examine the impact of electoral structure on Hispanics. We expect that structure will also continue to have little effect on the election of Hispanic women.

DATA AND METHODS

Our study is based on a survey of every United States city with a 1984 population of at least 50,000 and a minimum of 5 percent black or Hispanic population in 1980. Data were collected in May and June 1988 by a two-page questionnaire posted to city clerks, with follow-up telephone calls to the 10 percent of the initial respondents who did not return the mailed questionnaire.[11] All clerks replied, yielding 314 responses. In this analysis we use three different subsets of cities. When we analyze the representation of blacks, we include only the 239 cities with at least a 5 percent black population. When we examine Hispanic representation, we include only the 169 cities with the same population floor of Hispanics. And, when we examine Anglo representation, we include only those cities with at least a 5 percent Anglo population.[12] Our analysis of blacks is largely drawn from Herrick and Welch, who used the same data base.[13]

This group of cities provides considerable variation in electoral type. In the early 1970s, 63 percent of city councils elected their members solely at large, and another 15 percent used mixed systems, including at-large and district methods.[14] Over the years, however, more and more cities have dropped the at-large feature or combined it with district elections. By 1986, Renner reported that although at-large systems are the dominant form in cities under 50,000, only about one-half of the cities between 50,000 and 100,000 and less than half of all cities over 100,000 use them.[15] Reflecting the fact that cities with significant minority populations have been most apt to have at-large election systems challenged, only 35 percent of our 314 cities held purely at-large elections, 43 percent had mixed elections, 16 percent held single-member district elections only, 2 percent had multimember district elections, and the remaining 4 percent had other combinations of single-member, multimember, and at-large elections.

We asked each clerk to provide data on the number of at-large council members, the number elected in single-member districts or wards, and the number chosen in districts or wards electing more than one member. For each set of members, we asked the race or ethnicity and gender of each member. The categories included black men and women, Hispanic men and women, non-Hispanic white men and women, and "other" men and women.

We use two different analyses to examine the link between structure and representation. We first examined the proportionality of representation in cities employing at-large, single-member district, and mixed systems, using a ratio measure whereby the percentage of black men and women on the council is divided by the percentage of black men and women in the city population. Similar calculations were done for Hispanics and Anglos.[16]

Because the ratio measure of representation has methodological problems,[17] we also employ a regression technique used by Engstrom and McDonald.[18] The proportion of the city council that is black, for example, can be regressed on the proportion of the city population that is black, allowing one to see the relationship between the two factors at different levels of black population proportions. To examine how different electoral structures affect that relationship, we added dummy and interaction variables to the regression equation.[19]

We also add to this equation several variables designed to control for city demographic and structural characteristics that could account for minority and Anglo women's council membership. The socioeconomic levels of the minority community and of the entire community are both important. We use the city population median education, which was a significant predictor of women's council representation.[20] Karnig and Welch found that the education and income

Table 13.1

Representation of Black, Hispanic, and Anglo Women on City Councils among Cities of over 50,000 Population, 1988

	BLACK WOMEN	HISPANIC WOMEN	ANGLO WOMEN
Mean percent on council	5	2	18
Standard deviation	7	6	14
Range	0–29	0–20	0–60
Percent with more than 5 percent black (or Hispanic or Anglo) women	31	14	76
Percent with no black (or Hispanic or Anglo) women	67	86	23

The cities used in this analysis are those with more than 5 percent black population (for black women), 5 percent Hispanic population (for Hispanic women), or 5 percent Anglo population (for Anglo women).

of the black community was significantly related to black male, though not female, council representation. In examining black women's representation, we include the ratio of black and white median family income;[21] similarly, when examining Hispanic women's representation, we include the Hispanic/non-Hispanic income ratio. When examining Anglo women's representation, we simply use the community's median income.[22] The city council size, sometimes positively related to black and Hispanic council representation, provides another control.[23] We also control for the city's population size largely because our sample of cities varies considerably in that dimension.

FINDINGS

In Table 13.1 we present descriptive data on women's council representation. We see that black women compose about 5 percent of council membership in these cities, Hispanic women barely 2 percent, and Anglo women about 18 percent.[24] Most councils have no black or Hispanic women, and about one-quarter have no Anglo women. Women, therefore, are still a minority on most councils.

Council Membership and Population Proportions

Table 13.2 shows the ratio of black, Hispanic, and Anglo women's and men's council membership to their population proportion. A score of more than 1.0 means the council representation proportion for a given group exceeds its population proportion, and a score of less than 1.0 means the council proportion is less.

Table 13.2
Ratio of Council Representation to Population Percent by Gender and Ethnic
Groups, 1978 and 1988

	1978 (10%)	1988 (10%)	1988 (5%)
Black men (264, 189, 239)	1.26	1.43	1.42
Black women (264, 189, 239)	.16	.34	.33
Hispanic men (124, 111, 169)	.78	.82	.75
Hispanic women (124, 111, 169)	.11	.23	.19
Anglo men (365, 307, 311)	2.00	1.83	1.82
Anglo women (365, 307, 311)	.33	.48	.48

Source: The 1978 data, from Karnig and Welch, "Sex and Ethnic Differences," are based on all
cities of 25,000 and over with at least 10 percent black population (for the data on blacks), all
southwestern cities of 25,000 and over with at least 10 percent Hispanic population (for the
data on Hispanics), and a combination of these two sets for the Anglo data (some cities were
in both samples). The 1988 data are cities of 50,000 and over. See the text for the full description
of the 1988 data.

Numbers in parentheses are those for the 1978 sample, the 1988 sample with a 10 percent floor of
the relevant group (black, Hispanic, or Anglo), and the 1988 sample with a 5 percent floor.

Anglo women are represented at about one-half their population proportions,
black women about one-third, and Hispanic women at only about one-fifth. On a
more positive note, although the 1978 data are from cities of over 25,000 and the 1988
data are from cities over 50,000 and hence the two are not totally comparable, it appears that women of all ethnicities have significantly increased their representational
ratios. In deed, black and Hispanic women have doubled their ratios of representation
while white women have increased theirs by about 50 percent.

In contrast, black men only slightly increased their already high ratio, Hispanic
men stayed at about the same levels, and Anglo men's representational ratio decreased. Despite these changes, Anglo men are the most overrepresented group,
followed by black men. Hispanic men are underrepresented relative to their population but are more proportionally represented than white women, black women, and
Hispanic women, in that order. Since 1978, therefore, representation on urban city
councils has become much more reflective of urban populations, but it still has a considerable way to go to become fully representative.

Some research has indicated that in a variety of political offices, black women
are better represented relative to black men than Anglo women are to Anglo
men and Hispanic women to Hispanic men.[25] However, the findings of table
13.2 do not support these conclusions. Indeed, black women in 1978 fared
slightly worse (a ratio of about 1:8) than did Hispanic women (a ratio of about
1:7), who in turn did slightly worse than the Anglo women's ratio of about 1:6.
In 1988, all three groups have similar, and improved, ratios of female-to-male

Table 13.3
Election Type and Ratios of Representation to Population for Minority and Anglo Men and Women in Cities with 5 Percent or More Minorities,* 1988

VOTER GROUP	DISTRICT	MIXED	AT-LARGE	MULTI-MEMBER	ALL
Black women	.25	.30	.35	.87	.33
Hispanic women	.15	.17	.21	.14	.19
Anglo women	.45	.45	.50	.60	.48
Black men	1.96	1.32	1.37	.95	1.42*
Hispanic men	.74	.86	.67	1.01	.75
Anglo men	1.70	1.82	1.87	1.60	1.82

Note: See table 13.2 for a description of the case base for each analysis.

*Intra-election type differences significant at .05 if this was a sample.

representation (about 1:4).[26] Thus relative to their male counterparts, black and Hispanic women are about as far behind as Anglo women.

Election Structures and Council Representation

Women's substantial underrepresentation varies little among the major election types (see table 13.3). They are substantially underrepresented in all three. Black and Anglo women's representation comes closest to parity in the few multi-member district systems,[27] but of the three major systems, women's representation varies at most by 10 percent within each ethnic group. In all three groups, however, women are represented slightly better in the at-large than in the other two systems. Black women are somewhat better represented in mixed than district systems, but for Anglo and Hispanic women there is little difference between these two types.[28]

Structure makes by far the most difference to black men.[29] They are overrepresented in all three systems but are most overrepresented in single-member districts. In the small number of multimember districts, they are closest to their population proportions. Though Hispanic men do better in district and especially in mixed systems, the differences in their representation among these election types are also relatively limited.[30] The relative lack of effect of electoral structures on Hispanics is due in part to their opposite, though small, effect on the two genders.[31]

Regression Analyses of Electoral Systems and Representation

In another analysis, we have shown that the council representation of black women is not extremely responsive to their population proportions, although it is most responsive in at-large systems.[32] As the black female population proportion increased by 1 percent, the black women's council percent increases by about .33 percent in district systems, .31 percent in mixed systems, and .48 percent in at-large systems. Because of the negative constants for the at-large systems, black women are slightly more apt to be elected in district than in at-large elections when the black female population is fairly small, less than 5 percent. Above that, black women are somewhat more apt to be elected in at-large systems (a black female population of 5 percent translates into a total black population of about 9 percent). However, the maximum relative advantage of the at-large systems for black women is only about 4 percent.

In 1978, the representation of Hispanic women was unrelated to their population proportions. The following equations indicate that this has changed.

% Hispanic women councillors =

$-.12 + .20 \times$ % Hispanic women in population (district systems)
(1.30)   (.09)

$-.75 + .14 \times$ % Hispanic women in population (at-large systems)
(.97)   (.06)

$-1.11 + .39 \times$ % Hispanic women in population (mixed systems)
(.96)   (.11)

No matter which electoral system is used, as the Hispanic population increased, so does the representation of Hispanic women. In each case, the standard error is less than half the population coefficient, indicating that the relationship is probably not due to random fluctuations. However, the coefficients are small. The representation of Hispanic women is most reflective of population proportions in mixed systems, which combine single-member and at-large systems, though the negative constant also suggests that mixed systems are not very responsive in cities with small Hispanic populations. For example, in a population of about 10 percent Hispanic women, differences among electoral types are negligible. The average district system would yield a council of about 2 percent Hispanic women, a mixed system 3 percent, and an at-large system only 1 percent. But even in cities of about 60 percent Hispanic population, with about 30 percent Hispanic women, a mixed system yields only about 11 percent Hispanic women on the council, compared with 6 percent for the district and 3 percent for the at-large system.

The findings for Anglo women are straightforward and similar to what we found earlier using a slightly different case base.[33] In at-large systems the proportion of Anglo women on councils is responsive to their population proportions.

In mixed systems, the responsiveness is considerably less. Most interestingly, there is little effect from greater population proportions in district systems on the representation of Anglo women.[34] Thus, district systems do not translate Anglo population proportions into seats for Anglo women.

% Anglo women councillors =

9.34 + .17 × % Anglo women in population (district systems)
(8.20) (.23)

2.71 + .43 × % Anglo women in population (at-large systems)
(4.83) (.12)

7.26 + .24 × % Anglo women in population (mixed systems)
(5.20) (.13)

Other Predictors of Women's Representation

In a final analysis, we used regression to examine the impact of electoral structure, taking into account several other possible predictors of representation of each ethnic-gender group. In addition to the population proportions of the group and the type of election, these predictors included the population of the city, the ratio of black to white (or Hispanic to non-Hispanic) income, the proportion of people in the city who graduated from high school, and the total size of the council.

Only the black female population proportion and the council size are related to black female representation at a level that would be statistically significant at the .05 level if we were analyzing a sample (see table 13.4).[35] None of the election type variables or their interactions with black female population percent are significant, nor do they have standard errors less than the regression coefficient. Thus, other things being equal, black female representation seems little affected by election type. The black-white income ratio and educational levels of the community are also unrelated to the representation of black women.

The extent of Hispanic women's representation on the council is predicted poorly by our model (an R^2 of only .12). Only one of the coefficients for population proportions achieves standard levels of statistical significance, and only one other coefficient has a t value of more than 1 (the interaction term of the proportion of Hispanic women times mixed systems). Hispanic women's representation seems independent of all of these factors, except population percent.

The council representation of Anglo women is unrelated to their population proportion, a not surprising finding given the bivariate relationships. Anglo women are, however, significantly more likely to be found on councils in communities with more highly educated populations. Like black women, they are also slightly more likely to be found on larger councils, but only in at-large systems.[36]

Table 13.4
Predictors of Women's Representation in Each Ethnic Group

PREDICTORS	BLACK		HISPANIC		ANGLO	
	b	t	b	t	b	t
Sex-race population %	.43	4.05	.24	2.10	-.05	-.28
Council size	.15	1.68	-.06	-.59	.18	1.08
% high school graduates	.03	.55	.03	.64	.50	4.65*
Bl-Wh income ratio	-3.03	-1.03	-.11	-.10	.28	.96
South or Southwest	-.42	-.38	-.49	-.39	-1.07	-.63
Population size	-.00	-.58	.00	.61	.00	.42
At-large	.02	.01	.77	.39	2.61	.33
Mixed	.89	.42	-1.15	-.54	4.18	.50
Sex-race %x mixed	-.11	-.88	.19	1.07	-.06	-.26
Sex-race %x at-large	.07	.52	-.08	-.64	.02	.09
Constant	-1.88	4.56	-1.72	5.08	-23.65	8.39
R^2	.22		.12		.18	

Notes: The number of cases is 239 for the black representation analysis, 169 for the Hispanic, and 307 for the Anglo. The "b" is the standardized regression coefficient which indicates the difference in representation produced by each variable controlling for all the others. The "t" is a measure of statistical significance that some readers might find helpful. A "t" value of 1.96 or greater indicates statistical significance at the level of .05.

None of the election-type variables, including the interaction terms, are significantly related to representation of any of the women's groups. This finding reaffirms our conclusions that election type is mostly significant because of its effect on the election of black men.

CONCLUSIONS

As the 1980s began, we thought we understood the impact of different electoral systems on minority groups, and we did not really think about their impact on women as a group. As the 1990s begin, we realize that the task of achieving fair descriptive representation of every significant racial or gender group is much more complex than we had earlier thought.

The three major types of electoral structures have very little impact on the representation of black, Hispanic, and Anglo women. If anything, women of all ethnic groups fare better with at-large systems, but the differences we found, as in the past, are quite small. Of course, given the relative paucity of women in government, even small barriers can loom as important obstacles; still, it is difficult for us to argue that women are seriously impeded in their quest for council seats by any of the three major forms—district, at-large, or mixed.

Of course, some types of electoral structures make a more important difference. Many scholars have argued that proportional representation (PR) systems greatly facilitate the election of women.[37] National legislatures in countries with PR systems have much higher proportions of women members than do national legislatures employing single-member districts. PR systems also have an advantage in that they can produce heterogeneity in representation in the presence of racially polarized voting even without spatial segregation.[38]

Multimember district systems may be an incrementally useful innovation to consider in promoting representativeness. They have been completely ignored in previous urban research (undoubtedly being combined with single-member district cities in a "district" category), though conceptually they are distinct from single-member district cities. In these cities, election districts are used, but more than one person is elected from each. Though the fact that we have only five such cities in our sample mitigates our ability to draw solid generalizations, black and white women and Hispanic men are represented much closer to parity in those multimember districts than they are in any of the other systems. Anglo men remain considerably overrepresented, but less so than in the other systems. Black men are underrepresented slightly, but their representation is closer to parity than in the other systems. Only Hispanic women do not fare well in these cities. It would be useful to investigate smaller communities to see if these findings hold true with a larger number of cities.

Though all systems greatly underrepresent women of all ethnic groups on local councils, the answer to the question of which electoral system is fairer depends, at least for black women, on which set of issues and identity is more important to them.[39] If racial issues and identity are more important than gender for black women, district elections would appear to be "best." They provide somewhat more proportional representation for blacks, and to the extent that descriptive representation translates into action on the substantive issues of greatest concerns for blacks, having more black elected councillors, regardless of gender, would be desired. If women's issues are of equal or greater importance to black women, and if electing more women to the council means more attention to women's issues, then district elections do not necessarily allow for better representation of black women. Neither Hispanic nor Anglo women have the same cross-pressures in terms of considering which system is "best" because the consequences of electoral structure do not have a major effect on the representation of their gender group or their ethnic group.

In general, however, the contradictory consequences of these typical United States electoral systems on black men and black women, along with the generally low levels of women's representation among all racial and ethnic groups, provide more incentives to take another look at proportional representation systems for local governments.

NOTES

The authors thank Donna Gosch, David R. Johnson, and the City Clerks in the 314 surveyed municipalities.

1. Susan Welch, "The Impact of At-Large Elections on the Representation of Blacks

and Hispanics," *Journal of Politics*, November 1990, pp. 1050–76; Albert Karnig and Susan Welch, "Electoral Structure and Black Representation on City Councils," *Social Science Quarterly*, March 1982, pp. 99–114; Bernard Grofman, "Alternatives to Single Member Plurality Districts: Legal and Empirical Issues," in Bernard Grofman, Arend Lijphart, Robert McKay, and Howard Scarrow, eds., *Representation and Redistricting Issues* (Lexington, Mass.: Lexington Books, 1982, pp. 107–28); and Richard Engstrom and Michael McDonald, "The Election of Blacks to City Councils," *American Political Science Review*, June 1981, 344–55.

2. Welch, "At-Large Elections." In the early 1970s, black council representation in at-large systems was only about 40 percent of what one would expect based on black population proportions, according to Theodore Robinson and Thomas Dye, "Reformism and Representation on City Councils," *Social Science Quarterly*, June 1978, pp. 133–41. This parity ratio rose to 50 and 60 percent in the late 1970s (Engstrom and McDonald, "Election of Blacks to City Councils"; Karnig and Welch, "Electoral Structure and Black Representation"). These same studies found that black council representation in district systems increased from about 85 percent in the mid–1970s to over 90 percent later in that decade. Though current research indicates that mixed systems, those composed of both at-large and district elections, do not provide more black representation than purely at-large systems, research from the 1970s indicated that mixed systems fell between purely at-large and purely district systems in the degree of black representation afforded. Thus, in many cases, mixed systems were seen as compromise solutions.

3. Some suggest that Hispanics are slightly more proportionately represented in district systems (Delbert Taebel, "Minority Representation on City Councils," *Social Science Quarterly*, June 1978, pp. 142–52; Chandler Davidson and George Korbel, "At-large Elections and Minority Group Representation: A Re-Examination of Historical and Contemporary Representation on City Councils," *Journal of Politics*, November 1981, pp. 982–1005). Others suggest that Hispanics are represented slightly better in mixed systems (Susan MacManus, "City Council Elections Procedures and Minority Representation," *Social Science Quarterly*, June 1978, pp. 153–61). Yet others found that structure makes hardly any difference overall (Karnig and Welch, "Electoral Structure and Black Representation"; Fernando Guerra, "The Elections of Minorities and Women in Los Angeles and California," a paper presented at the Annual Meeting of the American Political Science Association, Atlanta, Georgia, 1989; and Charles Bullock and Susan MacManus, "Structural Features of Municipalities and the Incidence of Hispanic Council Members," *Social Science Quarterly*, December 1990, pp. 665–81.

4. Arnold Vedlitz and Charles A. Johnson, "Community Racial Segregation, Electoral Structure, and Minority Representation," *Social Science Quarterly*, December 1982, pp. 729–36; Douglas Massey and Nancy Denton, "Trends in the Residential Segregation of Blacks, Hispanics, and Asians: 1870–1980," *American Sociological Review*, December 1987, pp. 802–25; and Jeffrey Zax, "Election Methods and Black and Hispanic City Council Membership," *Social Science Quarterly*, June 1990, pp. 339–55.

5. Welch, "At-Large Elections."

6. Albert Karnig and Susan Welch, "Sex and Ethnic Differences in Municipal Representation," *Social Science Quarterly*, December 1979, pp. 465–81; Robert Darcy, Susan Welch, and Janet Clark, *Women, Elections, and Representation* (New York: Longman, 1987); and Susan Welch and Donley Studlar, "The Impact of Multi-Member Districts on the Representation of Women in Britain and the United States," *Journal of Politics*, May 1990, pp. 391–412.

7. Susan J. Carroll, *Women as Candidates in American Politics* (Bloomington: Indiana University Press, 1985); Wilma Rule, "Why More Women Are State Legislators," *Western Political Quarterly*, June 1990, pp. 437–48; and Darcy, Welch, and Clark, *Women, Elections, and Representation*.

8. Welch and Studlar, "Multi-Member Districts."

9. Karnig and Welch, "Sex and Ethnic Differences."

10. Rebekah Herrick and Susan Welch, "The Impact of At-Large Elections on the Representation of Black and White Women," *National Political Science Review*, forthcoming.

11. Donald Dillman, *Mail and Telephone Surveys: The Total Design Method* (New York: Wiley, 1978). The mailing procedure, suggested by Dillman, consisted of an initial mailing, followed three weeks later by a postcard reminder thanking those who had responded for their cooperation and urging nonrespondents to complete the questionnaire. Two weeks later a second copy of the questionnaire was sent. Telephoning was begun three weeks after the mailing of the second copy. Partly due to the brevity of the questionnaire, the response rate was incredibly high, exceeding that of the International City Management Association's 1986 survey of cities, which reported a 66 percent response rate.

12. These cities constitute approximately 85 percent of the 356 United States cities with over 50,000 population. In sampling, we eliminated cities with black, Hispanic, or Anglo populations so small that proportional representation would be difficult to achieve given the normal size (5 to 15) of most city councils. The specific cutoff used does not affect the substantive findings; we also examined these data using a population floor of 10 percent black, Anglo, or Hispanic.

13. Herrick and Welch, "Impact of At-Large Elections."

14. James H. Svara, "Unwrapping Institutional Packages in Urban Government," *Journal of Politics*, February 1977, pp. 166–75.

15. Tari Renner, "Municipal Election Processes: The Impact on Minority Representation," in *The Municipal Yearbook 1988* (Washington, D.C.: International City Management Association, 1988), pp. 13–22.

16. This ratio measure was used by Peggy Heilig and Robert Mundt, "Changes in Representational Equity: The Effect of Adopting Districts," *Social Science Quarterly*, June 1983, pp. 393–97. See also Albert Karnig, "Black Representation on City Councils: The Impact of District Elections and Socioeconomic Factors," *Urban Affairs Quarterly*, December 1976, pp. 223–42; Karnig and Welch, "Sex and Ethnic Differences"; Karnig and Welch, "Electoral Structure and Black Representation"; and Robinson and Dye, "Reformism and Representation on City Councils." To calculate the population percentage of women in each community, we apply the sex ratio in the United States, which is about 53 percent women and 47 percent men, to the percent black, Hispanic, or white in the community. Using these national male-female ratios overlooks variations from community to community, but these differences are minor.

17. Engstrom and McDonald, "Election of Blacks to City Councils"; Richard Engstrom and Michael McDonald, "The Effect of At-Large versus District Elections on Racial Representation in U.S. Municipalities," in Bernard Grofman and Arend Lijphart, eds., *Electoral Laws and Their Political Consequences* (New York: Agathon Press, 1986); and Karnig and Welch, "Electoral Structure and Black Representation."

18. Engstrom and McDonald, "Election of Blacks to City Councils."

19. The following equation was specified (let district cities be the omitted category):

$$\text{Pcblcn} = a + b_1 + b_2 \text{ mixed} + b_3 \text{ pcblpop} + b_4 \text{ pcblpop} \times \text{at1} + b_5 \text{ pcblpop} \times \text{mixed} + e$$

where

Pcblcn = percent of black council members

at1 = 1 if city uses only at-large election, 0 if not

mixed = 1 if city used both at-large and district, 0 if not

pcblpop = percent black population in city

Note that this formulation allows three separate equations to be specified within the overall equation. See Robert Friedrich, "In Defense of Multiplicative Terms in Multiple Regression Equations," *American Journal of Political Science*, November 1982, pp. 797–833. For example, for those cities with only district elections, the at-large and mixed system variables are both equal to 0, and black representation is specified by: Pcblcn = $a + b_3$ pcblpop. Similarly, we see that when the city has both at-large and district elections, the constant is represented by $(a + b_2)$ and slope by $(b_3 + b_5)$. We will use this regression formulation, substituting black, Hispanic, and white female council and proportions in the equation. See Herrick and Welch, "Impact of At-Large Elections."

20. Karnig and Welch, "Sex and Ethnic Differences."

21. Engstrom and MacDonald, "At-large versus District Elections."

22. Because of the high correlations between minority community characteristics and those of the whole community (such as median years of education), we use education as a measure of community socioeconomic status and income as a measure of minority socioeconomic status.

23. Taebel, "Minority Representation."

24. In each case, the data base is those cities with at least 5 percent of the relevant (black, Hispanic, Anglo) population.

25. Robert Darcy and Charles D. Hadley, "Black Women in Politics: The Puzzle of Success," *Social Science Quarterly*, September 1988, pp. 629–45.

26. We note that although in the 1970s, black women's congressional representation was better (relative to their male counterparts) than white women's, this situation was no longer so by the late 1980s. Congressional membership included only one black woman. After the 1990 election, black women again improved their representation. Black women are represented better in state legislatures relative to black men than white women are to white men. Black women are about 21 percent of all black legislators. See Joint Center for Political Studies, *National Roster of Black Elected Officials* (Washington, D.C.: Joint Center for Political Studies, 1990). The overall proportion of women in state legislatures is about 17 percent.

27. Herrick and Welch, "Impact of At-Large Elections."

28. None of these differences meet conventional tests of statistical significance. This situation is one where there is disagreement over the appropriateness of tests of statistical significance. Our units of analysis represent a universe, so such tests are not necessary. However, they give the reader a sense of how stable such differences are likely to be.

29. Karnig and Welch, "Sex and Ethnic Differences"; Herrick and Welch, "Impact of At-Large Elections."

30. If these data were a sample, the differences would not be statistically significant.

31. As found by Herrick and Welch, "Impact of At-Large Elections."

32. Ibid.

33. Ibid.

34. This finding is shown by the fact that the standard error of the Anglo women's population proportion exceeds the regression coefficient. These coefficients differ slightly from those found in Herrick and Welch ("Impact of At-Large Elections") because of the different case base used for white/Anglo women in the two studies. In the earlier work, only blacks and whites were being compared, so only cities with a 5 percent black population floor were used. Here a more inclusive set of cities is analyzed.

35. Here we use a one-tailed test because we expected a positive relationship for these two variables. An analysis of the council size variable reveals that it affects only the proportion of black women on the council in at-large systems.

36. This relationship supports previous findings of weak positive associations between the number of seats and women's representation (Welch and Studlar, "Multi-Member Districts").

37. Darcy, Welch, and Clark, *Women, Elections, and Representation*.

38. Refer to Joseph F. Zimmerman, "Enhancing Representational Equity in Cities" in this volume.

39. There has been an ongoing debate about the relevant salience of women's and black issues to black women. See Susan Welch and Lee Sigelman, "A Black Gender Gap?" *Social Science Quarterly*, March 1989, 120–33; Paula Giddings, *When and Where I Enter: The Impact of Black Women on Race and Sex in America* (New York: Bantam, 1984); and Linda LaRue, "Black Liberation and Women's Lib," *Transaction*, November/ December 1970, pp. 59–64. There is much evidence that black women are as committed to the goals of the women's movement as white women are. See Willa Mae Hemmons, "The Women's Liberation Movement: Understanding Black Women's Attitudes," in La Frances Rodges-Rose, ed., *The Black Women* (Beverly Hills, Calif.: Sage, 1980), pp. 285–300; Paula Reid, "Feminism v. Minority Group Identity: Not for Black Women Only," *Sex Roles*, February 1984, pp. 247–55; and Susan Marshall, "Equity Issues and Black-White Differences in Women's ERA Support," *Social Science Quarterly*, June 1990, pp. 299–314.

14

Electing Women to City Council:
A Focus on Small Cities in Florida

Susan A. MacManus and Charles S. Bullock III

Political scientists have neglected studying the barriers inhibiting women's election to city councils in small cities even though 84 percent of all municipalities have populations under 25,000.[1] The sheer number of small cities may explain why there is so little literature examining the conditions promoting the election of women in these locales. But could it be that small cities promote, rather than stymie, the election of more women to municipal office? What is the effect of election structures and political factors on women running for office in small jurisdictions? In this study, we examine the extent to which women officials *perceive* that various factors inhibit the election of women to city council and determine whether city size makes a difference in these perceptions. To explore these questions, we sent a questionnaire to a sample of women elected officials in 62 cities in 15 Florida counties, reflecting a diversity in rural-urban character, size, and city growth rate.[2] Of 160 questionnaires posted, valid responses were received from 85 (53 percent).

PREVIOUS RESEARCH

Most studies of female representation have focused on cities over 25,000 in population, with data gathered in the 1970s and early 1980s. Women have made extraordinary strides in capturing electoral positions during the past few years. Consequently, the earlier studies may not be generalizable to the 1990s. Furthermore, previous research focused on only a few election system characteristics and did not consider other structural and political factors that may be important for women's election to city councils.

Type of Council Election System

Karnig's and Walter's initial study in 1976 of female representation predicted that "voters would be more prone to support women, in multi-member [at-large] than in single-member districts."[3] The authors' rationale was that in multimember districts, voters would be less likely to see the outcome in zero-sum terms and, consequently, would be more apt to vote for a woman, perhaps out of a sense of fairness. Their study, based on data from 838 cities with populations over 25,000 collected in 1975, reported correlational coefficients that confirmed their hypothesis, although only weakly.

Subsequent studies also confirmed this positive, though weak, relationship between at-large elections and female city councillors, although several studies reported variations among different types of at-large systems. For example, Welch and Karnig concluded that "females are slightly more likely to be elected from [pure] at-large than at-large with residence requirements, and more likely to be elected from at-large with residence requirements than from district elections."[4] However, the association was not quite significant at the .05 level.

Based on previous research, we predict that the current method of electing council members will not be among the most frequently cited barriers to the election of women, regardless of the system currently in place.

Majority versus Plurality Vote Requirements

In the first study of municipal runoff elections, Fleischmann and Stein, using 1951–85 data from three large Texas cities, concluded that "minority and female front runners . . . were not disadvantaged in runoffs when compared to runoffs pairing candidates of the same sex and race."[5] Similarly, our large study of 211 southern city councils with 1980 populations over 25,000 (1986 data) found no relationship between this structural characteristic and female representational levels.[6] Our national study reported that plurality arrangements promoted the election of women only in the Midwest.[7]

Previous research suggests that women city council members will not identify the majority vote requirement as a barrier to the election of women in Florida cities.

Staggered versus Simultaneous Terms

It has been suggested that staggered terms negatively affect racial and ethnic minorities in pure at-large systems because they limit single-shot voting.[8] On the other hand, staggered terms might make it easier for a nonincumbent to gain name recognition and election in small cities. But simultaneous elections may make slating and group coalition building easier and also reduce campaign costs if group advertising is adopted.

Surprisingly, there have been few studies of the impact of staggered versus simultaneous terms on female representation on city councils. But of those who have studied the connection, none found a significant relationship between term structure and female city council representation.[9]

We hypothesize that few women local officials will identify this factor as a major deterrent to the election of female candidates.

Length of Council Term and Campaign Expenditures

Length of council term is another structural variable that rarely has been tested for its effect on the election of women to city councils. It has not turned out to be significant.[10] However, some believe that shorter terms may promote the election of women by increasing the number of open seats and/or reducing campaign costs.

Based on previous research, we expect that the length of the current city council term will not be viewed as a major barrier by a significant number of women elected officials surveyed. We also predict that there will not be a significant relationship between campaign expenditure and length of term.

We further hypothesize that there will not be a significant relationship between a council member's campaign expenditures and her recommendation that council terms be shortened.

Council Size

Previous research has suggested that smaller councils stymie the election of women to municipal office. This finding is based on the notion that the smaller the council, the greater the competition for office and the fewer the number of females elected. On the other hand, it has been argued that women have more difficulty getting elected to large councils, which are said to be more prestigious and important. However, no significant relationship has been found between council size and female representation levels.[11] We anticipate that local women elected officials will not identify council size as a major impediment to the election of women to city councils.

Costs of Running for Office

Are perceptions regarding the difficulty of fund-raising and the costs of running for office keeping more women from declaring their candidacies? Campaign reform advocates often suggest that candidacy rates would rise if filing fees were eliminated or reduced and campaign contributions were limited. To date, however, there has been no empirical examination of the degree to which these factors influence candidacy rates. However, Carroll's 1976 nationwide survey of women who ran as major party candidates for congressional, statewide, and state legislative offices reported that "money was mentioned far more frequently than any other problem" by women who sought office.[12] Other studies indicate that campaign spending levels have little significant impact on the success rate of women candidates for city council, at least in large cities.[13]

Smaller jurisdictions may offer an advantage to women candidates from the perspective of campaign costs. A body of research suggests that the smaller the jurisdiction, the lower the levels of campaign spending required because there is less need to use expensive media-based campaigns.[14] Campaign techniques emphasize volunteers, door-to-door, and other grass-roots strategies.

Relying on previous research and extensive coverage of efforts to limit campaign contributions and spending in the popular press, we hypothesize that campaign cost-related factors will be among the more commonly cited barriers by the women in our sample. Specifically, we anticipate that a sizable number of women elected officials will recommend the elimination of filing fees and the adoption of more restrictive campaign contribution laws.

We also predict that there will be a positive relationship between filing fees and identification of filing fees as a barrier.

Restriction on the Number of Terms

Unrestricted terms are said to promote the election of incumbents, thereby deterring the rapid entry of women into elective office. Studies examining the relationship between the proportion of incumbents and the percent of females on the city council have revealed that the relationship is not statistically significant. Nevertheless, there is still concern that unrestricted terms limit the number of open seats, thereby reducing the chance for sharp gains in women's and minorities' representation levels.

Therefore, we forecast that unrestricted terms of office will be identified as a barrier to the election of women by a sizable number of women city officials surveyed. We also surmise that women incumbents will be less apt to identify unrestricted terms as a barrier than will the nonincumbents. Challengers are more likely to call for limiting council member terms than incumbents.

Media Endorsements and Coverage

There has been little research on the importance of media in municipal elections, although newspaper endorsements have been found to make a difference in electoral outcomes in larger cities.[15] Newspaper endorsements have not been found to be discriminatory toward women candidates. In their longitudinal study of Austin, Texas, elections, MacManus and Bullock found no systematic bias in newspaper endorsements. In fact, the *Austin American Statesman* endorsed more female than male characters between 1975 and 1985.[16]

The general notion is that candidates in smaller jurisdictions are less dependent on extensive media-based campaign strategies, especially those involving television. Because media coverage of campaigns tends to be limited in small municipalities, particularly those in areas where the daily covers a metropolitan area, we hypothesize that a sizable number of women elected city officials will identify the lack of media coverage (newspaper and television) as a barrier to the election of women candidates.

We also expect that in towns where the local newspaper does not endorse city council candidates, a sizable proportion of the women elected officials will recommend greater newspaper and television coverage of city council races.

Partisan/Nonpartisan Elections

The Municipal Year Book 1988 reported that approximately 73 percent of all cities have nonpartisan elections.[17] Some election reform advocates have argued that adoption of partisan elections would increase female representation. They base their opinions on research that has identified a Republican, higher socio-economic, white, male bias among candidates elected in nonpartisan races.[18] Nevertheless, other studies have found that nonpartisan elections increase the number of women candidates or have some positive impact on the proportion of women elected to city councils, but these studies focused on large cities.[19]

The partisan/nonpartisan nature of city elections is also reported to affect a candidate's campaign tactics. According to Darcy, Welch, and Clark: "In partisan races, candidates can start from a base of loyal Democrats or Republicans, focusing first on arousing their partisan loyalties and support. . . . In a nonpartisan race, a candidate must build on other networks of friends, fellow workers, and associates."[20] However, there is a significant body of research showing political partisanship within nonpartisan systems.[21] Women tend to be more active in local political party organizations than men and are equally likely to be recruited to office by party leaders. Therefore, even in nonpartisan settings, they are apt to be able to make effective partisan appeals. Women candidates also are more likely than men to be involved actively in civic activities, especially in smaller communities. Consequently, they may be advantaged in small-town campaigns in nonpartisan settings.

For these reasons and because Florida's municipal elections are all nonpartisan, we expect to see very little support among local female elected officials for making elections partisan. We also expect there will be no significant difference between the views of Republican and Democratic women on this issue.

Timing of Municipal Elections

One frequent debate in the election literature is whether participation in local elections would be increased by holding municipal elections at a time separate from either presidential or gubernatorial elections. In smaller jurisdictions, especially those with limited media coverage of local election campaigns, it is probable that candidates, especially nonincumbents with low name recognition, would prefer holding city elections at a time unique to local government. However, among candidates who might perceive that the turnout of their supporters would be greater in presidential or gubernatorial elections, the preference might be to hold city elections simultaneous with those elections.

Basing our conclusion on little empirical evidence, we predict that few of our women city officeholders will identify election timing as a barrier to the election of women. However, those who identify timing as a barrier are likely to be from cities that do not hold their council elections at a time unique to local government.

Number of Women Candidates

Bledsoe's and Herring's study of women city councillors affirms what other scholars have found, namely that "the underrepresentation of women is due to a paucity of women candidates."[22] We agree and anticipate that the lack of women candidates will be perceived by our sample by mayors and councillors as the most serious obstacle to increasing female representation levels. We also forecast that the lower the proportion of women on a city's council, the more likely it is that a woman council member will identify the lack of women candidates as a major barrier.

City Size, Candidate Background, and Ambition

There are differing theories regarding the conditions under which women are elected to city council and the way in which city population size is related to the background characteristics of women elected officials. The desirability thesis maintains that women tend to be found in offices for which there is less prestige, fewer candidacies, and a far steeper path to higher elective office.[23] From this theory, we hypothesize that women are more apt to be elected in smaller towns, where the prestige of the position and the number of candidates competing for the position are lower.[24]

We also expect some differences in the ease of election by city size. We anticipate that councilwomen in larger cities have deeper roots in the community (length of residency) than those in smaller cities, especially since many of the smaller surveyed cities have been in the high growth areas of Florida. Thus, one might expect that it would be easier for a relative newcomer to win a council seat in a small town than in a larger city where it takes longer to establish name recognition and a sizable, effective campaign network. It is also not unreasonable to expect that women who have won election to city council in smaller cities may have had to run less often before finally winning.

The ambition that drives one to a position on a city council may not be quickly sated, so that women serve longer in larger cities. In a small community, the norm may be to do one's duty in the community and step aside, turning over an often thankless, poorly compensated job to some other active citizen. Increasingly, women retirees are taking their turns at these tasks.[25] On the other hand, it may be that the tenure of women holding office in smaller jurisdictions may be longer if there is less competition for council positions there.

One of our research objectives is to explore selected political antecedents of women serving in communities of different sizes. Our goal is to see whether their political histories differ significantly. We expect that they do.

THE RESULTS

The results reported in this study are based on the responses of 69 women city council members and 16 women mayors. The survey response rate for mayors was higher than for councillors—84 percent and 61 percent, respectively. Twelve of our mayors are elected separately by the voters (strong mayors), and four are selected by the city council (weak mayors). Among our 85 respondents, 54 percent are Republicans, 43 percent are Democrats, and 3 percent are independents. There are only four minority respondents, all councilwomen (three blacks and one Hispanic). Most of our respondents are from cities with some form of at-large election system (pure at-large, 44.7 percent; at-large by post, 35.3 percent; and at-large from districts, 5.9 percent). Another 3.5 percent are from cities with single-member district elections. The remaining 7.1 percent are from cities with a combination system (some at-large seats, some district-based seats).

Barriers to the Election of Women to City Council

Of the many elements that might be perceived to be impediments to the election of more councilwomen, only one was cited by more than a small number of the respondents. Table 14.1 shows that more than two-thirds of the women we surveyed believed that for there to be more members of their gender on city councils, there first must be more women candidates. Women elected officials from small cities were more likely to identify the lack of women candidates as a major barrier than were women from large cities, although the difference is not statistically significant.[26]

The obstacle placing second in number of citations was permitting officials to hold unlimited terms. This barrier was mentioned by one respondent in six. There was no significant difference between the responses of officials from small and large cities. However, there were differences between incumbents and non-incumbents, as predicted. Among incumbents, only 16 percent cited unrestricted terms as a barrier, compared with 33 percent of the challengers. The same pattern is sustained across both size groups. Among incumbent respondents from small cities, only one-fifth favored limiting the number of terms, compared with one-third of the challengers. All the respondents from large cities were incumbents, and none favored limiting the number of terms a council member can serve.

Just over a tenth of the women pointed to the method of electing council members as a barrier. Of those who saw current districting arrangements as hurdles to the election of women, three favored adopting an at-large format, one thought a mixed system (combination at-large, single-member district) would be friendlier to women candidates, and three opted for single-member districts. The

Table 14.1
Perceptions of Barriers to the Election of Councilwomen by City Size, 1990

WOMEN ELECTED OFFICIALS CITING BARRIERS

PERCEIVED BARRIERS	PERCENT IN ALL CITIES (n=85)	PERCENT IN CITIES UNDER 25,000 POPULATION (n=69)	PERCENT IN CITIES 25,000 POPULATION AND ABOVE (n=16)	LEVEL OF SIGNIFI- CANCE
Current Method of Electing Council	10.6%	8.7%	18.8% (n=3)	N.S.
Pure At-Large	3.7	3.1	6.2 (n=1)	N.S.
At-Large by Post	3.7	4.6	0	N.S.
At-Large from District	1.2	0.0	6.2 (n=1)	N.S.
Single-Member District	0.0	0.0	0	N.S.
Mixed (Combination)	1.2	0.0	6.2 (n=1)	N.S.
Majority Vote Require- ment	4.7	4.3	0	N.S.
Staggered Terms	2.4	1.4	0	N.S.
Length of Term	9.4	8.7	12.5 (n=2)	N.S.
Too Short	8.2	7.2	12.5 (n=2)	N.S.
Too Long	1.2	1.4	0	N.S.
Council Size Too Small	4.7	4.3	6.3 (n=1)	N.S.
Campaign Contribution Limits	7.1	5.8	12.5 (n=2)	N.S.
Too Low	2.4	2.9	0	N.S.
Too High	4.7	2.9	12.5 (n=2)	N.S.
Filing Fee(s)	4.7	5.8	0	N.S.
Unlimited Consecutive Terms	16.5	15.9	18.8 (n=3)	N.S.
Timing of Council Election	2.4	2.9	0	N.S.
Nonpartisan Elections	5.5	7.2	0	N.S.
Lack of Newspaper Coverage	10.6	11.6	6.3	N.S.
Lack of Television Coverage	7.1	7.2	6.3 (n=1)	N.S.
Lack of Female Candidates	69.4	71.0	62.5 (n=10)	N.S.

Notes: The significance tests were of the differences between the responses of women officials in cities under 25,000 in population and those in larger cities.

N.S. = not significant at the .05 level.

Figures in the table do not add to 100 percent due to multiple responses and, in some categories, missing data.

Source: Susan A. MacManus and Donna Camp Blair, "Survey of Female Mayors and City Councilmembers in a Sample of Florida Cities," March/April 1990.

three recommending change to an at-large system wanted to alter the type of at-large elections, since their cities already voted at-large. Two wanted to change from pure at-large (higher vote getters elected to available seats) to at-large by posts (candidates run for a specific position or numbered seat that has no geographical identity). One wanted to move her city in the opposite direction.

The lack of newspaper coverage was tied with council election method as the second most-cited barrier and was singled out by 11 percent of the respondents. Women in small cities cited this barrier slightly more often, but the difference was not statistically significant. As expected, newspapers in small cities are far less apt to make endorsements than are newspapers in larger cities. Among our small city respondents, only 36 percent reported that their major local newspaper endorses candidates, compared with 80 percent of our respondents in large cities.

The percentage of officials citing the lack of newspaper coverage as a major barrier to women's election to office was not significantly different for respondents from cities whose newspapers make endorsements than for those whose local newspapers do not make endorsements. These results suggest that new theories about candidate reliance on the media may need to be developed. The same is true for television. Only a small percentage (7.1%) of the respondents felt that television coverage of city government needs to be increased to help women's election to office.

Campaign cost barriers turned out to be less significant than we hypothesized. Only 7.1 percent identified campaign contribution limits as a major barrier; 2.4 percent indicated the limits were too low, and 4.7 percent responded they were too high. Filing fees were identified as a barrier by only 5 percent of our respondents, perhaps because filing fees in most (over 70%) of their cities is $25 or less. All respondents identifying this barrier reside in small cities. Unexpectedly, filing fees were not higher for respondents identifying the fees as a deterrent.

The "costs" of having to campaign frequently are evident in the statistics, which show that our respondents favor longer, rather than shorter, council terms. Over 8 percent think that terms are too short, compared with only 1 percent who think they are too long. Contrary to our hypothesis, there is no significant relationship between the amount a candidate spent in the most recent election and her propensity to identify length of term as a barrier to the election of more women candidates.[27] Among the 49 respondents who spent $500 or less, only four said changing the length of term would help more women get elected. Among the 32 who spent over $500, only three reported that changing the term would assist the election of women to office.

There were very few other surprises in our findings. As predicted, only a small percentage of our respondents cited any of the other election system characteristics—the vote requirement (majority or plurality), staggered terms, council size, the timing of municipal elections, or their nonpartisan structure—as significant barriers to the election of women to city council. There are no statistically significant differences by size.

Of the two women who said that changing the timing of the city council election might help more women get elected, one was from a city where elections are held in the presidential election year, and the other was from a city where local elections are held at a time unique to local government. Thus, our hypothesis that support for a change in election timing most often would come from women in cities where city elections were held in conjunction with other elections was not confirmed.

Our hypothesis that support for switching to partisan elections would not differ by party affiliation proved to be invalid. All women preferring a switch to partisan elections were Republicans, which may reflect the growing strength of the Republican party in Florida.[28]

There is essentially no difference between respondents from large and small cities on whether small councils deter the election of more women to office. In addition, our hypothesis that the lower the proportion of women serving on a city council, the more probable it was that the respondent would identify the need for more women candidates as a primary need was not confirmed. Although the percent of women council members was lower in cities where respondents identified the lack of women candidates as a major problem, the difference between small and large city respondents was not statistically significant.

It is not surprising that when asked to specify the one factor having the greatest potential for getting more women elected to city council, 60 percent of our respondents identified increasing the number of women candidates (see table 14.2). Eighteen respondents identified some other item as most important, but none of these factors were mentioned by as many as five individuals. Moreover, 16 women said that no change in the factors we investigated would increase the number of women in office. This view was held more often by women from small cities, although the difference was not statistically significant.

When given the opportunity to identify as many obstacles as they thought were important, sixteen respondents cited none. Just over half of the women cited one element, and another 13 mentioned two. Thus, more than 85 percent of the councilwomen noted only two or fewer impediments to the election of more women. There was no significant difference in the responses of women from large and small cities.

Based on Florida's population growth profile, women in small cities, as expected, had lived there significantly fewer years (17) on average than had women on the councils of larger cities (27 years). Although female incumbents in smaller cities also had shorter residencies in the state than did their sisters in larger cities, this difference was not statistically significant.

When we combine the average figures for years in the city before election and age at first election, we see dramatic differences in the proportion of the councillors' lives spent in the cities they serve. On average, councilwomen in large cities have lived there since age 14, and hence two-thirds of their lives were spent in the city. In small towns, the average councilwoman (current age 49) has lived there since her early- to mid-thirties (average, 32.6), thus the first

Table 14.2
Perceptions of the Most Important Change That Would Increase Women City Councillors by City Size, 1990

		WOMEN ELECTED OFFICIALS IDENTIFYING CHANGE		
MOST IMPORTANT CHANGE	PERCENT IN ALL CITIES (n=85)	PERCENT IN CITIES UNDER 25,000 POPULATION (n=69)	PERCENT IN CITIES 25,000 POPULATION AND ABOVE (n=16)	LEVEL OF SIGNIFI-CANCE
Current Method of Electing Council	2.4%	2.9%	0%	N.S.
Eliminate the Runoff Requirement	0.0	0.0	0	N.S.
Adopt a Runoff Requirement	2.4	2.9	0	N.S.
Change the Structure of Terms	0.0	0.0	0	N.S.
Change the Length of Terms	0.0	0.0	0	N.S.
Enlarge the Size of Council	1.2	0.0	6.3 (n=1)	N.S.
Limit the Number of Consecutive Terms	4.7	4.3	6.3 (n=1)	N.S.
Change the Timing of Council Election	0.0	0.0	0	N.S.
Adopt Partisan Elections	0.0	0.0	0	N.S.
Change Campaign Contribution Limits	4.7	2.9	12.5 (n=2)	N.S.
Eliminate the Filing Fee	2.4	2.9	0	N.S.
Mandate More Newspaper Coverage of City Elections	3.5	2.9	6.3 (n=1)	N.S.
Mandate More Television Coverage of City Elections	0.0	0.0	0.0	N.S.
Increase the Number of Women Running for Council	60.0	59.4	62.5 (n=10)	N.S.
None Identified	18.8	21.7	6.3 (n=3)	N.S.
Total	100.1	99.9	100.0	

Notes: The significance tests were of the differences between the responses of women officials in cities under 25,000 in population and those in larger cities.

N.S. = not significant at the .05 level.

Figures in the table do not add to 100 percent due to rounding.

Respondents were asked: "Of the following changes that might be made, which ONE factor do you think would be the SINGLE MOST HELPFUL in increasing the number of women elected to city council? (Check only one)."

Source: Susan A. MacManus and Donna Camp Blair, "Survey of Female Mayors and City Councilmembers in a Sample of Florida Cities," March/April 1990.

two-thirds of her life was spent elsewhere. Service in larger cities is associated with deeper roots in the community.

The analysis of the age of women when first elected to the council indicates that those who serve in large cities are younger than those in smaller municipalities. The average age at which women were elected in small communities was about 50 years while in large cities it was 41. Office-holding by younger women in larger cities suggests a strong commitment to a political career and ambition to move up to a higher office or a nonmunicipal post.

Size of city is also associated with tenure on the council. Councilwomen in larger cities had more seniority (six to seven years) than those in smaller cities (four years). Women serving in larger cities develop seniority while those in small towns rotate off. There are several possible explanations for this result. In small units, council service may be viewed as a civic duty that one adequately fulfills with a term or two and then steps aside. It is possible, though improbable, that women in small cities may have greater opportunities and leave the council to pursue other offices while councilwomen in larger cities are locked into their current position awaiting favorable conditions for moving up. Small-town women also may be more readily removed from office via the ballot if they take challenges less seriously and pay little heed to voter preferences on controversial issues.[29]

Contrary to our hypothesis, women in larger cities do not confront greater obstacles to election than do small-town councilwomen. Although incumbent women in large cities tended to have held public office previously, the difference from small-town officials was not statistically significant. Though the direction of the difference was as expected, women in large cities did not face significantly greater numbers of opponents in their most recent election than did women in small towns. This finding calls into question the "desirability of the office" theory.

To our surprise, there was also no difference in the average number of times women had run for office before winning election. For both groups, one in every two women had run once before being elected.

CONCLUSIONS

Our results reveal that successful female politicians, by substantial margins, believe enlarging the pool of women candidates is the most promising way to increase women city councillors. Very few see changing various electoral structures, reducing campaign costs, or mandating greater media coverage of city council elections as effective ways to increase the number of women elected. By an overwhelming majority, councilwomen and female mayors believe that for there to be more women officeholders, women must accept the challenge and become candidates. These opinions are the same regardless of city size.

It is possible that the views of our respondents—all of whom had tasted political success—differ from those of women who did not run or women who were defeated. Losers might attribute losses to a lack of campaign funds or to other elements we examined in this study. Women who do not run may opt out because of difficulties that they believe they would encounter or because they see structural features stacked against them.

Notions of ambition and opportunity may account for some differences between councilwomen in large and small cities. As expected, women serving in large cities have deeper roots in their communities. These women also appear to display greater ambition by winning office at an earlier age than their peers in small cities. One reason for the later entry of women into small-city elective positions may be that their candidacies were proffered in recognition of the recipient's status as a community leader. Another, even more plausible explanation, at least in Florida, is that older women can better afford the time to serve, having reared their families, retired, or become widowed. A disproportionate share of Florida's older women, especially immigrants from the northeast and midwest, live in small cities.

One thing is for certain. If women do not run, they cannot win, regardless of the size of the city, a specific electoral system structure, or the extent of local media coverage of election campaigns.

NOTES

The assistance of Donna Camp Blair of the University of South Florida is gratefully acknowledged.

1. The exceptions are Marilyn Johnson and Susan Carroll, "Statistical Report: Profile of Women Holding Office, 1977," in Center for the American Woman and Politics, *Women in Public Office*, 2nd ed. (Metuchen, N.J.: Scarecrow Press, 1978), pp. 1A–65A, and Susan A. MacManus, "Constituency Size and Minority Representation," *State and Local Government Review*, Winter 1987, pp. 3–7.

2. The sample respondents represent 62 cities out of all 92 with either a woman city council member or woman mayor in 15 Florida counties. These women were listed in the 1989 Directory of the Florida League of Cities. The sample closely mirrors Florida and United States cities at large. Eighty-four percent of all Florida and United States cities had 1987 populations under 25,000, compared with 81 percent of the cities represented by our respondents.

3. Albert K. Karnig and Oliver Walter, "Election of Women to City Councils," *Social Science Quarterly*, March 1976, p. 610.

4. Susan Welch and Albert K. Karnig, "Correlates of Female Office-Holding in City Politics," *Journal of Politics*, May 1979, p. 486. See also Charles S. Bullock III and Susan A. MacManus, "Municipal Electoral Structure and the Election of Councilwomen," *Journal of Politics*, February 1991, and Susan A. MacManus, "Determinants of the Equitability of Female Representation on 243 City Councils," a paper presented at the annual meeting of the American Political Science Association, September 1976.

5. Arnold Fleischmann and Lana Stein, "Minority and Female Success in Municipal Runoff Elections," *Social Science Quarterly*, June 1987, p. 384; Susan A. MacManus and Charles S. Bullock III, "Women on Southern City Councils: A Decade of Change," *Journal of Political Science* 17 (1989): 32–49; Charles S. Bullock III and Loch K. Johnson, "Sex and the Second Primary," *Social Science Quarterly*, December 1985, pp. 933–44;

and Bullock and MacManus, "Municipal Electoral Structure." For the runoff primary and women's recruitment in state legislatures, see Wilma Rule, "Why More Women Are State Legislators," *Western Political Quarterly*, June 1990, pp. 442, 444, and Rule's chapter on state legislatures in this volume.

6. MacManus and Bullock, "Women on Southern City Councils."

7. Bullock and MacManus, "Municipal Electoral Structure."

8. Chandler Davidson, "Minority Vote Dilution: An Overview," in Chandler Davidson, ed., *Minority Vote Dilution* (Washington, D.C.: Howard University Press, 1984), pp. 1–23.

9. Bullock and MacManus, "Municipal Electoral Structure"; and MacManus and Bullock, "Women on Southern City Councils."

10. Welch and Karnig, "Correlates of Female Office-Holding"; Bullock and MacManus, "Municipal Electoral Structure"; and MacManus and Bullock, "Women on Southern City Councils."

11. Welch and Karnig, "Correlates of Female Office-Holding"; and Susan Welch and Timothy Bledsoe, *Urban Reform and Its Consequences* (Chicago: University of Chicago Press, 1988).

12. Susan J. Carroll, *Women as Candidates in American Politics* (Bloomington: Indiana University Press, 1985), p. 50.

13. Peggy Heilig and Robert Mundt, *Your Voice at City Hall* (Albany: State University of New York Press), p. 73; and Theodore Arrington and Gerald L. Ingalls, "Race and Campaign Finance in Charlotte, N.C." *Western Political Quarterly*, December 1984, pp. 578–83.

14. Carroll, *Women as Candidates*; and Barbara Burrell, "Women's and Men's Campaigns for the U.S. House of Representatives, 1972–1982: A Finance Gap?" *American Politics Quarterly*, July 1985, pp. 251–72.

15. Lana Stein and Arnold Fleischmann, "Newspaper and Business Endorsements in Municipal Elections: A Test of the Conventional Wisdom," *Journal of Urban Affairs* 9, no. 4 (1987): 325–36.

16. Susan A. MacManus and Charles S. Bullock III, "Minorities and Women *Do* Win At-Large," *National Civic Review*, May/June 1988, pp. 231–44.

17. Charles R. Adrian, "Forms of City Government in American History," *The Municipal Year Book 1988* (Washington, D.C.: International City Management Association, 1988), pp. 3–11.

18. Carol A. Cassell, "Social Background Characteristics of Nonpartisan City Council Members: A Research Note," *Western Political Quarterly*, September 1985, pp. 495–501; and Welch and Bledsoe, *Urban Reform*.

19. Welch and Karnig, "Correlates of Female Office-Holding."

20. Robert Darcy, Susan Welch, and Janet Clark, *Women, Elections, and Representation* (New York: Longman, 1987), p. 32. See also Susan Welch and Donley Studlar, "Multimember Districts and the Representation of Women: Evidence from Britain and the United States," *Journal of Politics*, May 1989, pp. 391–412.

21. Cassell, "Social Background Characteristics"; Welch and Bledsoe, *Urban Reform*; and Timothy Bledsoe and Mary Herring, "Victims of Circumstances: Women in Pursuit of Political Office," *American Political Science Review*, March 1990, pp. 213–23.

22. Timothy Bledsoe and Mary Herring, "Victims of Circumstances: Women in Pursuit of Political Office," *American Political Science Review*, March 1990, pp. 213–23.

23. Karnig and Walter, "Election of Women to City Councils"; Johnson and Carroll, "Statistical Report"; and Welch and Karnig, "Correlates of Female Office-Holding."

24. A competing history is that women are more likely to succeed in larger cities for two reasons. First, larger cities are more cosmopolitan and less traditional. Second, in larger cities, there are more likely to be major support groups such as the League of Women Voters, the National Women's Political Caucus, and the National Organization for Women, which would strongly support women's candidacies. See Darcy, Welch, and Clark, *Women, Elections, and Representation.*

25. Susan A. MacManus, "It's Never Too Late to Run . . . and Win! The Graying of Women in Local Politics," a paper presented at the 1990 meeting of the Florida Political Science Association.

26. The small number of cases from cities with a population of 25,000 and above make it extremely difficult for differences by population size to achieve statistical significance.

27. There is, however, a statistically significant relationship between the amount of money the officeholder spent in the most recent election and the current length of her term.

28. From 1980 to 1990, there was a 38 percent increase in the percent of Republican registrants. See Susan A. MacManus and Ronald Keith Gaddie, "Reapportionment in Florida: The Stakes Keep Getting Higher," in George Blair and Leroy Hardy, eds., *Gerrymandering in the 1980s* (Claremont, Calif.: Rose Institute of State and Local Government, 1991).

29. Kenneth Prewitt and Heinz Eulau, "Political Matrix and Political Representation: Prolegomenon to a New Departure from an Old Problem," *American Political Science Review*, June 1969, pp. 427–41.

15

Cumulative Voting and Limited Voting in Alabama

Edward Still

As a result of settlements in a case against many Alabama county commissions, school boards, and city councils,[1] the Chilton County Commission, the Chilton County Board of Education, and three towns adopted cumulative voting (CV) plans, and 21 other towns adopted limited voting (LV) plans. This chapter examines the election results in those jurisdictions under the new voting systems.

BACKGROUND

Limited voting and cumulative voting are at-large systems, but each allows a minority group a better chance of electing its choice than the group would have in the plurality at-large system. Employing the cumulative voting system to fill five seats, each voter would have five votes to be cast for five different candidates. The voter could cast all five votes for one candidate or split them up among several candidates. In an LV system, the voter has fewer votes to cast than the number of seats to be filled.[2]

LV and CV lower the "threshold of exclusion," which is the proportion of the votes that a particular group must have to elect one candidate assuming that all other voters vote for their interests (i.e., strategically). The "threshold of exclusion" formulas are

$$\frac{V}{V+S}$$

for limited voting and

$$\frac{1}{1+S}$$

for cumulative voting, where V is the number of votes cast by each voter and S is the number of seats to be filled.[3] If a dominant group votes as a bloc, the "threshold of exclusion" is 50 percent in at-large elections and in single-member district elections.[4]

LV and CV in their application and their concepts are foreign to the experience of most Americans. As Dieter Nohlen pointed out: "There are two principles of representation: the majority/plurality one and the P.R. [proportional representation] one. These should be considered as two antithetical principles of political representation—politically, systematically, and with regard to the history of ideas. . . . Electoral systems should be classified and judged in accordance with the degree to which they meet the principle of representation that they are supposed to follow."[5]

Since most election systems in the United States are majoritarian, they are defended and attacked by reference to majoritarian principles. As long as the debate continues to be expressed in majoritarian terms, the participants will not think about systems such as CV or LV. Plaintiffs in vote-dilution suits are beginning to breach this barrier by using concepts of proportionality or civic inclusion even though they still couch their complaint in terms of "equal access" and usually want or settle for single-member districts.[6] The latter usually moves toward proportionality in results while preserving the outward form of majority/plurality systems and thereby providing a remedy with which both sides usually can be comfortable.

LV and CV meet the goals of proportionality or civic inclusion better than single-member districts. Empirical studies of existing LV and CV systems show they usually result in the election of racial minorities at a level close to the minority percentage in the population.[7] LV and CV allow voters to form "voluntary districts" with like-minded voters.[8] Although any districting system relies on an external (and often, relatively out-of-date) decision about grouping voters to form a district and elect an official, CV and LV allow voters to make that decision for themselves at each election. Districting relies on geographical proximity; CV and LV rely on a community of perceived interest. Under CV or LV, a like-minded group of voters has a greater chance of electing a legislator than under traditional plurality at-large voting. Therefore, not only dispersed ethnic minorities but also other groups without, or with minimal, elected representation (e.g., Republicans in Democratic-dominated states and vice versa, and women) have the opportunity to elect someone to represent them. In addition, there is no runoff primary election with CV and LV election systems, since all candidates are nominated in the first election. There is some evidence that CV and LV also allow for greater turnover of elected officials.

Table 15.1
Cumulative Voting Elections, Chilton County, Alabama, 1988

	BLACK PERCENT OF POPULATION	BLACK CANDIDATE'S PERCENT OF VOTE	NUMBER OF MEMBERS	BLACK'S RANK IN VOTE
Town of Centre	10.97	9.48	7	3
Chilton County Commission*	11.87	10.56	7	1
Chilton County Board of Education*	11.87	9.79	7	2
Town of Guin	10.30	8.43	7	6
Town of Myrtlewood	27.78	0	5	no black candidate

RESULTS OF THE CUMULATIVE VOTE ELECTIONS

The Chilton County Commission and the Chilton County Board of Education held cumulative voting primaries in June 1988 and general elections in November 1988. Three Alabama towns held cumulative voting elections in August 1988. Table 15.1 reveals little difference between the black percentage of the population and the black vote in these elections.

Chilton County Primary Election

Blacks in Chilton County were able to nominate one candidate to the county commission and a second candidate to the school board in the Democratic party primary election even though only 12 percent of the population and 11 percent of the registered voters are black. Tables 15.2 and 15.3 contain the results of the Chilton County Democratic party primary elections. On first examination, these tables appear incorrect because some candidates have more than 100 percent of all votes cast and the total of all votes cast equals 700 percent. The tables report each candidate's vote as a percentage of the number of voters. Since each voter has seven votes, the total should be 700 percent. By expressing the votes in this way, we can see the effects of the cumulative feature.

Aggregate data in a cumulative voting election, such as Chilton County, do not reveal how many people voted for a candidate but do provide a range. For instance, Agee, the winning black candidate, received one or more votes from

Table 15.2
Cumulative Voting, Democratic Primary Election, Chilton County Commission, 1988

CANDIDATES[1]	VOTES	PERCENT OF VOTES CAST[2]	NUMBER OF PLACES WITH BONUS VOTES[3]
*Agee	4820	105.48	6
Culp	3734	81.71	8
Patterson, K.	3437	75.21	7
Cleckler, A.W.	3123	68.34	8
+Cost	2344	51.29	3
Jackson	2227	48.73	3
+Cummings	2200	48.14	2
Smitherman	1582	34.62	2
Mims	1520	33.26	3
Cash	1167	25.54	3
§Asbury	1017	22.26	0
Martin	976	21.36	1
*Binion	884	19.34	1
Easterling	830	18.16	0
*Wilson	684	14.97	1
Bavar	667	14.60	1
Clackley	433	9.48	0
Cleckler, R.E.	235	5.14	0
Patterson, L.J.	108	2.36	0

* = Black candidate.
\+ = Incumbent.
§ = Female candidate.

[1] The first seven candidates listed won the primary election.
[2] This column contains the number of votes received by each candidate divided by the number of voters.
[3] This column contains the number of polling places in the county where each candidate received bonus votes.

15 percent or more of the Democratic voters in the county commission primary. Agee had to have received some multi-votes because his total vote is equal to 105 percent of the number of votes cast and he received "bonus votes" (i.e., extra votes in 6 of 12 polling places [see table 15.2]).[9] In the school board race, Hill (black) and Fox (white) also received more votes than there were voters (see table 15.3). One white woman won in the school board Democratic primary, and the other winners were incumbent white males.[10]

Analysis of the election results supports the hypothesis that blacks gave more than one vote for their candidates, that is, they "multi-voted." This behavior is the optimum one for a minority group wishing to elect a candidate in a cumulative vote system. The three black candidates for the county commission received a total of 12 percent of the Democratic votes, and the black candidate for the school board received the same percentage of votes. Blacks gave all of

Table 15.3
Cumulative Voting, Democratic Primary Election, Chilton County Board of Education, 1988

CANDIDATES[1]	VOTES	PERCENT OF VOTES CAST[2]	NUMBER OF PLACES WITH BONUS VOTES[3]
*Hill	4940	112.16	8
+Fox	4823	109.50	12
§Hayden	3804	86.36	10
+McGriff	3524	80.01	6
+Bice	3508	79.64	10
+Headley	2722	61.80	3
+Hall	2476	56.21	4
§Bowers	1810	41.09	2
Clements	1317	29.90	2
Cox	1022	23.20	0
West	866	20.12	0

* = Black candidate.
\+ = Incumbent.
§ = Female candidate

[1] The first seven candidates listed won the primary election.
[2] This column contains the number of votes received by each candidate divided by the number of voters.
[3] This column contains the number of polling places in the county where each candidate received bonus votes.

their votes to black candidates in the Democratic party primaries for seats on the county commission and the school board (see appendix tables 15A.1 and 15A.2). Black candidates were able to win seats with less than the "threshold of exclusion," that is, the votes they theoretically would need if whites adopted a strategy of nominating only whites. If whites—who were 82 percent of the electorate—had evenly spread their seven votes over the seven candidates, the resulting bloc vote could have defeated the one black winner.

In the Republican primary, all the candidates were white, and tables 15.4 and 15.5 show that several whites used the minority's best strategy; that is, they gave multiple votes to their favorite candidates. Gibson, a white woman candidate, received 152 percent of the vote while Kelley, a white male candidate, won 140 percent.

In the general election, four Democrats—one was the black candidate—and

Table 15.4
Cumulative Voting, Republican Primary Election, Chilton County Board of Education, 1988

CANDIDATES	VOTES	PERCENT OF VOTES CAST	NUMBER OF POLLING PLACES WITH BONUS VOTES
§Gibson	2193	152.17	19
Kelley	2029	140.79	15
Williams	1863	129.27	16
§Smith	1665	115.53	16
Parrish	1376	95.48	10
Cleckler	416	28.87	1
Beam	314	21.79	0
Geeslin	232	16.10	0

§ = Female candidate. The remainder were white males.

Table 15.5
Cumulative Voting, Republican Primary Election, Chilton County Commission, 1988

CANDIDATES	VOTES	PERCENT OF VOTES CAST	NUMBER OF POLLING PLACES WITH BONUS VOTES
Bryant	1991	130.78	13
Bean	1704	111.93	13
Kelley	1311	86.11	5
Plier	924	60.69	5
Hayes	861	56.55	2
Mims	758	49.79	2
§Gilliland	656	43.09	2
Headley	456	29.95	3
Lowery	452	29.69	1
Hayes	431	28.31	4
Easterling, F.	388	25.49	3
Littleton	385	25.29	1
Easterling, B.W.	209	13.73	0
Sparks	121	7.95	0
Washington	10	0.66	0

§ = Female candidate. The remainder were white males.

three Republicans were elected to both the county board and the board of education (see tables 15.6 and 15.7). Although no women were elected commissioners, two white women were elected to the school board. Only one incumbent was reelected commissioner while three incumbents were reelected school board members. Again, the black candidates were able to win election with a vote less than the 10.65 percent of the total number of votes cast in the county commission

Table 15.6

Cumulative Voting, General Election, Chilton County Board of Education, 1988

CANDIDATES[1]	VOTES	PERCENT OF VOTES CAST	NUMBER OF POLLING PLACES WITH BONUS VOTES
§Smith R	8690	77.01	8
*Hill D	7730	68.50	6
Williams R	7248	64.50	7
§Gibson R	7164	63.23	5
+Bice D	7087	63.49	2
+Fox D	6584	58.35	6
+Hall D	6391	56.64	4
§Hayden D	6013	53.29	0
+McGriff D	5586	49.50	2
+Headley D	4992	44.24	0
Kelley R	4819	42.71	2
Parrish R	3903	34.59	0
Cleckler R	1438	12.74	0
Beam R	1343	11.90	0

* = Black candidate.
+ = Incumbent.
§ = Female candidate.
R = Republican, D = Democrat.

[1] The top seven vote-getters were elected.

and school board elections. It appears that most of the electorate tended to vote along party lines and to multi-vote for their favorite candidates. An analysis of the votes for each party's candidates reveals a high correlation between the percentage of the precinct vote cast for each party's candidate for probate judge and the percentage of the precinct vote cast for the same party's candidates for the county commission and the board of education.[11] Even more striking is the nearly total racial polarization of the vote. Appendix tables 15A.3 and 15A.4 show the results of the regression analysis of the general election vote regressed against the racial registration figures.

The CV primaries and general election in Chilton County reveal that black Democrats and white Republicans were able to use their multiple votes to their particular advantage. For the first time, blacks and Republicans broke the white Democratic monopoly on the county commission and the board of education. Both minority groups (blacks and Republicans) used multi-voting to their advantage. White Democratic candidates, by contrast, received a much more uniform vote across the ticket than did Republican candidates. If racially polarized voting continues, white Democrats may find that multi-voting for some of their candidates, rather than voting for the whole ticket, will ensure a larger share of the seats on the county commission and school board.

Table 15.7
Cumulative Voting, General Election, Chilton County Commission, 1988

CANDIDATES[1]	VOTES	PERCENT OF VOTES CAST	NUMBER OF POLLING PLACES WITH BONUS VOTES
*Agee D	8705	74.57	6
Bryant R	8161	69.91	5
Kelley R	7945	68.06	5
Culp D	7110	60.91	5
Patterson D	6808	58.32	3
+Cleckler D	6282	53.81	3
Plier R	5701	48.84	3
Bean R	5564	47.66	3
+Cost D	5246	44.94	2
Jackson D	4802	41.13	2
Hayes R	4417	37.84	0
+Cummings D	4264	36.53	2
§Gilliland R	3364	28.82	0
Mims R	3348	28.68	0

* = Black candidate.
+ = Incumbent.
§ = Female candidate.
R = Republican, D = Democrat.

[1] The top seven vote-getters were elected.

LIMITED VOTING JURISDICTIONS

The 21 towns using limited voting can be divided into three groups. Blacks did not field candidates for the council in seven towns, at least one black candidate was elected without opposition in seven other towns, and there were black-versus-white elections in the remaining seven towns. As shown in table 15.8, blacks won one or more seats on the council in six of the seven black-versus-white elections. Table 15.8 also shows that the black vote (that is, the vote for black candidates) was a smaller percentage of the vote than the black percentage of the population. This finding could be caused by lower black registration rates, lower black turnout rates, or lower levels of solidarity of black voters. As table 15.9 reveals, the black registration rates in the counties in which these jurisdictions are located are lower than the white registration rates by 4 to 25 percentage points.

It is not possible to determine the black or white turnout rates for these small towns. However, the black support ratio (the ratio of the vote for black candidates to black population) compared with the white support ratio gives an indirect measure of turnout (see table 15.9). In Lowndesboro, where the black candidate lost, the white candidates had a support rate of 1.39, which was more than the number of white voters in the town. The black support ratio was only .16. Either the white population has grown much faster than the black population since

Table 15.8
Vote for Black Candidates in Limited Voting in Alabama Towns, 1988

TOWNS AND SEATS	BLACK PERCENT OF POPULATION	BLACK CANDIDATE'S PERCENT OF VOTE	BLACK CANDIDATE'S RANK IN POLL
5 seats, 1 vote			
Ariton	23.46	22.40	1
Goshen	26.30	16.33	3
5 seats, 2 votes			
Fulton	32.18	11.35	5
Lowndesboro	41.06	7.65	6
Silas	38.48	19.82	1
7 seats, 1 vote			
Dora	14.57	6.44, 3.35	7, 11
Kinsey	10.17	9.04, 7.35	5, 7

1980, or many black voters supported white candidates. Conversely, in the one town (Kinsey) where blacks were able to win two of seven seats with only one-seventh of the population, the black support ratio was approximately 60 percent higher than the white support ratio. Blacks in Kinsey either turned out at a higher rate than whites or were able to attract white support for their candidates. Given the pattern of racially polarized voting exhibited in cumulative voting elections in the same year, differential turnout rates are a more reasonable explanation.

Leaving aside racial proportionality, limited voting has the additional advantage of making it possible for a large part of the electorate to elect, at a minimum, one person to the council. At least 73 percent of the voters in the Alabama LV jurisdictions voted for a winner, compared with 61 percent in the CV election. The voter effectiveness percentage will depend, of course, on the particular conditions in the election. In the limited vote election, if there are many candidates with fairly even support in the electorate, the ratio could fall closer to or below 50 percent of the electorate.

SUMMARY AND CONCLUSIONS

Overall, the use of limited voting and cumulative voting had a positive effect in terms of direct black representation. Even in the presence of continued racial polarization, blacks were able to gain an equitable share of the seats on the Chilton County Commission and the Chilton County School Board.

Table 15.9
Racial Analysis of Votes in Contested Alabama Town, Limited Vote Elections,
1988

	BLACK SUPPORT RATIO IN TOWN*	WHITE SUPPORT RATIO IN TOWN*	COUNTY WHERE TOWN IS LOCATED	BLACK PERCENT OF VOTERS IN COUNTY	PERCENT OF BLACK POPULA- TION IN COUNTY	PERCENT BLACK REGIS- TRATION RATE	PERCENT WHITE REGIS- TRATION RATE
Silas	.33	.82	Choctaw County	41.30	43.6	67	73
Fulton	.16	.61	Clarke County	34.95	42.7	59	83
Ariton	.37	.40	Dale County	12.76	19.0	41	66
Kinsey	.25	.14	Houston County	17.01	23.1	48	71
Lowndesboro	.16	1.39	Lowndes County	70.15	75.0	47	60
Goshen	.17	.31	Pike County	31.08	35.4	56	68
Dora	.22	.35	Walker County	6.98	7.0	54	58

* The ratio of the group's vote to its population in the town.

Source of county data: Testimony of Dr. Gordon Henderson in Hawthorne
v. Baker, CV 89-T-381-S (M.D. Ala).

The biggest disappointment was the failure of blacks to field candidates in several towns. Jerome Gray, the Alabama Democratic Conference's field director, attributed this failure to fear and uncertainty on the part of black residents in these small, black-belt towns and the failure of his organization to cultivate leaders in such places. He believes that four years' experience with black councillors in neighboring towns will encourage more blacks to seek election to office in 1992.

As noted, the percentage of votes for black candidates came close to the black percentage of the population in most of the CV jurisdictions but in few of the LV jurisdictions. Whether these findings are a function of the size of the jurisdictions or of the election systems will have to be judged after we have more information about similar elections.

Even if we ignore the racial proportionality usually associated with these systems, they have the additional advantage of making it possible for 51 to 73 percent of the population to elect at least one person to the council. In addition, in the cumulative voting election other unrepresented minorities gained some representation or came close. The Republican party for the first time had some elected commissioners, white women (but no black women) were nominated, and the number of reelected incumbents decreased. Unfortunately, we did not have the data to make similar comparisons in the limiting voting system elections.

Each town that has adopted limited voting or cumulative voting is obliged by its settlement agreement to seek enactment of a state law confirming its election system. In addition, the Alabama Democratic Conference will be seeking legislation of general application that will allow municipalities to adopt limited voting or cumulative voting plans by enactment of an ordinance. From this small beginning, there may flow an increased interest in the use of limited voting and cumulative voting in Alabama's local governments.

APPENDIX

Table 15A.1
Cumulative Voting by Race, Chilton County Commission Primary Election, 1988 (Regression Analysis*)

PERCENT	WHITE VOTERS	BLACK VOTERS
Estimated Percent of Registered Electorate Voting	29.40	25.78
Estimated Percent Voting for White Candidates	99.52	−17.29**
Estimated Percent Voting for Black Candidates	0.48	117.29

* The proportion of the total registered voters who voted for candidates of one race was regressed on the proporton of the total registration of that race. The correlation coefficient was .44 for whites and .93 for blacks, significant at the .00005 level.

** Minus values occur when the regression estimate of black turnout is significantly lower than the black turnout.

Table 15A.2
Cumulative Voting by Race, Chilton County Board of Education Primary Election, 1988 (Regression Analysis*)

PERCENT	WHITE VOTERS	BLACK VOTERS
Estimated percent of Registered Electorate Voting	28.17	24.85
Estimated Percent Voting for White Candidate	99.82	−0.23**
Estimated Percent Voting for Black Candidates	0.18	100.23

* The proportion of the total registered voters who voted for candidates of one race was regressed on the proportion of the total registration of that race. The correlation coefficient was .84 for whites and .89 for blacks, significant at the .00005 level.

** Minus values occur when the regression estimate of black turnout is significantly lower than the black turnout.

Table 15A.3
Cumulative Voting by Race, Chilton County Commission General Election, 1988 (Regression Analysis*)

PERCENT	WHITE VOTERS	BLACK VOTERS
Estimated Percent of Registered Electorate Voting	59.21	37.38
Estimated Percent Voting for White Candidate	98.50	−14.72**
Estimated Percent Voting for Black Candidate	1.50	114.72

* The proportion of the total registered voters who voted for candidates of one race was regressed on the proportion of the total registration of that race. The correlation coefficient was .84 for whites and .89 for blacks, significant at the .00005 level.

** Minus values occur when the regression estimate of black turnout is significantly lower than the black turnout.

Table 15A.4
Cumulative Voting by Race, Chilton County Board of Education General
Election, 1988 (Regression Analysis*)

PERCENT	WHITE VOTERS	BLACK VOTERS
Estimated Percent of Registered Electorate Voting	56.89	36.92
Estimated Percent Voting for White Candidate	98.87	−4.65**
Estimated Percent Voting for Black Candidate	1.13	104.65

* The proportion of the total registered voters who voted for candidates of one race was regressed on the proportion of the total registration of that race. The correlation coefficient was .84 for whites and .89 for blacks, significant at the .00005 level.

** Minus values occur when the regression estimate of black turnout is significantly lower than the actual black turnout.

NOTES

1. *Dillard v. Crenshaw*, C.A. No. 85-T-1332-N (U.S. District Court, M.D. Ala.). The court approved the cumulative voting settlement in *Dillard v. Chilton County Board of Education*, 699 F. Supp. 870 (M.D. Ala., 1988), affirmed 868 F.2d 1274 (11th Cir., 1989), and two limited voting settlements in *Dillard v. Town of Cuba*, CV 87-T-1194-N (M.D. Ala.) (Order, 18 July 1988).

2. Edward Still, "Alternatives to Single-Member Districts," in Chandler Davidson, ed., *Minority Vote Dilution* (Washington, D.C.: Howard University Press, 1984), pp. 253–58.

3. Pamela Karlan, "Maps and Misreadings: The Role of Geographic Compactness in Racial Vote Dilution Litigation," *Harvard Civil Rights and Civil Liberties Law Review*, Winter 1989, p. 222; and Still, "Alternatives to Single-Member Districts," pp. 253–58.

4. The formulas for the threshold of exclusion for all four systems mentioned in the paragraph are the same:

$$\frac{V}{V+S}$$

For single-member districts and at-large systems, V and S have the same value, resulting in a threshold of 1/2. The same threshold formula applies to CV if one thinks of the voter as having only one vote divided into V fractional parts.

5. Dieter Nohlen, "Two Incompatible Principles of Representation," in Arend Lijphart and Bernard Grofman, eds., *Choosing an Electoral System: Issues and Alternatives* (New York: Praeger Publishers, 1984), pp. 83, 85, 88.

6. Karlan, "Maps and Misreadings," p. 222.

196 Edward Still

7. Richard L. Engstrom, Delbert A. Taebel, and Richard L. Cole, "Cumulative Voting as a Remedy for Minority Vote Dilution: The Case of Alamogordo, New Mexico," *Journal of Law and Politics*, Spring 1989, p. 469; Richard L. Engstrom and Charles J. Barrilleaux, "Native Americans and Cumulative Voting: The Sisseton-Wahpeton Sioux," *Social Science Quarterly*, June 1991; Leon Weaver, "Semi-Proportional and Proportional Representation Systems in the United States," in Lijphart and Grofman, *Choosing an Electoral System*, p. 191; and Karlan, "Maps and Misreadings," pp. 173, 227 n. 226.

8. Karlan, "Maps and Misreadings," pp. 226 and n.224.

9. *Bonus votes* means a number of votes greater than the number of voters. *Multivote* refers to the act of one voter casting multiple votes for a candidate in a CV election. Casting all of one's votes for one candidate is called *plumping*.

10. John Hollis Jackson, the attorney for both the Chilton County jurisdictions, reported that white candidates mentioned cumulative voting in their campaigns and asked voters to cast multiple votes for them.

11. Regressing the Democratic percentage of the county commission vote against the Democratic percentage of the vote for the probate judge yields a beta of .82 and an R^2 of .68, significant at the .00005 level.

16

Proportional Representation on New York City Community School Boards

Leon Weaver and Judith Baum

The degree of proportionality of representation of women and ethnic minorities on New York City community school boards produced by the single-transferable vote (STV) system of proportional representation (PR) and criticisms of the school governance system are the focal points of our analysis. The criticisms tend to color perceptions of the PR feature, and an appraisal is necessary to convey to the reader why, despite the demonstrable proportionality of results flowing from the PR system, there is considerable dissatisfaction with the governance system.

ORIGINS AND EVOLUTION

In 1969, the New York State Legislature politically decentralized part of the New York City school governance system, largely in response to widespread frustration with the city's inability to respond positively to demands for racial integration and improvement of schools in poor and minority districts. The ability of minorities to influence school management and institute school reforms was viewed as necessary to promote the educational achievement of minority students, but the desire for community control was not confined to the poor minority communities: there was increasing unrest citywide as the system declined in quality and increased in costs.

A hoped-for subsidiary result of decentralization was an increased participation of members of minority and disadvantaged communities in elections for other offices, since membership on a community school board was seen as a possible stepping-stone to the other city offices. There was, however, powerful local opposition to decentralization from professional unions and others, and as a result, the law that emerged was a compromise. Secondary schools were left under the control of the board of education appointed by the mayor and borough presidents. Elementary and middle schools were placed under the jurisdiction of 32 elected community school boards subject to oversight of the chancellor, who is appointed by the board of education and wields limited powers over personnel and finance.[1]

Another important feature of the compromise was that the nine-member community school boards would be elected by PR. One of the important influences in the lobbying process that led to the adoption of PR was provided by the late George Hallett, the longtime executive director of Citizens Union. Another important influence was the United Federation of Teachers, which preferred at-large elections and accepted PR as less threatening than the originally proposed subdistrict scheme.[2] The acceptance of PR by the state legislature was perceived as a move to calm certain groups' fears that decentralization would result in community school boards that are dominated by majorities or well-organized pluralities, to the virtual exclusion of ethnic minorities. It was hoped that PR, more than any of the possible alternative systems, would result in boards that reflect approximately the potential voting strengths of various groups in each district, thereby ensuring substantial participation by ethnic minorities.

COMPLAINTS AND CONTROVERSIES

During the two decades that the governance and electoral systems have been in effect, various complaints and controversies have posed the question of whether the demonstrable proportionality of the system is worth the negative trade-offs perceived by various critics. One of the most serious concerns is low voter turnout.

Obstacles to Voter Participation

Voter participation has fallen from its high of 14.0 percent in the first election to 7.2 percent in 1989. There are several reasons for this drop. First, changing city demographics saw an increase in families with two working parents and a proliferation of single-parent households. Parents, the natural constituency for school elections, have been too busy earning a living to be involved deeply in school governance. At the same time, many city dwellers were too old to have children in school, were young unmarried singles, or were parents, seeking excellence, who sent their children to private or parochial schools. Although this demographic shift occurred everywhere in the United States, it was accompanied in New York City by an influx of immigrants who spoke little English, were undergoing cultural displacement, and traditionally viewed schools as distant and authoritarian institutions. As a result, since so many New Yorkers were out of contact with city schools, few understood the issues in school board elections or felt impelled to vote.

Some critics also contend that the method of voting under PR tends to be an obstacle to voter participation in several ways:

1. The length of the ballot (typically 15 to 25 names) provides the voter with the task of learning about numerous candidates, a task with which many voters are unable or unwilling to cope.[3]

2. The preferential-vote feature, whereby each voter is entitled to indicate by numbered preferences his or her rankings of all the candidates nominated, further increases the burden on the voter. It is poorly understood, and little effort is made to educate voters on the method.

3. The counting process, with the perceived complications associated with the transferable-vote feature, is perceived as cumbersome and subject to error and fraud. Also some feel that this may happen to a greater degree than in other elections without the PR element because of the difficulties imposed by resource constraints in recruiting and training election administrators capable of conducting the PR count. Regardless of whether such perceptions are accurate or numerous, their existence is a cause of concern in several groups that take an interest in how the community school board's electoral system functions. Also, as long as these elections use paper ballots, concerns about their vulnerability to tampering will attach to the entire system, even though the paper ballots are only a concomitant and separable, rather than an inherent, feature of PR.

Turnout rates could presumably be increased by scheduling school elections concurrently with general elections, but such concurrent elections would not be acceptable to school advocates who are convinced that such a change would tend to increase the influence of professional politicians.

New Questions Raised

In recent elections, the vacuum left by reduced parent and other citizen participation has been filled increasingly by unions, political clubs, and professional politicians. These were the most organized vote-getters and soon saw the connection between school board membership and control over school system priorities, including patronage in the dispensing of jobs throughout the entire school hierarchy. Parents and other candidates representing general community interests found it more difficult than ever to break through to board membership. According to news reports and Council President Andrew Stein, only 30 to 35 percent of school board members were parents of students in the public school.[4] Of these members, still fewer had children attending schools in the district where they served. Regardless of the importance of minority representation, concerned citizens were questioning the validity of school boards in which a majority of the members did not have children in the schools.

After some dramatic revelations about incompetence and criminal misbehavior in several community school districts, long-sought state legislation to bar holders of other political office and school-system employees from local school board office was enacted, and stricter standards of campaign finance reporting, conflicts of interest, and ethical behavior were instituted. These changes took effect in the 1989 election after several lawsuits. The law was upheld in the courts, however, and several school board members gave up the political offices or school-system jobs that had caused conflicts of interest. Eight educators retained their jobs and gave up their school board seats.

Thus, by the time of the 1989 election, there had been a shift in the focus of attention and emphasis of citizens who take an interest in the schools. No longer were they primarily asking if the elected school boards mirrored the ethnic makeup of the voting population; instead they wanted to know if the elected members represented the interests of the children in the schools. Indeed, many of the allegations of fraud were brought against boards composed largely of ethnic minorities, although some boards dominated by whites were implicated equally in abuse of the school board office.[5]

In response to the dissatisfactions described above, several commissions were established to study corruption and mismanagement of the city school system, including the Joint Commission on Integrity in the Schools, the Temporary State Commission on Decentralization, and the State Commissioner of Education's Task Force.

Although questions about the representation of women had not been of great concern originally, such questions gained prominence as a result of the new attention to parent candidacies, which were seen as the antidote to self-interested politicians and professional unions, whose participation had become suspect.

In the 1989 community school board elections, there was unprecedented support from Chancellor Richard R. Green for parent candidacies and also a major advance in coverage of the elections from the city press and media. Nevertheless, the voter turnout fell to an all-time low, and complaints about the conduct of the election and the ballot counts continued.[6] Two elections were contested in the courts over handling of the paper ballots.

Evaluation of Criticisms

Evaluation of the above dissatisfactions would take us too far afield, but we offer the following comments as a first-phase sorting out.

It is necessary to distinguish between political behavior factors, such as generally low turnout in school elections, and factors inherent in the specific features of the representation and electoral system. Within these systemic features, we also must distinguish between those peculiar to and inherent in the particular form of PR used and other systemic features.

The length of the ballot (the number of candidates) is the result not of PR but of the method of nomination (by petition—in effect self-nomination) for which various system-design features might be substituted, such as a primary election or nomination by party conventions. We suspect that neither of these methods would be acceptable to the schools' constituencies, and we are not recommending them, merely citing them as widely used alternatives.

More realistic and desirable, in our view, would be a remedy available in the behavioral sphere, one that typically has evolved in similar PR systems in the country, that is, "slate" politics. Slating groups are de facto parties under another name and provide an important function: cutting the field of would-be nominees down to a manageable number on whom like-minded people can concentrate their support. The formation of pro-parent and pro-children slates of candidates seems the most feasible counterpart to the slating that probably is being done by professional politicians and unions. However, this prescription may not be easy to initiate. Slates initiated by unions or politicians also may carry parent labels.

Two features underlying the above-mentioned complaints are ascribable accurately to the PR system in use—the preferential vote (numerical rankings of candidates supported) and administrative problems with the count resulting from treating the numbered preferences as a single-transferable vote.

The putative additional burden on the voter imposed by the necessity of assigning numerical rankings to candidates will be minimized to some extent by slates. Opinions will differ concerning whether whatever additional burden remains would be much, if any, greater than if the simplest alternative voting system were employed, that is, a "9X" ballot in which the voter could vote for a maximum of nine candidates with no numbered preferences. Typically, many voters react in essentially the same way to both a preferential and nonpreferential ballot with a long list of candidates. Unless they take guidance on faith from a slate, they record only a few (perhaps only one) of their choices; and if numbered preferences are required, some voters will assign the numbers arbitrarily. In sum, the difference in behavior by voters in the two systems is not great.

Problems in administering the count in accordance with the STV principle, in addition to problems encountered in other elections, undeniably exist, but these can be demonstrably minimized to an acceptable level by such means as selecting only competent contractors to administer the count and providing the necessary resources to ensure recruitment and training of a competent staff.[7] Automating the count would also probably solve some of the problems but at the cost of others, such as greater difficulty of the lay public in monitoring the process.

PROPORTIONALITY

We analyze the degree of proportionality in school board elections from the standpoint of successful candidacies of women and minorities. Table 16.1 summarizes the spotty available data. Most of the comparisons that can be made are longitudinal ones with historical benchmarks in the same system and with census data.

Table 16.1
Community School Board Election Results, City of New York, 1970–1989 (Percent of Seats Won)

BOARD SEATS
HELD BY

	YEAR							
	1989	1986	1983	1980	1977	1975	1973	1970
WOMEN	54.0	49.0	48.0	41.0	39.0	42.0	41.0	34.0
MINORITIES	47.0	44.0	45.0(44)[a]	45.0[b](46)	37.0	35.0[b](36)	38.0	26.0
BLACKS	30.0	26.0	28.0	25.0 (20)[c]	24.0	20.0 (21)	24.0(21)	16.0
HISPANICS	16.0	17.0	17.0	20.0 (16)[c]	12.0	14.0 (15)	14.0	10.0
ASIANS	1.4	0.7	(0.3)	(0.3)[c]	0.7	1.0	0.3	0.3
WHITES[d]	53.0	56.0	55.0	55.0	63.0	65.0 (63)[e]	62.0	74.0

Note: Some percentages do not add to 100 because of rounding. Minor discrepancies between sources are ignored.

[a] Numbers in parentheses are census data. They are percentages of the total population except where otherwise noted.

[b] Obtained by adding the corresponding numbers below. Minority vote was not reported.

[c] Percentage of population age 20 and over or, in the case of Anker's data, age 18 and over.

[d] Percentages of whites for years 1975 and 1977 have been extrapolated from percentages of minorities.

[e] Anker gives this figure as 67 percent.

Women Candidates

Until the 1989 election, the number of women elected was not reported. The 1989 election was the first in which a majority of those elected—54 percent— were women. The only comparative standard available for the system is the 34 percent of women elected in 1970, the first PR election.[8] The 1989 percent is well above the national average of 33.8 percent.[9] The only available ethnic breakdown over time for women candidates is for blacks. The Joint Center for Political Studies reported that a substantial increase in successful black women candidacies accounts for the increase in blacks elected during the 1980s, as reflected in table 16.1. According to information provided by the National Association of Latino Elected and Appointed Officials, almost half of the Hispanic candidates elected in 1989 (19 of 39 whose gender could be inferred from names) were women.

The most probable explanation for the surge of successful women candidates in 1989 was the emphasis by various organizations on electing parents.[10] Successful parent candidacies are more apt to be women,[11] as compared with outcomes in prior elections, when lack of such emphasis tended to leave the field more open to politicians and schools' employees, whose motivations are presumably personal and political advantage.[12] It is reasonable to speculate that such candidacies probably contained a higher proportion of men than did the parent candidacies.

More recent and reliable census data must be awaited before it will be possible to apply to successful women candidacies tests of proportionality similar to those for candidacies of various ethnic groups.

Ethnic Minority Groups

The 1989 election witnessed a new high in ethnic minority groups directly represented on boards—47 percent, as compared with 53 percent for whites— reflecting a virtually steady increase in the minority percentages from a low of 26 percent in the first election of 1970.

Available and reasonably comparable census data suggest that the results summarized above are very close to proportionality as measured by both the total populations and those of voting age. In particular, the results of the elections in 1970, 1973, and 1983 were close to proportionality.[13]

CONCLUDING COMMENTS

The PR election system for the community school boards is functioning in practice much as its designers argued it would, by electing candidates of various elements of the community in approximate proportions to their voting strengths and in much closer proportions than in the single-member district system for city council and state legislative seats. Several knowledgeable observers speculate that an important reason for the closeness of the approximation is the tendency of unions, political clubs, and parent groups to try to give their slates ethnic and gender balance. The fact that the approximations are so close tends to cast doubt on the conventional wisdom that in the admittedly low turnouts, the ethnic minorities tend to turn out in lower ratios than whites.

Despite these results, there is considerable local opposition to PR and to other concomitant features in the present system. Although feasible alternatives are rarely discussed, the two most obvious alternatives would be a "9X" at-large system or a single-member subdistrict system as proposed by the influential Public Education Association, subject to the development of a reasonable subdistricting pattern that satisfies the requirements of the federal Voting Rights Act of 1965 as amended.

Presumably the election system will be one of the issues examined by the various commissions established to study the issues involved in the present law and practice of the "decentralization" philosophy reflected in the community school board system. In the meantime, the election system experience will continue to be watched by professional students of representation and electoral systems as one of those state-and-local-level experiments that James Bryce and others perceived to be a virtue of a federal system embodying the principles of decentralization and home rule.[14]

NOTES

1. Nancy M. Lederman, Jeanne S. Frankl, and Judith Baum, *Governing New York City Schools: Roles and Relationships in the Decentralized System* (New York: Public Education Association, 1987).

2. *Improving the Odds: Making Decentralization Work for Children, for School, for Communities* (New York: Manhattan Borough President's Task Force on Education and Decentralization, 1988), p. 51.

3. Jacqueline Montgomery, "Polls in Disarray," *New York Times*, May 17, 1989, p. A26.

4. Sarah Lyall, "In New York, Parents Lack Say in Schools," *New York Times*, January 16, 1989, pp. 1, B2.

5. *Findings and Recommendations of the Joint Commission on Integrity in the Public Schools* (New York: The Commission, 1990).

6. Voter turnout decreased from slightly over 14.0 percent in the first election of 1970 to 7.6 percent in 1986 to 7.2 percent in 1989. However, voting turnout in 1989 increased in 16 of the 32 districts.

7. New York City election officials contracted with a private firm for the counting of PR ballots rather than administering the count by city officials on an election-district basis, as in other elections.

8. Leonard Buder, "School Boards: More Women, Fewer Incumbents," *New York Times*, June 11, 1989, p. 40.

9. In its survey of school board members, the National Association of School Boards reported that 32 percent of board members responding were women. See "Here's Looking at You," *American School Board Journal*, January 1990, p. 34.

10. Thirty percent of the candidates identified themselves as parents; 40 percent of these candidates were elected. Buder, "School Boards."

11. The premises are that a substantial fraction of the parents are single ones and that these parents are predominantly women.

12. Successful candidates in this category dropped from between 85 and 90 to only 39 out of a total of 288 seats in the last election. Leonard Buder, "Judge Upsets School Board Limit," *New York Times*, April 26, 1990, pp. 1, 84, and Buder, "School Boards."

13. The most meaningful comparisons exist for the 1970–73 and 1980–83 periods. Except where otherwise noted, sources for table 16.1 are *Community School Board Elections, 1989* (New York: New York City Board of Education, 1989); correspondence from the late George H. Hallett (for 1970, 1973, and 1983); Joseph F. Zimmerman, "A Proportional Representation System and New York City School Boards," *National Civic Review*, October 1974, pp. 472–74, 493 (for 1970 and 1973); and Irving Anker, chancellor, memorandum to New York City community school boards entitled "Ethnic Patterns within the City of New York," October 8–9, 1973 (census data for 1973). The Joint Center for Political Studies (for the elections of 1980, 1986, and 1989 for blacks) and the National Association of Latino Elected and Appointed Officials (for the election of 1989 for Hispanics) reported numbers slightly and consistently less than those listed in the table, but the reported numbers reflect the same trends as shown in the table.

14. James Bryce, *The American Commonwealth* (New York: Macmillan Co., 1900).

PART V

OPTIONS FOR INCREASING THE REPRESENTATION OF WOMEN AND MINORITIES

17

Enhancing Representational Equity in Cities

Joseph F. Zimmerman

The democratic ideal is an electoral system neutral in terms of race, ethnicity, religion, sex, or other factors with the exception of the quality of the candidates. A system of this nature will not necessarily produce direct representation for women and underrepresented minorities in exact proportion to their respective percentages of the voting population but would provide a more broadly representative group of elected officials.

This chapter describes barriers to the election of minorities and women to city councils, the relative advantages and disadvantages of six electoral systems, and the increase in the number of legislative positions resulting from the establishment of a system of neighborhood governments in large cities.

BARRIERS TO ELECTION

The most blatant legal barriers to the election of women and underrepresented minorities to public office have been removed, yet the election of these groups is hindered by the remaining legal barriers and nonlegal barriers. In all states, important features of the electoral system are regulated by state laws, which often facilitate political party control of the nominating process and reelection of incumbents. Hence, promotion of the election of women and minorities may necessitate amendment of state election laws.

If the city employs the closed primary, political party leaders will determine the candidates whose names will appear on the primary ballot and on the general election ballot as well. If the primary system is open, women and underrepresented groups will have greater access to the ballot, since nominations are made by voter petitions.

Legal barriers also are found in city charters, which tend to be old and complex documents. A good charter facilitates citizen control of the municipality by providing voters with a readily available source of information on the powers, procedures, and structures of the government and authorizes mechanisms—the initiative, protest referendum, and recall—that can be employed by citizens to promote responsiveness by elected officials.[1] Voters in some or all types of municipalities in 44 states may adopt and/or amend a locally drafted charter. In six states—Alabama, Illinois, Indiana, Kentucky, North Carolina, and Virginia—amendment or adoption of a city charter can be accomplished only by enactment of a state law. Although a Vermont law authorizes the adoption by voters of a locally drafted charter, the law has not been utilized because bond counsels advise the law is unconstitutional.

The governance process would be improved in most cities if they adopted a charter based on the Model City Charter, which offers a choice of electoral systems.[2] One of the systems—proportional representation (PR)—is designed to produce direct representation for each group in proportion to its voting strength and is examined in detail in a subsequent section.

A significant nonlegal barrier to the election of minority and women candidates is incumbency. It is difficult in many local governments to defeat an incumbent because of his/her name recognition, campaign organization, and ability to raise campaign funds. Although not included in the Model City Charter, a charter provision could be adopted to increase the number of open seats in an election by limiting the number of consecutive terms that an elected official may serve. Several state constitutions limit the governor to a single term (Virginia is an example) or two consecutive terms (Alaska is an example). Voters in California, Colorado, and Oklahoma in 1990 approved constitutional amendments limiting the number of terms members of the state legislature may serve. The city charter in a number of municipalities restricts the number of terms the mayor may serve. The mayor of Atlanta, Georgia, for example, is limited to two terms. Women and members of minority groups would not have to battle as many incumbents for election to the city council if a limit on terms was included in the charter.

In medium to large cities with a small unicameral council adopted during the municipal reform movement, opportunities for the election of women and minorities might be enhanced by enlarging the size of the council. Many cities operate with a seven- or nine-member council. Increasing its size would enable underrepresented groups to sponsor candidates who would not have to compete against incumbents. The effectiveness of this strategy would depend in large measure on the type of electoral system employed and the number of members added to the council.

Another approach to facilitating the election of women and minority group members to office involves converting the unitary governmental system of a large city into a federated one with two tiers of elected governing bodies—the city council and neighborhood councils. The creation of subcity councils increases the number of elected officials, and in the first election, women and minority group members would not have to challenge incumbents.

ELECTORAL SYSTEMS

Six different electoral systems have been employed to elect local governing bodies in the United States, and a seventh system was used for 110 years to elect members of the lower house of the Illinois State Legislature.

The Single Member District System

The principal system utilized to elect members of city councils until the last decade of the 19th century was a single- or multimember ward plurality system, which facilitated boss and machine control of large cities. The typical city had a large bicameral city council with a common council and a board of aldermen. Richard S. Childs, an early municipal reformer, identified the following as major weaknesses of this system:

1. Ward elections confined each voter's influence over the governing body to the single member from his ward. He was denied having anything to say about the majority.

2. Ward elections notoriously produced political small fry who intrigued in the council for petty favors and sought appropriations for their wards in reckless disregard of city-wide interests and the total budget.

3. Ward boundaries got deliberately drawn to favor one faction or party or became obsolete by shifts of population, and redistricting was resisted, sometimes for generations, by the beneficiaries, resulting in gross inequalities of representation and elections of a majority of the council by minorities of the population.

4. The obscurities of the ward politics eluded scrutiny by press and public and facilitated development of self-serving political cliques.[3]

Numerous cities abandoned the ward system during the heyday of the municipal reform movement, but the single-member district system has made a comeback in recent years, particularly as the result of the enactment of the federal Voting Rights Act of 1965. The United States Department of Justice has been promoting the replacement of at-large plurality elections with single-member district elections in cities covered by the act.

The weaknesses of the system identified by Childs remain today. As Childs noted, each voter is restricted to voting for only one candidate for a council that may have 15 to 30 or more members; gerrymandering in particular is a major weakness, since the mapmakers often exercise more control over the successful candidates than the voters. The system also encourages minority groups to remain geographically concentrated in order to be able to elect one of their members to the council. Furthermore, the system can result in the election of a candidate by a minority of the voters if three or more candidates divide the votes and there is no provision for a runoff election between the two top vote-getters. The single-member district system with a provision for a runoff election continues to be an undesirable system because the runoff election is a special election in which voter participation tends to be low, resulting in the election of a council member by a minority of the voters in the district. In terms of minority group representation, the system may pit a black candidate against a Hispanic candidate and a white candidate, with the latter winning the election because the votes of the two minority groups are divided.

Utilizing 1988 data, DeSantis and Renner studied the impact of county electoral systems and discovered that district elections favored only black candidates.[4] The system tends to promote the election of one or more black candidates because blacks tend to be geographically concentrated in certain wards, but it may adversely affect Hispanic voters who often are dispersed more evenly throughout the city and may be able to exercise the balance of power between the two major political parties or groups in an at-large election.

The At-Large System

A major charge directed against the ward system by the early reformers was the neglect of citywide needs by the large city council, which routinely divided funds equally among the wards without regard to whether all funds appropriated to a ward for a given function were needed or whether there were unmet needs because of inadequate appropriations for other functions.

The solution to the problem, in the eyes of the reformers, was the replacement of the ward system by an at-large system and a sharp reduction in the size of the council. A small council, it was assumed, would be in the public spotlight and would be sensitive to the needs of all sections of the city.

By the 1960s, the at-large plurality council in a number of large cities was criticized by several political scientists on the ground it overrepresented white middle-class values.[5] These critics were joined by a growing number of black activists convinced that the at-large plurality system made it impossible or extremely difficult for a black to win a council seat. In addition, critics maintained that decisions were being made by a council unaware of and insensitive to the problems of poor neighborhoods and members of disadvantaged minority groups.

In adopting the at-large system, a number of cities recognized the need for neighborhood representation and incorporated a provision for a modified at-large system in the city charter. This system employs district residency requirements for members of the council. One member must reside in each district. If the two highest vote-getters in the latest election reside in the same district, only the top vote-getter is elected to the council. This modified at-large system will facilitate the election of a member of a minority group if it is geographically concentrated in a district but does not guarantee the election of such a candidate.

Combined At-Large and Ward Elections

Other cities responded to the complaints that the at-large council was unrepresentative of all neighborhoods by amending their charters to provide for the election of a number of council members at large and the election of the remainder of the members on a single-member district basis. Where this is employed, a majority of the council members typically are elected at large to ensure that priority is given to citywide needs, and a minority are elected on a ward basis to ensure that the special needs of the various neighborhoods are not neglected. A few cities provide for the election of a majority of council members by wards. A geographically concentrated minority under this system may be able to elect one of its members to the council. This system is similar to the at-large plurality system with residency requirements but differs in that the voters may not help to elect all members of the council.

Limited Voting

Although the single-member district system may be described as a limited voting system, since each voter may cast a ballot for only one candidate for the city council, the term *limited voting* has been restricted to a system in which a voter may cast a ballot for more than one candidate but for fewer candidates than there are seats to be filled, such as casting six votes for different candidates seeking election to a nine-member council.

This system is traceable to the concern, after the Civil War, that a single political party was totally dominating the election of candidates. To ensure direct representation for members of the minority party, the charter was amended to restrict each elector to voting for fewer candidates than the number of seats to be filled. The largest party typically will elect a majority, but not all members, of the council under this voting system.

A companion charter provision typically restricts each party to nominating fewer candidates than there are seats to be filled. In cities with nonpartisan elections, there is no need for a charter provision restricting the nomination of candidates.

Limited voting will guarantee direct representation for members of the largest minority party or group, with the extent of the representation dependent on the size of the council and the maximum number of candidates a voter may cast a ballot for. The system also can be employed on an at-large or a multimember district basis. (See Still's chapter in this anthology.)

Since voters are not allowed to express preferences and since each voter gives the same support to the candidate least favored as to the candidate most favored, the voter may contribute to the defeat of his favorite candidate. In consequence, this electoral system encourages bullet or single-shot voting—voting for only one candidate.

Limited voting is a crude system for securing minority representation and neither guarantees that each group or party will be fully represented in proportion to its voting strength nor prevents a minority from electing a majority of the council members if several strong slates of candidates divide the votes.

In a partisan election with limited voting, the majority party may influence the election of a minority council member by throwing votes to a favored minority party candidate, thereby encouraging all minority party candidates to curry the favor of the majority party. In a limited-vote election of magistrates in Philadelphia a number of years ago, the majority party divided its supporters into two groups and won both the minority and majority seats. And there is nothing to prevent the majority party from promoting the formation of two slates of candidates to divide the opposition vote.

Cumulative Voting

Like limited voting, cumulative voting seeks to enable the largest minority party or group to elect one or more of its members to a city council. Under this system, each elector has the same number of votes as there are seats on the council and may give all votes to one candidate or apportion the votes among several candidates in accordance with the intensity of the voter's preferences. To date, the system has been employed in the United States only to elect members of the Illinois House of Representatives from 1870 to 1980, since 1988 in Alamogordo, New Mexico, and in Chilton County and three towns in Alabama (see the chapters by Everson and Still). In Illinois, three representatives were elected in each senatorial district, and each voter could award three votes to a single candidate, grant two votes to one candidate and one vote to a second candidate, give one and one-half votes to each of two candidates, or assign one vote to each of three candidates.

Cumulative voting does not guarantee that a party or a group will be represented in accordance with its voting strength because parties or groups are unable to make their members follow instructions to the letter and also they may miscalculate their strength. Split-ticket voting, if of significant magnitude, will prevent proportionate representation.

Illinois experience reveals that the minority party can elect a majority of the members in a three-member district if the majority party miscalculates its strength and nominates three candidates instead of two, thereby splitting its vote and allowing the minority party to elect its two nominees.[6]

Proportional Representation: The Single-Transferable Vote

There are two types of proportional representation (PR)—the list system and the single-transferable vote system. The former is used in several European nations and Israel, but only the latter has been employed in the United States. The latter, which is explained in this chapter, is a type of preferential voting. Each elector places a number next to the name of each candidate, with a number "1" indicating first preference, number "2" second preference, etc.

The winners of the election are determined by a quota—the total number of valid ballots cast divided by the number of council members to be elected plus one. Assuming 100,000 valid ballots were cast to elect a nine-member governing body, the quota would be

$$\frac{100,000}{9+1} + 1 = 10,001.$$

This formula always produces the smallest number of votes that ensures a candidate's election regardless of how the votes are distributed among the candidates.

The next step in the election involves sorting the ballots by first choices. Candidates receiving a total of number "1" votes equal to or exceeding the quota are declared elected. Ballots exceeding the quota are transferred to the other candidates according to the second choices indicated. Following this step, the candidate with the fewest number "1" votes is declared defeated and his or her votes are transferred to the remaining candidates according to the next choices marked on them. If a second choice already has been elected or defeated, the ballots are distributed to the third choices. A new count is conducted, and candidates are declared elected if they have a total of number "1" and transferred ballots exceeding the quota. Elected candidates' surplus ballots are transferred to the remaining candidates. The process of declaring defeated the lowest candidate and transferring his/her ballots to the other candidates as indicated by the next choice continues until the full governing body is elected. Most ballots, either on first choice or by transfer, help to elect a candidate.

Surplus ballots can be distributed by two methods. Under the first method, candidates are not allowed to exceed the quota. On reaching the quota, surplus ballots are immediately given to the next choices indicated. Under the second method, the ballots of a candidate receiving a surplus of number "1" votes are reexamined to determine the distribution of number "2" votes. The surplus ballots are distributed proportionately according to second choices. If candidate A received 12,000 number "1" ballots and the quota is 10,000, the candidate has a surplus of 2,000 ballots. Assuming that candidate B was the number "2" choice on 6,000 of candidate A's number "1" ballots, candidate B would be given one-half of the surplus or 1,000 ballots.

The hallmark of a good electoral system is representational equity. Proportional representation meets this criterion by ensuring majority rule while guaranteeing minority representation. PR is based on the recognition that there are numerous factional divisions in a city and that it is essential to make it impossible for any faction or political party with a slight electoral majority to elect all members of a city council or school board. In the first election after the abandonment of PR by New York City, Democrats won 24 of the 25 city council seats in 1949, although they polled only 52.6 percent of the votes cast. Had PR been in effect, the party division would have been 13 Democrats, six Republicans, three Liberals, and three American Labor Party members.

In contrast to the single-member district system, the PR system allows a geographically dispersed minority to elect a candidate, since the constituency is based on interest and not on residence. In addition, the strength of a minority group is not dissipated if the group gives most of its number "1" votes to one of its candidates or scatters its votes among several of its candidates.

Although a minority group is fully represented under PR, the group cannot benefit from a split among opposition groups, as it can under limited voting and cumulative voting, and cannot thus elect a majority of the members of a council or school board. PR often is advocated because it provides representation for minority parties, but the system also provides the majority party with more seats than it would gain under a ward electoral system if the party members are concentrated in only a few wards.

Other PR advantages include the prevention of a popular name at the head of a party column from carrying weak or unqualified candidates into office and the elimination of the gerrymander because PR can be an at-large system. Zeller and Bone studied elections of the New York City Council by PR and concluded that the system "forced higher caliber candidates on both the majority and minority political organizations."[7]

Bullet or single-shot voting is common in at-large and limited voting electoral systems because additional choices might help to defeat a group's candidate. In a PR election, second and subsequent choices are examined and utilized only if the first choice has been elected or defeated. In consequence, the presence of many preferences on the ballot has no effect on the prospect of the first choice being elected. Under no circumstance can PR be employed to cancel or dilute invidiously the effectiveness of ballots cast by any group of registered voters. An electoral system that produces a council viewed by citizens as legitimate facilitates the implementation of city council policies dependent on the active cooperation of the citizenry.

How effective is PR in providing minority representation? In 1970, blacks exceeded 20 percent and Puerto Ricans 12 percent of New York City's population, yet there were no Puerto Ricans and only two blacks on the 37-member city council. In the same year, PR was employed to elect the 279 members of the newly established community school boards. Seventy-seven, or nearly 28 percent of the members, were black and Puerto Rican. Of these members, 44 were elected in six districts, and the remainder were elected in 15 of the other 25 districts. In the 1973 election, 110 (38 percent) of the candidates elected were black, Chinese, or Puerto Rican; these three groups composed approximately 36 percent of the population.

In the 1989 community school board elections, 138 (47.9 percent) of the 288 board members elected to office were members of minority groups—88 were black, 46 were Hispanic, and four were Asian. These boards were the first with women[8] constituting a majority of all members—156, or 54.2 percent. Less than half the members (140) were incumbents, and 40 percent were parents of public school children.

PR makes it more difficult for the mayor to win council support for a particular program, and the mayor may have to make concessions to groups and areas that he often could ignore in the past. Mayor Fiorello H. LaGuardia of New York City wrote that the PR-elected city council was "annoying and exasperating." But he added: "Is not every executive subjected to criticism, or even, if you please, to be harassed by the legislative body? I am glad that I am living under a system of government that permits an executive to be criticized, even if that criticism extends to the point of unjustifiable abuse."[9]

A FEDERATED CITY

The early municipal reformers promoted functional consolidation and the creation of a strong mayor by abolishing elected boards and commissions and transferring their responsibilities to the mayor. Furthermore, the reformers desired to reduce the political power of ward-based councilmen by replacing the large bicameral council with a relatively small unicameral council elected at large. The reformers generally were successful in achieving their goals, but critics charged the system was overcentralized and unresponsive to the special needs of poor neighborhoods.

Many large cities responded to the criticism by adopting administrative decentralization. New York City, for example, has long employed administrative decentralization to improve the delivery of services to neighborhoods. To provide greater citizen input into the city's policy-making process, voters in 1963 approved a charter amendment providing for the appointment of community planning boards by each of the five borough presidents, and a total of 62 were appointed. Renamed *community boards* by a 1969 charter amendment, each board subsequently was authorized to appoint a district manager to chair a district service cabinet composed of representatives of city agencies delivering services to the neighborhood. Although community boards facilitate greater citizen input into the city's policy-making process, the boards remain advisory, and their members are appointed.[10] In poor neighborhoods, city hall is viewed by many citizens as light-years away from the residents.

Two new groups of reformers emerged in the 1960s. One group was composed primarily of blacks who argued that large units of government do not necessarily plan better, achieve a higher level of service and more economies, or tax more equitably than small units. Furthermore, they argued that economies of scale do not have to be sacrificed to achieve responsiveness. Employing the colonial analogy, Milton Kotler maintained: "The absolute rule of Negro communities by outside forces has reached the highest degree possible without precipitating rebellion. At the point when practically all decisions affecting public life are made on the outside, a politically confident and conscious people aspiring to be free, must insist upon a share in local rule."[11]

The second group—public choice theorists—advanced arguments in favor of the existing system of fragmented local governments in a given area. They are convinced that a large number of units in an area promote citizen participation, governmental responsiveness to citizens, and choice of residential location on

the basis of services provided and taxes levied by the various governments.[12]
The arguments of the public choice theorists, of course, can be employed to
support the conversion of a large unitary government into a system of neighborhood governments.

Neighborhood Governments

American political traditions favor citizen participation, decentralization of
political authority, and small units of local governments. Replacement of a single
large city government by neighborhood governments, however, would not be
feasible because there are many governmental services and products that can be
provided more economically and efficiently on a wider geographical scale.

The creation of a two-tier system of local government in large cities, however,
could be a major structural improvement that would make many governmental
officers subject to greater control by voters. In a federated city, the upper tier
would retain responsibility for major areawide functions that can be performed
best on a large-area scale. Functions closest to the citizens, such as health and
education, could be the responsibility of lower-tier units. Responsibility for
several functions could be shared on a wholesale-retail basis. Water supply and
refuse disposal could be the responsibility of the citywide government while
water distribution and refuse collection could be the responsibility of the lower-
tier units.

The creation of a federated city would provide increased opportunities for
women and minority group members to be elected to office, since each lower-
tier government would be governed by a directly elected council. In neighborhoods with several racial and ethnic groups, employing PR to elect the council
would be desirable to ensure that each group has direct representation on the
council. Like most cities, each neighborhood government could have an elected
strong mayor or a professional manager appointed by the council.

A system of multifunctional neighborhood governments should make the governance system more responsive to the special needs of residents in each neighborhood, increase public officers' accountability to residents, and help to
legitimize government in neighborhoods with many alienated citizens. Uniform
citywide policies in a number of functional areas would be replaced by policies
that an elected council has custom-tailored to the conditions prevailing in each
neighborhood.

The establishment of a system of neighborhood governments also should have
the advantages of relieving the mayor and council of the citywide government
of the minutiae and problems they must deal with as the result of pressure from
individual neighborhoods, absolving them of blame for administrative failures
in programs transferred to the neighborhood governments, and permitting citywide officials to devote more time to the study and solution of major problems.

SUMMARY AND CONCLUSIONS

Providing representation equity for all groups in a local government is a complex and difficult task necessitating several changes in the governance system of the typical city. Implementing the essential changes often will require amendment of state election laws as well as local government charters.

The two most important changes that would promote the election of women and minority group candidates are the adoption of single-transferable vote PR or a semiproportional representation system, and the establishment of a federated city. If a local government continues to utilize the single-member district system, it is essential that the state constitution be amended to incorporate redistricting criteria that will prevent partisan, ethnic, and/or racial gerrymandering.

Opportunities for the election of women and minority group candidates also could be enhanced in many local governments by increasing the size of the governing body and limiting the number of consecutive terms a member may serve. Since service on local governing bodies often is the principal entry path to elections to the state legislature or the United States Congress, an increase in the number of women and minority group members at the state and national levels is to a great extent dependent on increasing opportunities for underrepresented groups to elect their members to local governing bodies.

NOTES

1. For details, see Joseph F. Zimmerman, *Participatory Democracy: Populism Revived* (New York: Praeger Publishers, 1986).

2. *Model City Charter*, 7th ed. (Denver: National Civic League, 1989).

3. Richard S. Childs, *The First 50 Years of the Council-Manager Plan of Government* (New York: National Municipal League, 1965), p. 37.

4. Victor DeSantis and Tari Renner, "Minority and Sexual Representation in American County Legislatures: The Effect of Election Systems," paper presented at the annual meeting of the American Political Science Association, Atlanta, Georgia, August 21-September 3, 1989, p. 14.

5. Edward C. Banfield and James Q. Wilson, *City Politics* (Cambridge: Harvard University Press and M.I.T. Press, 1963), pp. 139–42.

6. George S. Blair, *Cumulative Voting: An Effective Electoral Device in Illinois Politics* (Urbana: University of Illinois Press, 1960), pp. 103–4. For information on the Alabama experience, see Edward Still, "Cumulative Voting and Limited Voting in Alabama," in this volume. See also Richard L. Engstrom, Delbert A. Taebel, and Richard L. Cole, "Cumulative Voting as a Remedy for Minority Voter Dilution: The Case of Alamogordo, New Mexico," *Journal of Law and Politics*, Spring 1989, pp. 469–97.

7. Belle Zeller and Hugh A. Bone, "The Repeal of P.R. in New York City: Ten Years in Retrospect," *American Political Science Review*, December 1948, p. 1127.

8. *Community School Board Elections: 1989* (Brooklyn: New York City Board of Education, June 14, 1989). The number of school boards was increased to 32 after the 1970 election. See also Richard L. Engstrom, "District Magnitudes and the Election of Women in the Irish Dáil," *Electoral Systems*, August 1987, pp. 139–48.

9. "Mayor LaGuardia on P.R.," *National Municipal Review*, April 1940, p. 275.

10. For additional details, see Zimmerman, *Participatory Democracy*, pp. 145–55.

11. Milton Kotler, "Two Essays on the Neighborhood Corporation," in Joint Economic Committee, *Urban America: Goals and Problems* (Washington, D.C.: United States Government Printing Office, 1967), p. 176.

12. See Charles M. Tiebout, "A Pure Theory of Local Expenditures," *Journal of Political Economy*, October 1956, pp. 412–24, and Robert L. Bish and Vincent Ostrom, *Understanding Urban Government: Metropolitan Reform Reconsidered* (Washington, D.C.: American Enterprise Institute for Public Policy Research, 1973).

18

Electoral Barriers to Women

R. Darcy

It is difficult to understand why democratic political institutions have managed so thoroughly to exclude women from political life. Women are the majority in many countries, have the same political ability as men, and achieved full political rights 50 or more years ago; political institutions appear open, free, and democratic. The result should have been the full incorporation of women into positions of political leadership—not their almost complete exclusion. We review the research seeking to find an explanation for this situation and to coax from this research practical ways to bring women into elective office at a faster rate.

WOMEN AND POLITICAL INSTITUTIONS

In the 1950s, a United Nations Economic and Social Council (UNESCO) team headed by Maurice Duverger, a French political sociologist, investigated the political role of women.[1] The team hypothesized two explanations for the failure of democratic institutions to incorporate women fully: elite opposition, which they labeled the male conspiracy; and voter hostility to women candidates. Researchers in the 1970s and 1980s explored each of these hypotheses and generally reported negative results.

The Male Conspiracy and Voter Hostility

One immediate explanation for the absence of women from political life is the opposition of men who dominate and control access. The evidence of a male conspiracy seemed obvious, since it was men who decided not to grant women the right to vote when drafting 18th-century constitutions and who repeatedly voted to deny women suffrage for another century. Since it was men who dominated the political parties, it seemed plausible to blame them for the failure to nominate and elect more than a handful of women candidates once women's suffrage was achieved. Furthermore, male political leaders have made remarks such as, "The only time to run a woman . . . is when things look so bad that your only chance is to do something dramatic."[2] Thus, when a woman fails to gain a nomination or fails in an election, the blame often falls on male prejudice.

On the other hand, political elites have not appeared implacably hostile to electing women during the past decade. In Great Britain, the major parties develop national lists of candidates, including substantial numbers of women, from which local party organizations are encouraged to select their nominees. The Labour party and Liberal Democrats have affirmative-action requirements calling for women to be on constituency nomination shortlists,[3] and the Conservatives encourage this approach. In the United States, the two political parties have special training, recruitment, and funding operations for potential women candidates. In other European nations, the political parties are making even stronger efforts to find and elect women political candidates. Male-dominated political parties in India, Norway, and Spain have set quotas for women candidates in an attempt to raise the proportions of elected women.[4] The Israeli Labor convention set a quota for women at 25 percent, although they gained only 10 percent of the "safe" seats, and special efforts have been made to recruit women candidates in South Korea.[5] In Taiwan, the constitution requires minimal representation of women in the Legislative Yuan.[6]

Altruism is not the dominant motive. The realities of competitive politics suffice as an explanation. Party elites are pragmatic and, confronted with feminist claims and the fact that the majority of voters are women, avoid giving their opponents an issue by making an effort at nominating some women. Similarly, electing a few women officials is one way for developing nations to demonstrate they are modern and progressive.

Studies of American congressional and state legislative races find newly re-cruited women candidates gaining the same type of winnable nominations as new men candidates. Women candidates at the state legislative and congressional levels run well-funded campaigns.[7] Considerable research in other nations also fails to document political parties and political elites currently discriminating against women.[8] Lack of evidence for elite discrimination, despite considerable effort to find it, shifts the burden of finding evidence to those who believe it still persists.

Voters support women candidates. An examination of thousands of state legislative and congressional races over many years shows women candidates do not get fewer votes than men. In fact, voters tend to respond better to women. Voters remember or recognize women's names more frequently, and they have more positive views of women than of men candidates.[9] Generally, the small numbers of women candidates and elected officials are not due to current voter hostility to political women.

SYSTEMIC RESPONSE TO WOMEN SEEKING
POLITICAL OFFICE

Instead of voter hostility and an elite male conspiracy, the explanation for the small number of women getting elected is more prosaic. Women in large numbers began only recently in the early 1970s to seek elective political power through established political parties. Because of the large proportion of male incumbents and the slow rate that politicians turn over, the proportion of women in public office tends to grow slowly.

The Suffrage Movement

The present struggle for women's political representation is often viewed as a fourth stage of a long struggle for political rights. The first stage of the struggle—characterized by Mary Wollstonecraft (1759–97) in Britain, William Thompson (1775–1833) in Ireland, and Marquis de Condorcet (1743–94) and Charles Fourier (1772–1837) in France—provided intellectual arguments that women should share in the new political rights being won in the American and French revolutions.[10] The second stage—characterized by John Stuart Mill (1806–73) in Britain and the Seneca Falls Convention with its Declaration of the Rights of Women (1848) in the United States—began the political action to achieve political and social rights for women.[11] The third stage was the worldwide suffrage movement between about 1880 and 1930 that achieved political rights for most women in democratic countries. By the end of this process, most democratic governments had granted (or restored) most or all political rights to women.

An examination of these earlier movements and what the women involved intended to do with their political rights reveals an absence of any vision of using their vote to compete in established ways for political power. Women did not intend to seek nominations of established parties for office or struggle to gain influence within the political parties. Instead, the goal was to use their vote in three other ways. First, they believed their attempts to lobby elected officials would be more effective if they had the vote, since officials would have to pay attention to the representatives of voting women. Next, they intended to use two new political devices—the initiative and the referendum. Finally, some suffrage leaders tried to establish a new political party to contest for political power from the outside.[12]

Common to each of these strategies was the idea that political power as exercised by political parties and political institutions was corrupt. Women were going to find new ways to bring about needed reform. The concern was the women's reform agenda rather than competing with men within the existing political parties for positions of political authority. As a result, very few of the women who worked to bring suffrage to Great Britain or the United States used their votes to gain elective office. Instead, they worked on the fringe of politics—serving as appointees or limiting themselves to local offices or work in reform groups. The "firsts" showed that women could gain election: Constance Mar-kievicz, first woman elected to the United Kingdom Parliament (from Dublin, 1918), Rebecca Latimer Felton, first woman in the United States Senate (from Georgia, 1922), and Jeannette Pickering Rankin, first woman in the United States House of Representatives (from Montana, 1916). Women elected to local gov-ernment were the exception to the generalization that women avoided elected office.[13]

With the publication of Simone de Beauvoir's *The Second Sex* (1949), Maurice Duverger's *The Political Role of Women* (1955), and Betty Friedan's *The Feminine Mystique* (1963), European and North American men and women began the process of questioning the lack of real progress for women despite the gain in political rights and the achievement of a number of "firsts."[14] It was only in the late 1960s and early 1970s that there was large-scale recognition that women were excluded from positions of power and that the remedy was to be found in electing women in substantial numbers to political office. One reason for the low representation of women in elected office is that elective office was histor-ically not the goal of women activists, who chose to pursue other priorities through other means.

The Political System's Response to Women

It is believed by many that politics reflects the wider society. Women—denied access to education, denied equal treatment in the economy, restricted in their vocational choices, and denied equal promotional opportunities—were handi-capped in their attempts to enter politics. This assessment is certainly correct. The corollary that many have drawn, however, is not correct, at least not in the short term. This corollary is that change in access to social and economic roles for women will result in more women getting elected to public office.

Let us look at the recruitment process for the United States House of Rep-resentatives. Members of Congress come from a narrow stratum of society, with less than .0002 percent of the adult population currently serving. Most were elected to other offices before their election to Congress, and many started their careers as lawyers. In the past, women were denied admission to law school or restricted to quotas as low as 5 percent of the students admitted, thereby reducing the number of women in the eligible pool of candidates for entry-level political offices, such as the state legislature. As a result of this discrimination, the number of women "eligible" to run for Congress was small. Today, law schools no longer discriminate against women, and half or more of the students admitted are women, as are almost half of the students graduating.[15]

Does equal opportunity for law school positions today affect the eligible pool from which lower-level candidates are selected? Not really. The number of lawyers in the United States today is approximately 500,000, and the number of new lawyers is about 25,000 each year, or 5 percent of the total. Even if half of these new lawyers are women, the total pool of lawyers will change very slowly, with the proportion of women increasing about 2.5 percent each year. If women are half of the new lawyers, eventually half of all lawyers will be women—but that change will take decades, since currently only 13 percent of the lawyers are women.

Men constitute approximately 95 percent of the members of Congress, and most members serve for several decades before retiring. After each election, only about 15 percent of the members are new. Even if half of these are women, it will increase the proportion of women by only 7.5 percent, and it will take over a decade to bring the proportion of women elected to Congress up to half. But because of the slow growth in the proportion of women in the eligible pools—the legal profession, for example—growth in the proportion of women elected will not reach half of the newly elected members of Congress for decades. Using the 1984 percentage of .0505 women in the House of Representatives as a base and the most conservative assumptions, we projected that the proportion of women in the House in 1988–89 would reach .0646 percent. The actual figure was .062 percent just before the 1990 elections. Because of the slow growth of women in the eligible pool and the slow turnover of the male-dominated membership, the most conservative growth projections are only barely conservative enough for the slow growth rates in women's congressional representation.

Table 18.1 shows the 10-year growth of women members in the national legislatures of Australia, Israel, and 19 European and North American nations. Table 18.2 contains similar data on the growth of women members in the lower houses of 50 American state legislatures.[16] Progress has been very slow, and for some countries and states there has been virtually no progress. In 10 of the 19 countries, the percentage of women remained less than 10 percent in 1989— twenty years after the start of the latest wave of the women's movement. In Israel, the proportion of women dropped over the decade. The average annual growth was one-half of 1 percent. Similarly, representation of women in eight states is below 10 percent, and in four states there has been a decline in the proportion of women. The best prediction for the percent of women in a 1989 legislature is the percent of women in the legislature in 1981 plus 5 percent, reflecting little over one-half of 1 percent growth per year. This growth rate is approximately what was projected using the most conservative growth models.[17]

Changes in European society and American society are close to bringing about equality of opportunity for young women beginning their education and careers. But this equality of opportunity will translate very slowly into changes in the overall proportions of women in leadership roles because the new people, for whom the changes are taking place, constitute only a small portion of society. For some time into the future, political roles will be dominated by people coming of age before equality of opportunity for both genders.

226   R. Darcy

Table 18.1

Growth in the Proportion of Women in the National Legislature (Lower House) in Europe, Australia, Israel, Canada, and the United States, 1977–89

Country	Percent of Women 1977	1989	(Election)	Percent Growth	Percent Growth Per Year
Australia	0.0%	6.1%	(1987)	6.1%	.61%
Belgium	7.5	8.5	(1987)	1.0	.10
Canada	3.6 (1979)	9.6	(1984)	6.0	1.20
Denmark	16.7	30.7	(1988)	14.0	1.27
Finland	23.0 (1975)	31.0	(1985)	8.0	.80
France	1.4	5.7	(1988)	4.3	.39
Germany	7.3	16.0	(1987)	8.7	.87
Greece	3.3	4.3	(1985)	1.0	.13
Ireland	3.3	7.8		4.5	.38
Israel	6.6	5.8	(1988)	−0.8	−.07
Italy	8.5 (1976)	12.9	(1987)	4.4	.40
Luxembourg	6.7	10.9	(1984)	4.2	.60
Netherlands	14.0	21.3	(1986)	7.3	.81
Norway	23.9	38.5	(1989)	11.9	.99
Portugal	9.6 (1981)	10.0	(1987)	0.4	.07
Spain	5.4	7.8	(1986)	2.4	.27
Sweden	21.5	28.0	(1985)	6.5	.81
United Kingdom	2.9	6.5	(1987)	3.6	.36
United States	4.1	6.4		2.3	.19
Mean:	8.9%	13.9%		5.0%	.55%
Median:	6.7	9.6		4.4	.40
Standard Deviation	7.2	9.8		3.7	.39

Sources: Author's calculations from Isabella Prondzynski, *Women in Statistics: Women in Europe Supplement #30* (Brussels: Commission of European Communities, 1989), p. 14; Maria Weber, "Italy," in Joni Lovenduski and Jill Hills, eds., *The Politics of the Second Electorate: Women and Political Participation* (London: Routledge and Kegan Paul, 1989), p. 196; personal communications from Avraham Brichta of the University of Haifa, Michael Marsh of Trinity College, Dublin, Ian McAllister of the University of New South Wales; Janine Brody, *Women and Politics in Canada* (Toronto: McGraw-Hill Ryerson, 1985), p. 4; Vicky Randall, *Women and Politics*, 2d ed. (Houndsmill, Basingstoke, Hampshire, England: Macmillan Education, 1987); and Elina Haavio-Mannila et al., eds., *Det Uferdige Demokratiet: Kvinner i Nordisk Politikk* (Oslo: Nordisk Ministerrad, 1983).

ELECTING MORE WOMEN

Increasing the rate by which women come into political life requires increasing the proportions of women among new candidates, increasing the turnover rate of older incumbents, and decreasing the turnover rates of newly elected women incumbents.

Table 18.2
Growth in the Proportion of Women in the Lower Houses of U.S. State Legislatures, 1981–89 (N = 50)

State	Percent of Women 1981	Percent of Women 1989	Percent Growth
Alabama	5.7	6.6	0.9
Alaska	10.0	22.5	12.5
Arizona	20.0	36.6	16.6
Arkansas	4.0	8.0	4.0
California	12.5	17.5	5.0
Colorado	29.2	33.8	4.6
Connecticut	21.1	22.5	1.4
Delaware	17.0	14.6	- 2.4
Florida	10.0	13.3	3.3
Georgia	8.3	12.2	3.9
Hawaii	19.6	21.5	1.9
Idaho	11.4	26.1	14.7
Illinois	15.8	17.7	1.9
Indiana	8.0	11.0	3.0
Iowa	16.0	19.0	3.0
Kansas	14.4	26.4	12.0
Kentucky	8.0	6.0	- 2.0
Louisiana	1.9	2.8	0.9
Maine	23.8	31.1	7.3
Maryland	17.7	24.8	7.1
Massachusetts	8.7	18.7	10.0
Michigan	14.5	18.1	3.6
Minnesota	14.1	20.1	6.0
Mississippi	1.6	5.7	4.1
Missouri	12.2	16.5	4.3
Montana	13.0	21.0	8.0
Nebraska*	10.2	16.3	6.1
Nevada	12.5	23.8	11.3
New Hampshire	30.2	32.5	2.3
New Jersey	8.7	10.0	1.3
New Mexico	7.1	15.7	8.6
New York	9.3	12.0	2.7
North Carolina	15.8	17.5	1.7
North Dakota	15.0	17.9	2.9
Ohio	9.0	14.1	5.1
Oklahoma	10.8	6.9	- 3.9
Oregon	31.6	18.3	-13.3
Pennsylvania	4.9	7.3	2.4
Rhode Island	10.0	14.0	4.0
South Carolina	7.2	9.6	2.4
South Dakota	11.4	18.5	7.1
Tennessee	5.0	10.1	5.1
Texas	7.3	10.6	3.3
Utah	8.0	14.6	6.6
Vermont	23.3	32.6	9.3
Virginia	8.0	12.0	4.0
Washington	27.5	32.6	5.1
West Virginia	14.0	18.0	4.0
Wisconsin	18.1	31.3	13.2
Wyoming	22.5	28.1	5.6
Mean	13.3	17.9	4.6
Median	12.5	17.6	4.0
Standard Deviation	7.1	8.2	5.0

Regression Equation: $r = .813$, $R^2 = 66\%$
1989% = 5.334 + .948 (1981%)

Sources: Author's calculations from *National Directory of Women Elected Officials 1981* (Washington, D.C.: National Women's Political Caucus, 1981) and *National Directory of Women Elected Officials 1989* (Washington, D.C.: National Women's Political Caucus, 1989).

*Unicameral legislature.

Electoral Barriers to Women

Even a superficial examination of the electoral arrangements for selecting the world's legislatures finds one factor standing out. Women are much more apt to run and be elected in multimember districts than in single-member districts and are much more likely to be elected at large or on a national list than in districts.[18] The evidence is much less clear at the local level (see Welch and Herrick's chapter in this volume). There are several reasons multimember election systems facilitate the election of women. First, when there are many candidates to be nominated for a legislature, it is very difficult for party organizations not to include at least some women. If only one candidate is to be nominated, it can be assumed that balance will be achieved by nominating a woman somewhere else. A second reason is that when a number of candidates are to be nominated by a political party, it is reasonable for the party organization to adopt rules for their selection. Many European political parties require minimum proportions of women on candidate lists, including Norway, where the rules are directly responsible for that country having the highest proportion of women elected to a national legislature. When only one candidate is to be nominated in a district, such quotas are impossible to enforce.

On a practical level, women need to recognize their electoral stake in multimember districts and party list election systems, as well as party rules requiring a minimum number of women candidates. Currently, discussions of electoral reform in Israel and South Korea have included the effect that alternative plans will have on women's representation.

Electoral Change and Political Turnover

A major factor slowing the movement of women into political office is that the offices are already held by men. For each seat gained by women in a national legislature, a seat must be lost by a man. Political elites and national legislators, however, have a tendency to hold their seats for a long time, thereby slowing women's gains. Any disruption that increases turnover of national legislators should benefit women.

The 1980 Canadian election produced a Liberal government with 52 percent of the seats in Commons, but the 1984 election resulted in a major defeat for the Liberals, dropping them to 14 percent of Commons. The Tories' share of the seats went from 37 to 75 percent. This massive turnover produced a Parliament with a majority of new members.[19] One consequence was the increase in the proportion of women from 5.0 percent in 1980 to 9.6 percent in 1984. That the new women were overwhelmingly Conservative is due to opportunities created by that party's changed fortunes, not to some distinctive Conservative goodwill toward women. The massive turnover created opportunities for women, and their numbers virtually doubled.

The same change occurred in Sweden. Until the 1976 elections, the Left

Table 18.3
Changes in the Proportions of Women Members of the Swedish Riksdag by Party Group and Election, 1976 and 1982

GROUP	AFTER 1976 ELECTION ALL MEMBERS	DECREASE/ INCREASE IN WOMEN PROPORTIONS	AFTER 1982 ELECTION ALL MEMBERS	DECREASE/ INCREASE IN WOMEN PROPORTIONS
Left Coalition	-3.4%	-5.1%	+6.9%	+14.9%
Center-Right Coalition	+2.9	+8.6	-6.9	- 6.7

Regression Analysis:

%change in women's proportions in the Riksdag = .2278 + 1.93796 (% change of party)

N=20 r = .789 p<.0001 (all parties, 1974–1982). R^2 = 62%

Source: Author's calculations from Elina Haavio-Mannila et al., eds., *Det Uferdige Demokratiet: Kvinner i Nordisk Politikk* (Oslo: Nordisk Ministerrad, 1983), p. 262.

Coalition of Social Democrats and Communists held a majority of seats in the Riksdag. The 1976 election produced an electoral shift that gave control to a Center-Right Coalition, but the 1982 election changed control back to the Left Coalition. How did these electoral shifts influence the representation of women? As table 18.3 indicates, the proportion of women increased within the center-right parties when these parties were making gains and decreased within the left parties when the Left Coalition was suffering losses (1976). Conversely, the proportion of women decreased within the center-right parties when the Center-Right Coalition was losing seats and increased within the left parties when these parties were making gains (1982). A regression analysis of all parties in the elections between 1974 and 1982 shows that party gains or losses can explain 62 percent of the variation in women's gains or losses within the party.[20] Women have more opportunities for gains among parties gaining seats and fewer opportunities among parties losing seats.

Evidence from Canada and Sweden shows the relationship between turnover (produced in this case by election reversals) and gains in the representation of women. Big electoral gains, either for the Left or the Right, should result in gains for women on the winning side; big electoral losses, again either on the Left or the Right, should result in losses for women on the losing side. Political stagnation, as in the United States House of Representatives, slows women's gains.

Rules restricting the number of terms that can be served or making it easier for incumbents to be defeated—such as limitations on incumbent fund-raising—will speed the election of women. In September 1990, Oklahoma voters approved an initiative petition restricting state legislators to 12 years in office, and in

November 1990, voters in California and Colorado approved similar initiative proposals. Legislative turnover will increase in these states, since the number of incumbents contesting elections will be reduced. The result should be an increase in the proportion of women state legislators.

The tendency of national legislators to stay in office once elected has another side. In Ireland, the United States, and Sweden, research reveals that women legislators are less apt to run for reelection than are men.[21] This fact has a severe impact on the numbers of women serving. If an elected woman holds her seat, as her men colleagues do, women will have a growing base upon which to build their representation. On the other hand, if women do not hold their seats, keeping their numbers depends on the difficult process of electing new women candidates, and the result can be stagnation or even decline in women's representation. Keeping women members in service can have a greater effect on levels of women's representation than would the election of new women. Since women are the newer element in political bodies, their electoral staying power should be greater than that of men. A priority must be to find why women do not hold their seats as long as men, with strategies devised to remedy the situation.

CONCLUSION

The success most Europeans and North American democracies have had in almost completely excluding women from participation in national legislatures, despite more than a half century of formal political equality, is evidence of a major flaw in our democratic institutions.

Changes are occurring that will eventually lead to a more equitable distribution of political power. But if we are going to depend on social change to produce political change, the process will be very slow, with progress noticeable only over decades. Political progress for women depends on nominating greater proportions of women for political office and increasing the rate of political turnover among existing officeholders. This goal can be accomplished by making politics more competitive, reducing incumbency advantages, exploring electoral systems that advantage women, and altering party rules to require greater representation of women among party candidates. Once elected, women need to stay in office, on average, as long as men. Early retirements of women elected officials, when not accompanied by similar early retirements among men, reduce women's gains in representation.

Historically, election systems were not designed to keep women out of office; the causes of women's low representation go much deeper. But election systems can facilitate or impede attempts to remedy the underrepresentation of women. Electoral arrangements giving incumbents nearly insurmountable advantages prevent women from making gains. Electoral systems that diffuse responsibility for candidate nominations frustrate efforts to establish affirmative-action programs or quotas for women candidates. It is probably unrealistic to expect countries— such as Canada, the United Kingdom, or the United States—to adopt proportional representation for the sole purpose of facilitating the election of women, desirable as that goal may be. But aspects of the election system that strengthen older incumbents, discourage women officeholders, and restrict nomination opportunities can be questioned and changed. This task will be a formidable one, but the alternative is additional decades during which women will be absent from all but a few elective offices.

NOTES

The author thanks Donley Studlar, Pippa Norris, Avraham Brichta, Karen Beckwith, and Wilma Rule for their helpful and critical comments. Chen Sheng analyzed some of the data.

1. Maurice Duverger, *The Political Role of Women* (Paris: United Nations Economic and Social Council, 1955).

2. Quoted in Peggy Lamson, *Few Are Chosen* (Boston: Houghton Mifflin Company, 1968).

3. Joni Lovenduski and Pippa Norris, "Selecting Women Candidates: Obstacles to the Feminisation of the House of Commons," *European Journal of Political Research*, September 1989, pp. 533–62.

4. Robert Darcy, Susan Welch, and Janet Clark, *Women, Elections, and Representation* (New York: Longman, 1987).

5. R. Darcy and Sunhee Song, "Men and Women in the Korean National Assembly: Social Barriers to Representational Roles," *Asian Survey*, June 1986, pp. 670–87.

6. Janet Clark, "Electoral Systems and Women's Representation in Taiwan: The Impact of the Reserved Seat System," paper presented at the 1989 annual meeting of the American Political Science Association, Atlanta, Georgia, and Bih-er Chou, Cal Clark, and Janet Clark, *Women in Taiwan Politics: Overcoming Barriers to Women's Participation in a Modernizing Society* (Boulder, Colo.: Lynne Rienner, 1990).

7. Darcy, Welch, and Clark, *Women, Elections, and Representation*.

8. Donley Studlar and Ian McAllister, "Political Recruitment to the Australian Legislature: Towards an Explanation of Women's Electoral Disadvantages," *Western Political Quarterly*, June 1991.

9. Darcy, Welch, and Clark, *Women, Elections and Representation*. See also Studlar and McAllister, "Political Recruitment to the Australian Legislature," and Elina Haavio-Mannila et al., *Det Uferdige Demokratiet: Kvinner i Nordisk Politikk* (Oslo: Nordisk Ministerrad, 1983). Some evidence of voter hostility also can be found. See Michael Marsh, "Electoral Evaluations of Candidates in Irish General Elections, 1948–82," *Irish Political Studies*, vol. 27, 1987, pp. 65–76, and Jonathan Kelley and Ian McAllister, "Ballot Paper Cues and the Vote in Australia and Britain: Alphabetic Voting, Sex, and Title," *Public Opinion Quarterly*, Summer 1984, pp. 452–66.

10. Mary Wollstonecraft, *Vindication of the Rights of Women*, ed. Carol H. Poston (New York: Norton, 1975). The original edition was published in 1792. See also William Thompson, *Appeal of One-Half the Human Race, Women, against the Pretentions of the Other Half, Men, to Retain Them in Political and Thence in Civil and Domestic Slavery* (London: Virago, 1983). The original edition was published in 1825.

11. John Stuart Mill, *The Subjection of Women* (Cambridge: MIT Press, 1970). The original edition was published in 1869.

12. Verta Taylor, "Social Movement Continuity: The Women's Movement in Abeyance," *American Sociological Review*, October 1989, pp. 761–75.

13. Patricia Hollis, *Ladies Elect: Women in English Local Government, 1914–1965* (New York: Oxford University Press, 1987).

14. Simone de Beauvoir, *The Second Sex* (Paris: Gallimard, 1949); Duverger, *Political Role of Women*; and Betty Friedan, *The Feminine Mystique* (New York: Dell, 1963).

15. Darcy, Welch, and Clark, *Women, Elections, and Representation*.

16. For a scatterplot of 1971–75 data, see Irene Diamond, *Sex Roles in the State House* (New Haven: Yale University Press, 1977), p. 27. For a table containing 1974–84 data, see Wilma Rule, "Why More Women Are State Legislators: A Research Note," *Western Political Quarterly*, June 1990, pp. 437–48.

17. Darcy, Welch, and Clark, *Women, Elections, and Representation*, p. 132.

18. Ibid.

19. Eric Mintz, "The Canadian General Election of 1984," *Electoral Studies*, April 1985, pp. 71–75.

20. The changes were calculated as follows:

Where for each party delegation elected,

$$\% \text{ change in women} = \frac{(\text{current women} - \text{previous women})}{\text{previous women}} \times 100$$

$$\% \text{ change of party} = \frac{(\text{current number} - \text{previous number})}{\text{previous number}} \times 100.$$

21. R. Darcy, "Election of Women to Dáil Eireann: A Formal Analysis," *Irish Political Studies*, vol. 3, 1988, pp. 63–76; R. Darcy and James Choike, "A Formal Analysis of Legislative Turnover: Women Candidates and Legislative Representation," *American Journal of Political Science*, February 1986, pp. 237–55; and U. Frankstram and G. Gustafsson, "Kvinnor i Kommunalpolitiken," preliminary discussion paper presented at the annual political science conference, Umeå University, Sweden, October 11–12, 1984.

Select Bibliography

Alonzie, Nicholas O. "Distribution of Women and Majority Judges: The Effects of Judicial Selection Methods." *Social Science Quarterly*, June 1990, pp. 316–25.

Atkins, Burton, Matthew R. DeZee, and William Eckert. "The Effect of a Black Candidate in Stimulating Voter Participation in Statewide Elections: A Note on a Quiet 'Revolution' in Southern Politics." *Journal of Black Studies*, December 1985, pp. 213–25.

———. "State Supreme Court Elections: The Significance of Race." *American Politics Quarterly*, April 1984, pp. 211–24.

Beckwith, Karen. "Women and Election to National Legislatures: The Effects of Electoral System in France, Italy, and the United States." *Rivista Italiana Di Scienza Politica*, vol. 20, 1990, pp. 73–103.

Bogdanor, V., and D. Butler, eds. *Democracy and Elections: Electoral Systems and Their Political Consequences*. Cambridge: Cambridge University Press, 1983.

Brams, Steven J., and Peter C. Fishburn. "A Note on Variable-Size Legislatures to Achieve Proportional Representation." In Arend Lijphart and Bernard Grofman, eds., *Choosing an Electoral System*, pp. 175–77. New York: Praeger Publishers, 1984.

Bullock, Charles S., III, and Loch K. Johnson. "Sex and the Second Primary." *Social Science Quarterly*, December 1985, pp. 933–44.

Bullock, Charles S., III, and Susan A. MacManus. "Municipal Electoral Structure and the Election of Councilwomen." *Journal of Politics*, February 1991, pp. 75–89.

———. "Structural Features of Municipalities and the Incidence of Hispanic Council Members." *Social Science Quarterly*, December 1990, pp. 665–81.

Burrell, Barbara C. "The Political Opportunity of Women Candidates for the U.S. House of Representatives." *Women and Politics* 8, no. 1, 1988, pp. 51–68.

Carroll, Susan J. *Women as Candidates in American Politics*. Bloomington: Indiana University Press, 1985.

Cole, Richard L., Richard L. Engstrom, and Delbert A. Taebel. "Cumulative Voting in
    a Municipal Election: A Note on Voter Reactions and Electoral Consequences."
    Western Political Quarterly, March 1990, pp. 191–99.
Darcy, Robert, and Charles D. Hadley. "Black Women in Politics: The Puzzle of
    Success." *Social Science Quarterly*, September 1988, pp. 629–45.
Darcy, Robert, Susan Welch, and Janet Clark. "Women Candidates in Single- and Multi-
    Member Districts: American State Legislative Races." *Social Science Quarterly*,
    December 1985, pp. 945–63.
————. *Women, Elections, and Representation*, 2nd ed. Lincoln: University of Nebraska
    Press, 1991.
Derfner, Armand. "Vote Dilution and the Voting Rights Amendments of 1982." In
    Chandler Davidson, ed. *Minority Vote Dilution*, pp. 145–63. Washington, D.C.:
    Howard University Press, 1984.
Diamond, Irene. *Sex Roles in the State House*. New Haven: Yale University Press, 1977.
Duverger, Maurice. "Duverger's Law: Forty Years Later." In Bernard Grofman and
    Arend Lijphart, eds., *Electoral Laws and Their Political Consequences*, pp. 69–
    84. New York: Agathon Press, 1986.
————. *The Political Role of Women*. Paris: United Nations Economic and Social Coun-
    cil, 1955.
Engstrom, Richard L. "District Magnitudes and the Election of Women in the Irish
    Dáil." *Electoral Systems*, August 1987, pp. 139–48.
Engstrom, Richard L., and Charles J. Barrilleaux. "Native Americans and Cumulative
    Voting: The Sisseton-Wahpeton Sioux." *Social Science Quarterly*, June 1991,
    pp. 387–93.
Engstrom, Richard L., and Victoria M. Caridas. "Voting for Judges: Race and Roll-Off
    in Judicial Elections." In William Crotty, ed., *Political Participation and Amer-
    ican Democracy*, pp. 171–91. Westport, Conn.: Greenwood Press, 1991.
Engstrom, Richard L., Delbert A. Taebel, and Richard L. Cole. "Cumulative Voting as
    a Remedy for Minority Vote Dilution: The Case of Alamogordo, New Mexico."
    Journal of Law and Politics, Spring 1989, pp. 469–97.
*Findings and Recommendations of the Joint Commission on Integrity in the Public
    Schools*. New York: The Commission, 1990.
Fund for Modern Courts. *The Success of Women and Minorities: The Selection Process*.
    New York: Fund for Modern Courts, 1985.
Graham, Barbara Luck. "Do Judicial Selection Systems Matter? A Study of Black
    Representation on State Courts." *American Political Quarterly*, July 1990,
    pp. 316–36.
Grofman, Bernard. "Alternatives to Single Member Plurality Districts: Legal and Em-
    pirical Issues." In Bernard Grofman, Arend Lijphart, Robert McKay, and Howard
    Scarrow, eds., *Representation and Redistricting Issues*, pp. 107–28. Lexington,
    Mass.: Lexington Books, 1982.
————, ed. *Political Gerrymandering and the Courts*. New York: Agathon Press, 1990.
Grofman, Bernard, and Arend Lijphart, eds. *Electoral Laws and Their Political Con-
    sequences*. New York: Agathon Press, 1986.
Grofman, Bernard, Michael Migalski, and Nicholas Noviello. "Effects of Multimember
    Districts on Black Representation in State Legislatures." *Review of Black Political
    Economy*, Spring 1986, pp. 65–78.
Haavio-Mannila, Elina, Drude Dahlerup, Maud Eduards, Esther Gudmondsdottir, Bea-

trice Halsaa, Helga Hernes, Eva Hanninen-Salmelin, Bergthora Sigmundsdottir, Sirkka Sinkkonen, and Torild Skard. *Unfinished Democracy: Women in Nordic Politics.* New York: Pergamon, 1985.

Hallett, George H., Jr. "Proportional Representation with the Single Transferable Vote: A Basic Requirement for Legislative Elections." In Arend Lijphart and Bernard Grofman, eds., *Choosing an Electoral System*, pp. 113–25. New York: Praeger Publishers, 1984.

Jacobson, Gary. *Money in Congressional Elections.* New Haven: Yale University Press, 1980.

Jacobson, Gary, and Samuel Kernell. *Strategy and Choice in Congressional Elections.* New Haven: Yale University Press, 1981.

Lakeman, Enid. "Electoral Systems and Women in Parliament." *Parliamentarian*, July 1976, pp. 159–62.

———. *Power to Elect: The Case for Proportional Representation.* London: Heineman, 1982.

Lenz, Timothy, and Anita Pritchard. "Legislators' Perception of the Effects of the Change from Multi-Member Legislative Districts." *State and Local Government Review*, forthcoming.

Lijphart, Arend. "Trying to Have the Best of Both Worlds: Semi-Proportional and Mixed Systems." In Arend Lijphart and Bernard Grofman, eds., *Choosing an Electoral System*, pp. 207–13. New York: Praeger Publishers, 1984.

Lijphart, Arend, and Bernard Grofman, eds. *Choosing an Electoral System: Issues and Alternatives.* New York: Praeger Publishers, 1984.

Lyons, W. E., and Malcolm E. Jewell. "Minority Representation and the Drawing of City Council Districts." *Urban Affairs Quarterly*, March 1988, pp. 432–47.

MacManus, Susan A. "Constituency Size and Minority Representation." *State and Local Government Review*, Winter 1987, pp. 3–7.

MacManus, Susan A., and Charles S. Bullock III. "Minorities and Women *Do* Win At-Large." *National Civic Review*, May/June 1988, pp. 231–44.

Massey, Douglas, and Nancy Denton. "Trends in the Residential Segregation of Blacks, Hispanics, and Asians: 1870–1980." *American Sociological Review*, December 1987, pp. 802–25.

Messina, Anthony, Laura Rhodebeck, Frederick Wright, and Luis Fraga, eds. *Ethnic and Racial Minorities in Advanced Industrial Democracies: Social, Economic, and Political Incorporation.* Westport, Conn.: Greenwood Press, 1992.

Mladenka, Kenneth. "Blacks and Hispanics in Urban Politics." *American Political Science Review*, March 1989, pp. 165–91.

Moncrief, Gary S., and Joel A. Thompson. "Electoral Structure and State Legislative Representation." *Journal of Politics*, February 1992, pp. 246–56.

———. "The Move to Limit Terms of Office: Assessing the Consequences for Female State Legislators." Paper presented at the annual meeting of the Western Political Science Association, Seattle, Washington, March 1991.

Moreland, Laurence, Robert Steed, and Todd Baker, eds., *Blacks in Southern Politics.* New York: Praeger Publishers, 1987.

Niemi, Richard G., and Laura R. Winsky. "Membership Turnover in the U.S. State Legislatures: Trends and Effects of Districting." *Legislative Studies Quarterly*, February 1987, pp. 115–23.

Niemi, Richard G., Jeffrey S. Hill, and Bernard Grofman. "The Impact of Multi-Member

Districts on Party Representation in U.S. State Legislatures." *Legislative Studies Quarterly*, Autumn 1985, pp. 441–55.

Norris, Pippa. "Women's Legislative Participation in Western Europe." *Western European Politics*, October 1985, pp. 90–101.

Pitkin, Hannah. *The Concept of Representation*. Berkeley: University of California Press, 1967.

Rae, Douglas. *The Political Consequences of Electoral Laws*. New Haven: Yale University Press, 1971.

Renner, Tari. "Municipal Election Processes: The Impact on Minority Representation." In *The Municipal Yearbook 1988*, pp. 13–22. Washington, D.C.: International City Management Association, 1988.

Rule, Wilma. "Electoral Systems, Contextual Factors, and Women's Opportunity for Election to Parliament in Twenty-Three Democracies." *Western Political Quarterly*, September 1987, pp. 477–98.

———. "Why More Women Are State Legislators: A Research Note." *Western Political Quarterly*, June 1990, pp. 437–48.

———. "Why Women Don't Run: The Critical Contextual Factors in Women's Legislative Recruitment." *Western Political Quarterly*, March 1981, pp. 60–77.

Saint-Germain, Michelle. "Does Their Difference Make a Difference? The Impact of Women on Public Policy in the Arizona Legislature." *Social Science Quarterly* 70, no. 4, pp. 956–68.

Simms, Marian, ed. *Australian Women and the Political System*. Melbourne: Longman Cheshire, 1984.

Still, Edward. "Alternatives to Single-Member Districts." In Chandler Davidson, ed., *Minority Vote Dilution*, pp. 253–58. Washington, D.C.: Howard University Press, 1984.

Studlar, Donley T., and Ian McAllister, "Political Recruitment in the Australian Legislature: Toward an Explanation of Women's Electoral Disadvantages." *Western Political Quarterly*, June 1991, pp. 467–86.

Taagepera, Rein, and Matthew Soberg Shugart. *Seats and Votes: The Effects and Determinants of Electoral Systems*. New Haven: Yale University Press, 1989.

Thernstrom, Abigail M. *Whose Votes Count?* Cambridge, Mass.: Harvard University Press, 1987.

Uhlaner, Carole, and Kay Schlozman. "Candidate Gender and Congressional Campaign Receipts." *Journal of Politics*, February 1986, pp. 30–50.

Weaver, Leon. "The Rise, Decline, and Resurrection of Proportional Representation in Local Governments in the United States." In Bernard Grofman and Arend Lijphart, eds., *Electoral Laws and Their Political Consequences*, pp. 139–53. New York: Agathon Press, 1986.

———. "Semi-Proportional and Proportional Representation Systems in the United States." In Arend Lijphart and Bernard Grofman, eds., *Choosing an Electoral System*, pp. 191–206. New York: Praeger, 1984.

Welch, Susan. "The Impact of At-Large Elections on the Representation of Blacks and Hispanics." *Journal of Politics*, November 1990, pp. 1050–76.

Welch, Susan, and Timothy Bledsoe. *Urban Reform and Its Consequences*. Chicago: University of Chicago Press, 1988.

Welch, Susan, and Donley T. Studlar. "Multimember Districts and the Representation of Women: Evidence from Britain and the United States." *Journal of Politics*, May 1990, pp. 391–412.

Wright, J.F.H. *Mirror of the Nation's Mind: Australia's Electoral Experiments*. Sydney: Hale and Iremonger, 1980.

Zeller, Belle, and Hugh A. Bone. "The Repeal of P.R. in New York City: Ten Years in Retrospect." *American Political Science Review*, December 1948, pp. 1127–48.

Zimmerman, Joseph F. *Federal Preemption: The Silent Revolution*. Ames: Iowa State University Press, 1991.

———. "The Federal Voting Rights Act and Alternative Election Systems." *William & Mary Law Review*, Summer 1978, pp. 621–60.

———. *Participatory Democracy: Populism Revived*. New York: Praeger Publishers, 1986.

———. "A Proportional Representation System and New York City School Boards." *National Civic Review*, October 1974, pp. 472–74, 493.

Index

African-Americans. *See also* Minorities
—congressional success: Congress, 18–
   21, 33, 34–35; percentage needed
   for success, 35; permanancy of
   success, 36
—election to government: city councils,
   156–58; county councils, 148–50;
   Florida legislature, 88–90;
   judgeships, 131, 132; social bias
   and, 26–28; state legislatures, 59,
   60–65, 76, 81, 88–89, 105–6, 116,
   121
—men's election in states with single-
   member legislative districts, 62
—men's election to government: city
   councils, 158; Congress, 41–42;
   county councils, 146; state
   legislatures, 58, 59, 61–63, 88–89,
   121
—population, South and non-South, 32–
   33
—representation/population ratio: city
   councils by election type, 156–58;
   Congress, 41; county councils, 152;
   state legislatures, 62–63
—women's election in state with
   multimember legislative districts, 61
—women's election in states with single
   primary, 66

—women's election to government: city
   councils, 156; Congress, 41–42;
   county councils, 146; offices in
   Pennsylvania, 83–84; state
   legislatures, 49, 59, 122
—women's representation/population
   ratio: city councils, 156, 157;
   Congress, 42; county councils, 152;
   state legislatures, 62–63
Anglos
—election to government: Arizona
   legislature, 120–22; city councils,
   156–57; Congress, 41–42; county
   councils, 148–50; judgeships, 129;
   state legislatures, 50, 59, 92–93,
   121
—men's election to government: state
   legislatures, 67; in states with single-
   member legislative districts, 67
—representation/population ratios: city
   councils, 156–57; Congress, 41;
   state legislatures, 122
—women's election to government: city
   councils, 151; senate, Florida, 93;
   socioeconomic state factors, 65–66;
   state legislatures, 65–66
Asians
—election to Congress, 23–24, 41–42

Contributors

JUDITH BAUM is Director of Information Services for the Public Education Association in New York City. She is coauthor of *Governing New York City Schools: Roles and Relationships in the Decentralized System*, published by the Public Education Association in 1987, and has been responsible for updating and publishing the triennial *Manual for Candidates in the New York City School Board Elections* since 1980. She has chaired the Citywide Community School Board Elections Committee since 1985. The committee is a broad coalition of public school professionals and advocates who advise and monitor implementation of the city's community school board elections every three years.

CHARLES S. BULLOCK III holds the Richard Russell Chair of Political Science at the University of Georgia. He is past president of the Southern Political Science Association and past chair of the Legislative Studies Group and currently is a member of the Executive Council of the American Political Science Association. He has published extensively on the impact of election structures on the election of women, Hispanics, African-Americans, and incumbents.

M. MARGARET CONWAY is a Professor of Political Science at the University of Florida. She is the author or coauthor of several books, including *Political Participation in the United States* (1985, 1991) and *Political Parties: Stability and Change* (1984). She also has published articles in a number of journals, including *American Political Science Review*, *Journal of Politics*, *Public Opinion Quarterly*, and *Political Behavior*.

R. DARCY is Professor of Political Science and Statistics at Oklahoma State University. He is coauthor with Janet Clark and Susan Welch of *Women, Elections, and Representation* (1987) and with Richard Rohrs of *Guide to Quantitative*

History (1991). He also has authored or coauthored four dozen journal articles, book chapters, and research notes on elections, statistical methods, and women in politics. Darcy has been a visiting professor at a number of universities including Queen's University, Belfast; University College, Galway; and the University of New South Wales.

VICTOR DESANTIS is a faculty member at the University of North Texas and previously was Director of Survey Research and Data Coordinator for the International City Management Association. Currently, he is completing a Ph.D. in political science at American University. His main research interests are legislative institutions and local government economic development.

RICHARD L. ENGSTROM is Research Professor of Political Science at the University of New Orleans. His articles on election systems have appeared in *American Political Science Review*, *Journal of Politics*, *Electoral Studies*, and other journals. He has served as a Fulbright Professor at the National Taiwan University and at University College, Galway, and as a Senior Fellow of the Institute of Irish Studies, Queen's University, Belfast.

DAVID H. EVERSON is Professor of Political Studies and Public Affairs at Sangamon State University. He is the author of *American Political Parties* (1980) and several other books and also edits *Comparative State Policies*.

SANDRA A. FEATHERMAN is Vice Chancellor for Academic Administration, University of Minnesota/Duluth and is the author of numerous articles on ethnicity and voting behavior, women and politics, and the design of electoral systems. She has been an expert witness in a vote-dilution case.

BERNARD GROFMAN is Professor of Political Science and Social Psychology in the School of Social Sciences at the University of California, Irvine. He is a specialist in mathematical models of collective decision-making and the political consequences of electoral laws, with over 100 published articles on topics such as jury verdict choice, reapportionment and voter turnout, and coalition-formation models. During the last decade he has served in 11 states as an expert witness in redistricting litigation or as a court-appointed reapportionment expert.

LISA HANDLEY is a Research Analyst for Election Data Services Incorporated, a redistricting and political consulting firm in Washington, D.C.

REBEKAH HERRICK is a Ph.D. candidate at the University of Nebraska. Her research interests include Congress and mass behavior, and currently she is focusing on her dissertation, entitled ''Unconventional Political Participation and Personality: An Exploration of the Effects of Extraversion on Modes of Political Participation.''

SUSAN A. MACMANUS is Professor and Chair of the Department of Government and International Affairs at the University of South Florida, Tampa. Her research interests include urban and minority politics, public policy analysis, and public budgeting and finance. Her articles on women and politics have appeared in *Journal of Politics*, *Western Political Quarterly*, *Social Science*

Quarterly, *Women and Politics*, *Journal of Political Science*, and in various edited volumes. Her most recent book, *Doing Business with Government* (1992), includes discussions of the difficulties women business owners have in contracting with governments at all levels.

PIPPA NORRIS lectures in the Department of Politics at Edinburgh University. Recently she was a visiting scholar at the University of California, Berkeley, and Harvard University. Her research interests focus on the comparative study of women and politics, British elections and parties, and American elections. She is the author of *Politics and Sexual Equality* (1990) and *British By-elections* (1990), coauthor with Ivor Crewe of *Electoral Change since 1945*, and joint editor of the *Yearbook of Elections and Parties, 1991* and the *Bibliography of Political Studies, 1990*. Her current main research project, with Dr. Joni Lovenduski, is a British candidate study.

GEORGIA A. PERSONS is an Associate Professor of Political Science in the School of Public Policy at the Georgia Institute of Technology. She has published many articles on black electoral politics and recently edited *Dilemmas of Black Politics: Issues of Leadership and Strategy* (1991). She also conducts research in the area of public policy/regulatory policy.

ANITA PRITCHARD is an Associate Professor of Political Science at Florida Atlantic University. She has published articles in the areas of congressional voting decisions, presidential-congressional relations, women in politics, and representation and electoral systems.

TARI RENNER is an Assistant Professor in the Graduate Center for Social and Public Policy at Duquesne University. He previously was the Senior Statistical Analyst for the International City Management Association and was responsible for the design, implementation, and analysis of the association's research projects. His primary research areas are urban politics and the electoral behavior of American political subcultures.

WILMA RULE is an Adjunct Professor of Political Science at the University of Nevada, Reno. Her major research interests are the legislative recruitment of Anglo and minority women and the effect that electoral systems have on women's political opportunity. She has published articles in *American Political Science Review*, *Administrative Science Quarterly*, *Western Political Quarterly*, and other scholarly journals.

MICHELLE A. SAINT-GERMAIN is a Research Associate in the Southwest Institute for Research on Women at the University of Arizona. Her research focuses on women and public policy. She has conducted studies of elected women and public policy in the United States and Central America and of older Anglo and Hispanic women and preventive health care.

EDWARD STILL is an attorney practicing in Birmingham, Alabama. He has been counsel for parties in numerous voting rights cases in Alabama and Florida. He has presented several papers on limited and cumulative voting at annual meetings of the American Political Science Association and is the author of "Alternatives to Single-Member Districts" in Chandler Davidson, ed., *Minority Vote Dilution* (1984).

LEON WEAVER was an Emeritus Professor at Michigan State University and a founding member of the Section on Representation and Electoral Systems of the American Political Science Association. He was the author of monographs and other technical literature on electoral systems, with emphasis on alternative systems. These publications include interpretive studies of nonpartisan elections and proportional and semiproportional electoral systems in the United States; empirical studies of the Hare system (single-transferable vote) of proportional representation in Cambridge, Massachusetts; majority-preferential voting and minority representation systems in Michigan; and cumulative voting in Alabama.

SUSAN WELCH is Professor of Political Science and Dean of the College of the Liberal Arts at Pennsylvania State University. She has published widely on issues of representation for women and minorities. She is coauthor with Lee Sigelman of *A Dream Deferred: Black Attitudes toward Race and Equality* (1991) and currently is preparing a revision, with R. Darcy and Janet Clark, of *Women, Elections, and Representation* (1987).

JOSEPH F. ZIMMERMAN is Professor of Political Science in the Graduate School of Public Affairs of the State University of New York at Albany and a former chair of the Section on Representation and Electoral Systems of the American Political Science Association. His books include *The Federated City* (1972), *State-Local Relations: A Partnership Approach* (1983), *Participatory Democracy: Populism Revived* (1986), and *Federal Preemption: The Silent Revolution* (1991).